PADDLE
THE NILE

SARAH DAVIS

EXPEDITION
PUBLISHING

www.EXPEDITIONPUBLISHING.com

Cover design and layout: Josie Dickinson, JKD Design
Typesetting and page assembly: Toni Esser, Tesser Book and Print Design
Editorial Consultant: Ross Addison
Cover photo: Nadim Elmessiri
Back cover photo: Richard McGibbon
Author photo: James Anderson

ISBN paperback: 978-0-6454898-1-1

ISBN ebook: 978-0-6454898-0-4

A catalogue record for this work is available from the National Library of Australia

EXPEDITION
PUBLISHING

Published by Expedition Publishing
www.expeditionpublishing.com

Travelling the length of the Nile is no mean feat; filled with adventure, challenges and dangers. Sarah completed this momentous journey with determination and strength. Paddle the Nile is a gripping and motivating read.

Levison Wood — Author, Photographer, Explorer

Paddle The Nile is an inspirational book about a dream that came alive. Sarah showed so much resilience, strength and spirit in an environment that was unpredictable. This book will motivate you to go and make your dreams come true.

Bruce (Hoppo) Hopkins — Bondi Rescue Lifeguard

Risking what many said is impossible did not sway Sarah from daring to deliver on her dream. Her book is much more than an account of the actual epic journey. Paddle the Nile transported me into the heart and mind of a person who truly lives to challenge the limits of our human potential. Being an adventurer myself, I resonate with what it took to 'put the paddle in the water'. Sarah takes you through the entire two-year journey, from concept to completion. She is a role model for us all.

Jerry Dunn — America's Marathon Man

Sarah's compelling account of her Nile expedition includes encounters with hippos, crocodiles and death-defying rapids. Paddle the Nile takes you to heart of Africa, with all its charm and challenges, beauty and brutality. If you're going on an adventure there's going to be risk, it's how you manage that risk that will be the difference between success and failure.

Luck will take you so far but is overrated when it comes to dealing with locals toting AK-47s and being incarcerated within a dubious judicial system. Having a plan and a cool head when facing adversity requires a special mindset and Sarah's story is full of overcoming adversity in its many forms.

Strap yourself in for a high-octane ride down one of the world's greatest rivers …

Lloyd Figgins — International Security Advisor and Author of The Travel Survival Guide

This is a remarkable adventure and lesson in following your dreams, however impossible they might seem. What follows is an epic journey filled with drama, fun, cultural insights and endless challenges.

Alastair Humphries — Adventurer, Author and Keynote Speaker

This book is dedicated to two people.

To my mum, Angela Davis, for her endless love and support despite
the stress and worry she has endured with all my exploits.

To my great mate Brad Deeth, 23 November 1972 – 3 January 2019.
Rest in peace, my beautiful friend.

PADDLE THE NILE

AUTHOR'S NOTE

The stories in this book reflect my own recollection of events, and are written from my perspective. Where possible the people mentioned in this book have been contacted prior to publication for permission to use their name(s) in this recollection. Some names and identifying characteristics have been changed to protect the privacy of those depicted. Dialogue has been re-created from memory.

PADDLE THE NILE

CONTENTS

PADDLE THE NILE

PROLOGUE

Steve Pavlina

The Nile is Africa's longest river and disputed to be the longest river in the world at 6,693 kilometres in length[1]. This mighty river has two tributaries: the White Nile and the Blue Nile. The longer White Nile rises in central Africa, with its most distant source being in either Rwanda or Burundi — the jury is still out on which it is. For my expedition, I chose what many consider to be the Rwandan source.

In a tributary of the Rukarara River, deep in the Nyungwe Forest, the Nile begins to make its way through Rwanda, Tanzania and Uganda, via Lake Victoria. It continues north to South Sudan and then up through Sudan.

In Khartoum, the capital of Sudan, it is joined by the Blue Nile, which starts some 1,400 kilometres earlier in Lake Tana in the Ethiopian highlands before making its way to this confluence. The joined rivers head up to Egypt. North of Cairo, it becomes two branches, which empty into the Mediterranean Sea, marking the end of this incredible river.

My plan was to complete a source-to-sea human-powered descent of the Nile from Rwanda to Egypt, except for a section through South Sudan that was deemed too risky from a security and political standpoint. That still left me with approximately 5,300 kilometres to cover.

I was going to need people with me. And as much as possible, I wanted them to be local people — for the deeper cultural experience I hoped it would create and compensate for the local knowledge I lacked.

I anticipated that from start to finish, it would take me at least five months, considering rest days and time to plan and prepare each section.

In the military, there is the well-known adage which says that 'no plan survives first contact with the enemy'. Expeditions are no different – no plan survives contact with – well, pretty much anything. It was certainly the case in my expedition. While things didn't always go to plan, what eventuated was an epic, life-changing adventure.

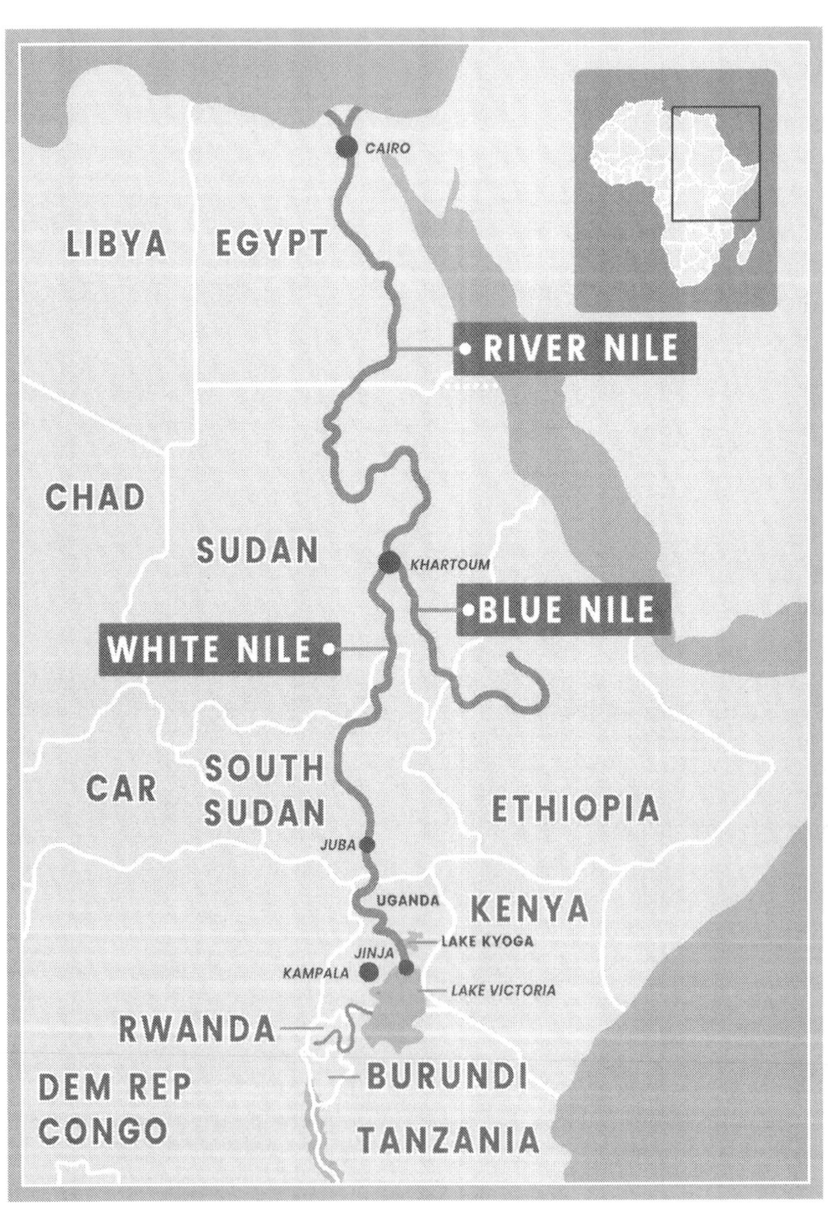

PADDLE THE NILE

PART 1

January 2016 to October 2018

Before paddles hit the water

CHAPTER ONE
THE IDEA

*If you want to be happy, set a goal that commands your thoughts,
liberates your energy and inspires your hopes.*

Andrew Carnegie

The enormous, extremely irate hippo charged us again. We frantically tried to paddle our raft to safety, but we weren't fast enough. I felt a tug and glanced behind to see she had sunk her enormous teeth into the back of our raft and had hold of it. She wanted to rip us apart! And this was only day six on the water. Little did I know it was going to be one of many incidents on this incredible adventure.

The path to this terrifying encounter started some two and a half years earlier in far safer surrounds at home in Australia, when I had a distinctly lower heart rate.

It was New Year's Day 2016, and the sun was about to rise at Bondi Beach in Sydney. I watched the pinpoint of light on the horizon grow; the warm hues radiated across the sky. A new day and a new year. The reset button had been pressed.

I reflected on the challenges of the year now behind me. I'd broken off a friendship that had become toxic and pushed me to the edge. Then a romantic relationship had ground to a halt. And the heavy black cloud of depression also visited me once again. It was a year I was glad to bid farewell.

So, while I felt the warmth of the new-day sun on my face, my focus slowly drifted to the good things the year had brought. Even though I was still brushing myself off emotionally and feeling tender, I was happy. I had clawed my way out of the pit of depression and was relieved to watch 'the black dog' fade into the distance. I had a rewarding job, was healthy, and I felt utterly free for the first time in a long while. There was much to be grateful for, and I smiled, savouring this feeling.

I now had a blank canvas to fill, and that excited me, but what I also experienced was a restless, nagging feeling this wasn't '*it*'. That there had to be more to my life. Staring down the barrel of twenty-odd years of corporate life, each consisting of 48 weeks of work interspersed with four weeks' leave, filled me with horror. It made me feel trapped and claustrophobic.

I was never particularly motivated by promotions. Sure, my ego liked the idea of important-sounding titles, and the pay rise would have been welcomed, but there wasn't enough intrinsic motivation to chase it. I wanted to create a life that made me feel truly *alive*, one that brought a mix of purpose, excitement and challenge. I was still trying to find my place in this world. To not feel like the square peg being rammed into the round hole, and to stop twisting myself into a shape that fitted in.

It had always been my life outside of work that brought satisfaction and joy. It was where I challenged myself, set goals and pursued them fervently.

These goals were mostly in sport — surf lifesaving competitions, triathlons, ocean swimming, half-marathons, marathons, and ocean surf ski paddling.

It also fed my highly competitive nature and gave me a sense of achievement and direction. Beyond that, I lived for travel. I craved getting off the beaten track, away from the masses, backpacking and going on adventures.

The need for change was clear. The answer, however, to the question as to what I was going to do, was not so obvious. It's hard to be what you can't see. And nothing I'd seen had jumped out at me or given me something to aspire to.

During the first few months of 2016, I began to gain clarity and focus, and I came across some people who had achieved 'firsts'. They weren't your classic explorers or adventurers. You know, those ex-military Bear Grylls-types, or people who'd been scaling mountains since they could walk.

One was a woman who had completed a kayaking expedition down the Amazon, yet she didn't have a background in kayaking or expeditions, just a willingness to leap into the unknown and give it her absolute best, backed up with some fierce determination.

This triggered something in me — that's what I wanted to do! To go on an expedition not done before. Suddenly I could *see* it; I could see what I wanted to do and be. I'd always read books by explorers and adventures, but it never occurred to me that I could be the 'explorer'. These people made me realise that it was something I might be able to do. They were ordinary, everyday people with big, audacious dreams. It felt like I was finally paying attention to a voice that had been whispering to me all along.

Butterflies of excitement bubbled up just thinking about going on a monumental adventure. I'm not proud to admit it, but my ego also relished the idea of achieving a 'first'.

The next question was, what was I to do?

It had to involve paddling, as this was my main sport. I had started paddling after becoming a volunteer surf lifesaver at North Bondi Surf Life Saving Club. Since then, as well as surf ski paddling (using a form of kayak for paddling through the surf), I'd also been lucky to compete in ocean ski races around the world, and it had evolved into a sport I loved.

With that decided, it was time to do some research. At first, I tried to find somewhere close to home that I could paddle. *Kayaking around Australia?* A few people, including a woman, Freya Hoffmeister, had beaten me to it. She had also made her way around South America. That was impressive!

The Amazon? Also done.

With my geography failing me, I decided to look up what the world's longest river was ... The Nile.

Could this be it?

What made my heart beat faster was that my first search failed to find any woman who had gone from the Nile's source to the sea, self-powered. A knot of excitement started to build, and I got goose bumps. This combined two things I loved – kayaking and travelling. And the icing on the cake was that it would be through Africa, a continent I adored.

This was it. I was going to paddle the Nile!

I couldn't remember any other big decision giving me a sense of such unquestionable certainty.

I'd normally be looking at the pros and cons, deliberating, looking at the facts and making sure it was the right decision. And this decision had every reason to put me in the 'barking mad' category, with a list of cons longer than my arm. But it felt right, for reasons I couldn't explain. Despite the inherent risks and uncertainty, along with the fact that I had no idea how I was going to pull it off, I felt comforted and confident in my decision.

Now I had my cunning idea, next was working out how the hell I was going to do it. There's no book or internet site for anything like this. No simple 'Ten steps to organising an expedition in Africa'. As I would discover, it required tons of research, finding experts in the field, reading and working it out for myself.

Ahead of me were times of near crippling self-doubt and feeling that I had bitten off way more than I could chew — but I was ready to give it my best shot.

CHAPTER TWO
PLANNING

As you start to walk on the way, the way appears.

Rumi

An early win was talking to Pete Meredith, who was mentioned in two insightful books I read. One was *Living the Best Day Ever* by Hendri Coetzee about the *Settle the Nile* expedition that went from Lake Victoria to the Mediterranean Sea. The other was *Walking the Nile* by Levison Wood, about his incredible expedition walking the length of the Nile. Both books gave me valuable insights and increased my excitement for the trip, thanks to their descriptions of the countries, the people, the challenges and the environment.

Pete was an integral member of the expedition with Hendri and had provided advice to Levison. He is renowned for his rafting and kayaking expertise, having been involved with, and led, countless expeditions. Without him and his advice, I wouldn't have had a clue where to start. This was a significant turning point in organising this trip.

He told me what was involved, how long it would take, the river conditions, the weather, some of the equipment required, the authorities to engage with, challenges to expect, and costs en route. These conversations with Pete, and many others after, along with more research, helped me gradually develop the plan.

The plan was broken into bite-sized chunks, with each one taking me one step closer to my goal. The process of planning, organising and slowly creating something from nothing was rewarding, and I loved it.

By now a few months had passed since my epiphany, and it was May 2016. While this was all wildly exciting, I forced myself to pause and contemplate what was involved. And it seemed like a good idea to do a reconnaissance trip before fully committing to this crazy idea.

I already had a ten-day trip planned in August to go horseriding across the desert in Namibia, so I decided to spend a week in Uganda, trying white water kayaking, checking out what the Nile was like and talking to the local people.

This trip confirmed my overwhelming desire to undertake this expedition. The thought of spending months in Africa, making my way down the mighty river filled me with excitement.

It also scared the shit out of me. Having seen the monster rapids — one called the *Dead Dutchman* (you don't have to be Sherlock Holmes to deduce why) — and hearing numerous stories of crocodile and hippo attacks, I was terrified. To reduce the risk of fear stopping me, I decided to create some 'community accountability' — by telling everyone my plan I'd be less likely to back out of it.

Before doing that, I decided to brand the expedition. I wanted to be taken seriously and differentiate myself to hopefully attract a following and much needed sponsorship.

Naming my adventure *Paddle the Nile* seemed to be the obvious choice. I drafted a logo and had it professionally created, registered my domain (www.paddlethenile.com) and created my website. I invested in a promotional video, created social media accounts to share my endeavour, and hoodies and T-shirts were printed in readiness.

There was another key decision to be made.

I was about to go on a jolly through some developing countries dealing with – among many challenges – extreme poverty. I had to give back somehow. This was too big an undertaking not to do some good and fundraise. After much deliberating and investigation, I picked CARE Australia as the charity I would support. They are part of the global humanitarian aid organisation, CARE International, which is focused on ending world poverty.

I chose them not just because of the incredible life-changing work they do, but because they put women and children at the centre of all their initiatives and operate in the countries I was set to travel to. I also began engaging with foreign officials, sending letters to the various bureaucrats for each country. These were the people I needed to approve my expedition or provide support. Being a dual national, both the British and Australian Embassies in the countries I was set to visit were notified of my intent.

By early 2017, I was also making progress on other elements of the plan. This included working out which time of year to go, what equipment to take, which courses I needed to do, such as Remote First Aid, searching for sponsorship and applying for grants. When I wasn't planning, I was working full-time and doing intense ocean ski training ahead of a big 53-kilometre race in Hawaii in May.

As the middle of 2017 approached, I was ready to share my dream. The thought of telling everyone, publicly committing to it, felt like a pivotal yet daunting moment. I was putting myself out there with absolutely no guarantees I could even make it to the start line, let alone finish this expedition. The odds were stacked against me, having never been on — let alone organised — anything like this, and it was going to take me into an environment filled with all manner of potentially lethal situations.

Yet at the same time, the thought of not at least trying to get this trip off the ground felt wrong. I knew I had to give it a shot or regret it forever.

In June 2017, having spent hours procrastinating, with my finger hovering over the 'Post' button, I finally shared my dream with Facebook and all my friends. It was official. I was going to attempt to paddle the length of the Nile. *Go me!*

The response I received was fantastic. Everyone was excited to hear of my plans and looking forward to following my journey. One person responded, 'I will keenly follow how you intend to avoid crocs and hippos.' *Yeah, you and me both.*

Mum wasn't exactly thrilled at first — a few unsupervised internet searches threw up horror stories of crocodile attacks, hostile situations and more. Once I explained the precautions I was taking, along with why this trip was important to me, she supported me 100 per cent. I'll be forever grateful to her because I know it wasn't easy watching me carry out this goal.

In July 2017, I went on a two-week reconnaissance trip to Sudan and Egypt. I wasn't sure what, if any, support I was going to get. However, there was no need for concern, as everyone I spoke with was excited and incredibly supportive of my plans.

I met with the British and Australian embassy delegates. There were also meetings with government officials as well as CARE representatives to find out about the work they were doing and see if there might be an opportunity to visit some of the their projects. Finally, I met with local paddlers, who I hoped would join me on my journey or help find paddlers to join the trip.

Back home, my attentions turned to fundraising. Raising money for charity turned out to be easier than finding sponsors for the expedition. The latter proved to be an exercise about as fruitful as banging my head against the proverbial brick wall. I kept sending out emails, having meetings, hitting up everyone in my network and beyond … with limited success.

I did manage to secure my primary sponsor, Shaw and Partners Financial Services, who generously came on board as soon as I announced my plans. I knew the co-CEO, Earl Evans, who was a fellow paddler and supporter of North Bondi Surf Life Saving Club. Having Shaw and Partners as my main sponsor was a huge win, but what meant so much to me was the belief they showed in what I was doing. Additionally, Nurmi Accountants and Mayo Hardware came on as financial sponsors.

What really blew me away were my friends who donated money and equipment (even my dentist and gastroenterologist donated). Having never been married, but seeing this as my 'big day' (or big six months), I decided to set up a gift registry as a way of getting some of the equipment. It allowed people to see what their money went towards. The fact that my friends were willing to put their hands in their pockets was humbling — it reduced me to tears.

There was a selection of equipment suppliers as well: Big Water Rescue Equipment, Kathmandu, Braca-Sport, Bennett Paddles, Canoe Innovation, Vaikobi, Borika Mounts and NuZest.

Nile River Explorers were going to loan me the rafting equipment and assist with accommodation in Uganda, and Peak Dynamics offered to do some psychological testing to monitor how I dealt with the stress during the trip. Getting these sponsors helped build my confidence.

There were countless trips to doctors and specialists. We didn't need the wheels falling off in the middle of nowhere during this expedition. I became a human pin cushion with all the vaccinations I needed, and was given an impressive selection of prescriptions for the medications to take with me. Most were standard meds, such as antibiotics, but it also included PrEP to prevent HIV in a worst-case situation of rape in countries where HIV is prevalent.

In November 2017, I competed in the World Surf Ski Championships. This was a 22.5-kilometre race in Hong Kong that proved to be the pinnacle of my sporting career. I represented Australia and took out top spot on the podium for my category. After this race, I scaled back my time on the water.

I focused on building muscle rather than working on my paddling fitness, knowing the latter would build during the expedition, besides, I already had a good base. I didn't want to risk developing overuse injuries from paddling before I even started. Instead, I hit the gym to get my 'Popeye' on and bulk up. This would help prevent injuries and ensure I had plenty of muscle reserves.

By now I had dropped to four days a week at work, as it wasn't possible to train, plan and work full-time. I also needed to develop a risk management plan for the trip. Finally, we were in my area of expertise, having spent close to 20 years in the field of risk management. It did cause a chuckle when people found out what I did. There is a certain irony that someone who manages risk professionally would take on an expedition filled with many deadly dangers.

There was also 'life admin' to be done. Cheery things like getting a will in place and setting up a power of attorney. Then sorting out direct debits, cancelling memberships, putting stops to health insurance, and advising banks that I'd be smashing my credit cards overseas.

Among all of this, I needed to set a date for this adventure to begin. And I eventually did. I announced, with some trepidation, that, on 18 October 2018 paddles were going to hit the water. It sounded good; however, I wasn't sure how I'd make this target, given all I still needed to prepare. Setting a date created a sense of urgency that cranked up my preparation and planning.

I managed to get some media coverage. It started with an article in the local paper. This led to a TV interview with the ABC (Australia Broadcasting Corporation) News filmed with me and the interviewer on kayaks on Sydney Harbour, which was fun! Then there were articles in some adventure magazines, along with a couple of podcast interviews.

The purpose of getting media exposure was to attract sponsors and donations to CARE, as well as increase my social media following. The impact, however, was limited, and getting sponsorship proved near impossible. So instead, I had to start digging into my savings to buy equipment and pay for the trip.

I hosted a fundraising event at the local sailing club. A few friends got involved, but my mate Brad Deeth was instrumental. Brad and I worked together, so our daily proximity meant he heard first-hand all the highs and lows of organising this expedition. He was an absolute gem and always knew the right thing to say when I despaired about the problems I was facing. He got what I was doing and was behind it 100 per cent, even putting on a fundraiser at work. I was so thankful for his support, as well as his friendship.

Shaw and Partners put a considerable chunk into the donation pot. They kindly named CARE Australia the charity for their annual client event. It was an event with over 1,000 guests at the Art Gallery of New South Wales, in Sydney. Earl invited me to share a little of my journey and about CARE Australia. Speaking in front of such a large crowd was slightly nerve-wracking, but well worth it. Shaw and Partners matched the funds raised on the night, taking the total to A$16,115 (Australian dollars). Earl presented me with one of those enormous novelty cheques – I'd always wanted one!

My biggest coup was Australian actor Hugh Jackman being snapped in one of my *Paddle the Nile* hoodies. That was pretty cool. He's a member at North Bondi Surf Life Saving Club, and one of his close friends who I know, forwarded the details of my trip to him. Hugh was happy to have a chat and hear more about my plans. He, and his wife Deborra-Lee Furness, donated to CARE Australia, and I gave him a hoodie in return.

Despite the progress, there were still key action items to be ticked off, such as getting the in-country teams in place. These were the people who would be joining me on the water. For the rafting section from the source in Rwanda through to the final rapids in South Sudan, I needed three experienced rafters. This was critical. Some people had approached me, but they lacked the experience.

I had advertised on adventure websites, and even contacted the Australian Army, who were potentially keen but couldn't commit because I wasn't able to categorically say when it would start or how long it would take. Other 'minor' issues, such as having the required approvals, were no closer to being resolved. It got to a point where trying to do all this remotely from Australia was proving tricky. Progress was grinding to a halt while the planned start date drew ever closer.

So, I decided to chance it and go to Africa, hoping everything could be sorted on the ground there. With much apprehension, I booked my one-way ticket to Uganda and handed in my notice at work. It was time to get packing and head to Africa for one last push to turn this seemingly impossible dream into a reality.

About a month before leaving, I received an official letter from Australia's Department of Foreign Affairs and Tourism asking me to reconsider my plans. Having been engaging with them for over a year, during which they had been nothing but supportive, even arranging meetings for me in Cairo, this came as a big surprise.

It was a jolt to open the letter and read their request, making my stomach flip and forcing me to question myself and my plans. I'm naturally fairly compliant, and to go against a government directive felt wrong. I could have really done without this!

The last thing I wanted to be seen as was that reckless fool ignoring advice, getting into trouble, and causing the government substantial costs to send in the cavalry.

However, they didn't know the level of preparation that was going into this and the detailed risk management plans I'd developed. I looked at it from their perspective and guessed it was primarily some arse-covering, so if anything did go wrong, they could say they had warned me. I had to back myself and my preparation. Their lack of support, however, meant the assistance I had been promised in getting the approvals for Egypt was no longer available. *Bollocks*. I uneasily ignored their letter, ate some chocolate and got on with things.

Come 26 September 2018, I was at the airport. My life in Sydney was packed up, I was gainfully unemployed and had nowhere to live. My excessive 57 kilograms of luggage was checked in. And as I was handed my boarding pass, I heard a familiar, 'Hello there!'

To my surprise, four friends were there to see me off, all wearing *Paddle the Nile* t-shirts. I couldn't believe my eyes. Tears rolled down my cheeks through a big, appreciative smile. We had a coffee together, final group photos, and then it was time to really say goodbye and head to departures.

I felt like a base jumper doing their first jump, having never strapped a parachute to their back – ill prepared and taking a total leap of faith with potentially dire consequences.

When I'd initially come up with this dream, I was excited. As the departure date had loomed, everyone kept asking me, 'Are you excited?' 'Excited?' Are you kidding me? Stressed? Too right. Overwhelmed and daunted? Now you're talking …

In the run-up to leaving, I repeatedly said to myself, 'Sarah, next time you feel the need for fulfillment, give yourself a good talking to, go back to bed and wait for it to pass.' I felt I'd conned myself into something I couldn't get out of.

Naturally, people thought I'd be itching to get going. Here I was, about to set off on an incredible journey following my big, bold dream. It was just that the reality of my dream was sinking in, and I was scared shitless.

I was so far out of my comfort zone I couldn't see it. There was still so much to arrange. *What have I been doing for the last two years? What was I thinking even coming up with this harebrained idea?*

There was nothing to do but suck it up and get on with it. Worst case, I reasoned, if I couldn't make it happen, I would have a holiday in Africa for a couple of months. For now, it was time to sit back and enjoy the flight, as much as I could.

CHAPTER THREE
REACHING AFRICA

Of the gladdest moment in human life, methinks,
is the departure upon a distant journey into
unknown lands.

Sir Richard Burton

Two stops and 30-something hours later, I touched down in Uganda. Despite my apprehensions, it was wonderful to be there. I went straight to Jinja, about 125 kilometres and a three-hour drive from the airport, and to Nile River Explorers (NRE). This was where I'd stayed on my first reconnaissance trip, and the familiarity gave me comfort. It was from here I hoped to find my team for the rafting sections and complete the final preparations. It felt like a massive step forward, trusting that now I'd get the momentum going again and have paddles finally hitting the water.

My plan had been to camp here in my own tent. However, after a lengthy journey, I was keen for a little more luxury. I also wasn't entirely convinced all my gear would fit in my small tent. Today didn't feel like the day to give it a shot. Luckily at the campsite they had safari tents that were big enough to stand up in, with twin beds, so I happily booked one.

I slept like a log that night and enjoyed the treat of waking up naturally — no alarm. After a shower, I made my way to the deck of the restaurant at NRE and sat with a coffee in hand overlooking the mighty Nile. I heard the monkeys chattering and watched them jumping from tree to tree. A couple of tropical birds glided through the air in graceful circles. I sat there quietly, watching the Nile meander past, listening to the wildlife, and soaking it all in. It was a view I could never tire of. It was like taking a big breath, slowly letting it out, shoulders dropping and the tension evaporating.

It began to sink in that I was actually here. Here in Africa.

After the frantic lead up, I felt relieved and utterly free. It was a liberating feeling. The pace of life had instantly slowed, and the constant distractions and buzz were gone. I cut myself some slack and had a couple of days of downtime before buckling back down to organising.

Jon Dahl, the owner of NRE, and one of the head rafting guides, Davey O'Hara (both of whom I'd spoken to before coming out) came to have a chat. With his relaxed manner, Jon gave me the much-needed confidence that I was going to be able to pull this off and he was willing to do whatever he could to help. This included giving me the accommodation at NRE for free, which was very kind. He and Davey were a wealth of knowledge and experience. Meeting them made me more at ease — even if Davey did share stories of ferocious crocodiles that made me shudder. There were other familiar faces from my last trip that made me feel at home.

After a couple of days, I met Paulo Babi, who Jon had told me was interested in being the lead rafting guide. We met at NRE, and as he approached, I was struck by his broad, warm smile. He was in his late thirties and stood about five foot nine. We sat at one of the tables overlooking the Nile. Paolo was quietly spoken but had an enthusiastic and positive disposition. We chatted, but I didn't want to press him too hard about joining the trip, so we sat and enjoyed a juice until I broached the subject.

'So, Paulo, Jon mentioned that you might be interested in joining the trip. Are you keen?' I held my breath.

'Yes, it would be good,' he replied, to my enormous relief.

Now I had my lead guide, and not just any guide — Paulo had been a rafting guide on the Nile for over two decades. He had been Uganda's top freestyle kayaker and represented his country at two world championship events.

He took part in the first descent of the Akagera River from its source in Rwanda (a section we'd be covering), led by Pete Meredith. Having someone with all this experience was reassuring. His nickname was *Mbati*, which means *duck*, coming from his ease and ability on the water. He was always eager to help and had an endless stack of 'dad jokes' ready to use as entertainment.

It was so valuable to have his first-hand experience. He even agreed to ask his fellow rafters and kayakers if there was anyone interested in joining us. I needed two more, including one to double as our safety kayaker.

While Paulo was seeking some fellow adventurers, I cracked on with getting official approvals and other tasks. There were days it went well, but plenty with no progress, even steps backwards that had me feeling like throwing in the towel (but, instead, reaching for chocolate once again). It was frustrating and stressful. I continually repeated my mantra 'control the controllables'. There was no point focusing on things outside of my control or influence — easier said than done!

I knew a hefty goal like this was never going to come easy. If it was, there'd be no sense of achievement. Things happened when they were meant to, and until then, it was a dance between *making* and *letting* it happen. One morning, on opening my email, I received a boost. Some months before leaving for Africa, I was honoured to meet with Dick Smith AC, after writing to him. He is a well-loved Australian, record-breaking adventurer, generous philanthropist, political activist and highly successful entrepreneur.

He was going to donate to the expedition. I was incredibly thankful to have this donation as it was much needed and it created a greater belief in my mission.

Even though I had more people 'in my corner', I still felt like an outsider on my one-woman crusade, but this was a familiar feeling. As an only child, and one who had been single a long time, doing things solo was my *modus operandi*. My only child status created some supportive traits and some less so. I think it helped me be self-motivated, independent and self-reliant, traits that were beneficial in pulling off this expedition.

The downside of growing up without siblings includes me being pretty selfish, shocking at compromising, and not reacting well when things don't go my way. Plus, things like going out for a tapas meal is my idea of hell. Sharing. *What? No, no I don't do that.*

I'm not always the most enthusiastic team player and generally feel comfortable taking responsibility and getting on with things, which is in part due to the way I was brought up. That was the example my mother and grandmother set. They were both very independent, single parents after less than friendly divorces, and got on with what needed to be done. So that's what I was doing here, getting on with it. However, it was times like this when a co-driver would have been appreciated.

While I may have been without a co-driver, I had plenty of support. Jon Dahl generously lent me all the rafting equipment on top of the gratis accommodation. There was Natalie Lonsdale, who was part of Hendri Coetzee's *Settle the Nile* expedition. She had become the first woman to complete a descent of the Nile from Lake Victoria.

A special showing of the film documenting the *Settle the Nile* expedition was put on at Jinja Basecamp. This was the meet and greet location for NRE rafting trips and provided great backpacker accommodation. Everyone who came along provided valuable advice. It was a fabulous evening, and I was so appreciative of the warm reception and all the support given. I felt reinvigorated by it.

After the event, someone gifted me a bunch of energy bars and gels. Nicci and Paul, the owners of Jinja Basecamp, gave me some vacuum-packed fatty meat and assisted me with some of the logistics.

Back at NRE, I met a chap called Rob Davies, a Brit who owned a shop in Jinja. His mum was visiting from the United Kingdom and staying at NRE. At the height of my angst and stress, they took me to a local restaurant for dinner. To be out with them, sharing stories and chatting about everything that wasn't *Paddle the Nile* was a lovely distraction, while enjoying a delicious rack of ribs and chips.

Gradually, things started falling into place. The next substantial step was getting my team together – the 'Dream Team'. Paulo had finally recruited two of his fellow rafting guides to join our expedition. The first I met was Koa. I was struck by his beautiful wide smile and good looks. He was athletically built and radiated confidence. Koa was a former kayaking student of Paulo's and a competitive white water kayaker, as well as rafting guide. He would be our safety kayaker when needed.

Then there was Peter, Paulo's half-brother. Peter was an international rafting guide and another very handy kayaker. He was known as 'Little Peter', as he was only about five foot four and could get away with being a teenager despite being in his thirties. This was matched by a crazy sense of humour that was set to have me in stitches regularly. What I didn't know then was how calm and extremely capable he would be in the life-threatening situations ahead of us.

Having the team complete was an enormous relief and allowed me to sleep a little better. Things were looking up!

Before setting off, I decided to get some rafting practice in. Jinja is known as Uganda's adventure capital and was the perfect spot for it. I'd had a few cracks at rafting over the years, but I thought getting a fresh feel for it would be sensible.

I'd done several courses before arriving in Africa, including the Swift Water Rescue Technician course, which involved learning how to perform rescues in white water individually and in teams, as well as understanding the dangers and risks of fast-moving water. Basically, it was three days of having water forced into every orifice. I wanted to make sure if there was an issue in the rapids, I wouldn't be completely clueless. It was a valuable course but brought home just how dangerous rapids can be.

So, it was time to get out there on the white water and hope I enjoyed it, otherwise large sections of this expedition were going to be deeply unpleasant. I was nervous at the thought of facing one of my fears: these massive rapids.

Years back, I'd had a near-drowning experience competing in powerful surf at the Australian Surf Life Saving titles up on the Gold Coast in Queensland. It was the swim race, and while trying to get out through surf, I was pummelled by a set of waves and took what I thought was going to be my last breath as a colossal wave loomed over me. I managed to finish the race, hyperventilating, but the experience had a lasting impact; I really struggle to hold my breath underwater. You potentially need this skill in the rapids if you come out of the raft, because you can get pinned underwater by the powerful currents and turbulence.

I'd also researched how to stay calm in pressure situations and to not panic. I discovered that, physiologically and mentally, we react differently depending on whether we view a situation as either a threat or challenge. If you see it as a threat, you're on the back foot, you don't want to be there, blood leaves the periphery, reducing anaerobic power; your thinking gets fuzzy, and your decision-making skills take a dive.

When you look at something as a challenge, the blood pumps to your muscles, you're on the attack, you're focused and in a positive emotional state. It facilitates better decision-making and effective cognitive functioning. You believe you can meet the demands of the situation.

Now was my chance to try and put it into practice.

Heading into this rafting trip, I reframed the situation from 'threat' to 'challenge'. I kept thinking about how it was going to be fun. I was *choosing* to be here and *choosing* to enjoy it.

After an on-land safety briefing, followed by a short trip to the 'put-in', we got on the water. Paulo was our guide, and we began with a few drills on the 'flatwater'. Then we were straight into it. The first was a Grade V* rapid with an eight-foot drop. After Paulo's instruction, 'Get down!' we sat inside the bottom of the raft and hung on. We dropped down and rodeoed our way through the rapids. *This is awesome!*

There were lulls and flatwater in between the sections of white water where we drifted along, caught our breath and let the adrenaline levels drop. Paulo entertained us with his repertoire of jokes while we meandered, taking in the lush scenery, watching the river birds and catching sight of the odd monkey. A couple of times we jumped in for a swim before psyching ourselves up for the next section.

After plenty of immense rapids, it was time to get out and enjoy a well-earned BBQ. I smiled *all* the way down and loved every minute. It had been a day of exhilarating adrenaline-fuelled fun! I was relieved that I had enjoyed it, and the approach of treating it as a challenge worked. It was a good confidence boost, and when my head hit the pillow that night, I was exhausted and went to sleep smiling.

---

*Rapids are rated depending on their difficulty and danger from Class I (the easiest) to Class VI (the most dangerous and difficult).

This was nice because I was stressing about everything else.

A big-ticket item still to sort out was getting approvals to complete my trip. For some countries such as Uganda, it was as simple as getting a tourist visa, which I already had. For others, it required specific government-backed letters of support, which were difficult to obtain. It was an undocumented process that required endless researching, emailing and phone calls.

For Rwanda, the tourism section of the Rwandan Development Board (RDB) needed to give me the permissions. For Tanzania, a trip to the Tanzanian Embassy in Kampala, Uganda's bustling capital, confirmed my tourist visa was adequate. While in Kampala, I went to the South Sudanese Embassy and got the visa application form to begin securing the required approvals.

The RDB initially had been super responsive to my emails, but as I got closer, all I heard was crickets. So, I just adopted the African way of assuming that it would all come together. *Keep going until someone tells me I can't.* This 'wing it' mentality was foreign to me and added to the tension.

A week before heading to Rwanda, I received a reply from the RDB to my emails asking me to arrange a 'fixer' in Rwanda. A fixer is someone who knows the local lay of the land, has contacts to arrange logistics, is someone the authorities are familiar with, and can deal with any issues that come up. A good fixer is worth their weight in gold. They recommended a wonderful English woman, Joanna Nicholas, from Rwandan Adventures, who specialise in adventure holidays in Rwanda.

She was a tour operator who'd lived there for years, so she was able to help with the logistics to get us to the start. She also arranged medivac insurance for the guys and me. I already had multiple insurance policies, but this gave me additional peace of mind. It was fantastic to have Joanna on board, but I really didn't expect to need her much once we were on our way. Oh, how wrong I was! Another vital part of the planning was food. This first section was going to take us to some remote areas with limited food resupply points. Having enough sustenance was crucial. Otherwise, I was likely to have a mutiny on my hands.

There had to be enough food for four people for three weeks. It needed to be food that wouldn't go off, didn't take up much space or require much cooking, as well as providing adequate daily calories and nutrition. And it needed to be available in Uganda. This was unexpectedly hard. Using a trusty spreadsheet and the website *Calorie King*, I worked out the supplies we needed. This included oats, Nutella, peanut butter, pasta, rice, couscous, raisins, protein powder (now that was challenging to find, but I managed to discover some in Kampala), a few tins of beans, biscuits, noodles, oil, tea, coffee, Coffee Mate (coffee whitener), tins of corned beef, energy bars, cup-of-soups, sugar, plus washing up liquid and sponges.

I moved from a tent to one of the larger rooms, which quickly started to resemble a supermarket. We also needed plastic bowls to eat out of and basic cutlery to eat with. I gathered my team together for a couple of meetings, and prior to going food shopping, I asked the guys if they had any dietary restrictions. No, they were all good. Paulo assured me my food choices were fine. But, even with my spreadsheet predicting we were going to need about 80 kilograms of food, I was still concerned as to whether we had the right food and enough of it.

At another team meeting, I asked the guys about their medical backgrounds. 'I was dropped on my head as a kid,' Peter said, smiling.

'Any lasting issues?' I asked, not sure whether he was being serious.

He chuckled and said, 'No!'

I checked if they had passports or the necessary travel documents. We were going to need to get a travel document for Koa, who had never left Uganda. I then asked if there was anything else they might need or concerns they had. Silence.

Did they have any contacts with cars I could hire to get us to the start? Did they know anyone with a tent we could borrow for them, as I had not been able to find one in Kampala to buy? Possibly.

I had to gently prod them to get replies, which they seemed slightly reluctant to share. Frank and direct discussions weren't their way. Rather than push them too much, I suggested they think about it and come back to me. This included agreeing to how much I was going to pay them. Koa seemed to be their spokesperson, and when we reconvened, he shared their answers to my questions and raised any concerns. It meant things took a little longer to get organised, but we got there.

Before heading off, I needed to fully test all my shiny new equipment. I was Miss 'All the Gear and No Idea'. Seriously. I'd done some testing prior to leaving Sydney to ensure everything worked, but I needed to be completely familiar with it all before heading into remote Africa. Our lives were going to depend on some of it.

There was getting the stove going, which was way tougher than it should have been, trialling the water filter, getting highly proficient with the GPS and double-checking the satellite phone and the solar equipment. The route, broken into 50-kilometre stretches, had to be mapped out and loaded into the GPS, which was a long and painful process.

I felt a bit of a twat with all this new gear, along with a brand-new PFD (personal floatation device, aka lifejacket), throw bag, helmet and clothing. It was all necessary but felt excessive in a country where the majority live in basic conditions. Many don't have access to electricity, child malnutrition is an issue, and the education and healthcare system is lagging significantly, and sanitation is in need of improvement.

Over 40 per cent of the population live on US$1.90 (US dollars) or less per day[2]. This put things in perspective. Many are living a hand-to-mouth existence to meet basic physiological needs of food, shelter, clothing, and health care.

When it comes to health, according to World Health Organisation (WHO) data published in 2018, life expectancy in Uganda is 60.2 years for men, 64.8 years for women — ranking Uganda 159th in the World Life Expectancy. Yet the population growth is large, with women, on average, each having a whopping 5.6 births.

Shortly before heading off, I had fun talking about my plans to a group of school kids from an international school in Kampala who were staying at Jinja Basecamp. I was inundated with questions, including how I'd deal with crocodiles, what would happen if my paddle broke? And why wouldn't I just fly?

But one girl blew me away with her insightful comment, 'To do something like this, you need self-belief.' At ten years old, she got it. I felt in need of more of that self-belief. Even with everything in place — the team, the food, the equipment, and our plan — there were still many moments of self-doubt.

One positive of self-doubt was the level of preparation it drove and the lack of complacency it created. I had to acknowledge that but not let the worry take over. It was time to focus on all the planning that had been done, the endless research, the team with me, the people here in Uganda at the end of the phone if needed and be confident that we'd deal with anything that came up along the way.

So, I kept taking action, working through the to-do lists and this distraction took some power away from the doubts. The reality, however, was that I was edging ever closer to paddles hitting the water. *This expedition might actually happen.*

PART 2

The Source to Lake Victoria

Hungry hippos and an unexpected detour

CHAPTER FOUR
TO THE SOURCE + DAY 1

No man is more unhappy than he who never faces adversity. For he is not permitted to prove himself.

Seneca

Three and a half weeks after touching down in Uganda, we were set to make our way to Rwanda. I was stoked to have progressed so far and so quickly. The guys had found a people carrier and driver to take us and all our gear to Kigali, the capital of Rwanda. On top of the food, electrical and communications equipment, clothing, first aid kits and medical supplies, and camping gear, there was the raft, the frame to go on it, oars and paddles. I'd hired a creek boat (a type of whitewater kayak) and paddles. This would be used by Koa to scout the river ahead to find us a safe route through the rapids.

Early on 22 October 2018, we loaded up our copious amount of gear and set off to Kigali. It was happening! I was reservedly excited. This was a tremendous leap forward, but there were still permits to obtain for this section. I sat in the back of the car, pulled out my phone, put my headphones on, played some tunes and sunk into my seat. Back in May, I'd plucked a start date of 18 October 2018 out of the air. To be pretty much on target was as surprising as it was gratifying.

The first couple of hours all went well. I watched the country blurring past us as we made our way to the border — its rich red earth reminded me of home — my mind occasionally doing a check of whether I had everything. The guys chatted among themselves and with the driver and his co-driver.

After about two hours, the driver pulled over. The car was overheating. They poured water into the radiator and steam gushed out. This didn't bode well. I optimistically reasoned that the addition of water had solved the issue.

But no. After another 20 minutes we stopped again, and more water was added. This was repeated until we made it to a town and performed a pit stop at a garage to see what could be done. This turned out to be the start of one car problem after another.

We continued on our way with our driver determined to make it so he would get paid. I was quite Zen about it, confident that we'd get there, somehow. We stopped again and the driver opened the boot. I then heard glass breaking.

What have we got that's glass?

With a sharp intake of breath, it suddenly dawned on me. My relaxed attitude evaporated, replaced with, shall we say, heated dismay.

I realised it was the pot of very special glue needed to patch the raft if it was ripped, for example, on some rocks. I had been given a stern lecture by one of the senior rafting guides on the level of care the glue needed. 'Don't let it get too hot, too cold or leave it in the sun. Treat it like a baby,' I was instructed. Now this precious glue was seeping into the tarmac. I tried not to lose my cool; it was an accident after all. My response went something along the lines of, 'The glue! I don't *FUCKING* believe it!' accompanied by a less than friendly glance at the driver.

I didn't say anything more; I sat back in my seat and took a few deep breaths. I thought this was remarkably controlled considering I was going to have to replace this glue somehow.

My response, however, didn't go unnoticed — no one made a sound or uttered a word for well over an hour once we were back on the road. According to Peter, the driver was terrified of me. This was not my intention.

After a final attempt to get the car to limp its way to Kigali, the driver finally waved the proverbial white flag and admitted that his car was not going to make it. He called a friend and a long wait ensued for another vehicle to come and meet us.

We were met by driver number two in car number two. All the gear was unloaded and reloaded, which took about an hour, during which a large crowd gathered to watch these strange goings on with a bunch of equipment that was unfamiliar to them. Then, somewhat behind schedule, we were off again. This car worked perfectly.

Under the cover of darkness, we reached the border between Uganda and Rwanda. We queued to get our stamps for leaving Uganda before joining the next queue to get our stamps and entry into Rwanda. In the background, our driver skilfully negotiated with officials to let us proceed without the standard full inspection of our gear, which saved time. We arrived in Kigali around midnight. The ten-hour, 590-kilometre journey had taken us 16 hours.

I'd booked us into a hostel for the night, where we were due to meet another driver and car the following day. Happily, we didn't have to unload/reload that night. We were shown to our rooms and collapsed, exhausted.

We stayed two nights and a day in Kigali, which gave me time for final preparations and to obtain the permits to allow us to go to the source of the Nile — our starting point. *Fingers crossed.*

I woke up the following day to find texts from Peter and Koa looking for guidance on what to do. *Really?* It felt like a 'Mum, we're up, what shall we do?' moment. I met them for breakfast and told them the plans, which were me running around like a headless chicken (quicker to go solo), while they chilled once they'd unloaded the car. Me making sure they were fed and watered. Them looking bored. I loved those guys to pieces, but it did feel like having three teenage kids at times.

Together we went and found somewhere to buy a large gas cylinder to be used with a burner stove. It simply screwed onto the cylinder and turned it into a single-stove gas burner to cook on. This was Peter's and much easier to use than the stove I had with me.

I got a *boda boda** into town and exchanged some Tanzanian money, got some maps, bought a toothbrush for Koa, who had forgotten his, sorted a Rwandan SIM card, had an interview with a local newspaper and then went to the crucial meeting with the tourism section of the Rwandan Development Board at 4pm.

We were due to head to the source early the next morning and needed the permits — not cutting it fine at all. It was a highly productive meeting, and they were super supportive. Not only did I get the required permits, but I was also given a signed letter from the Head of Tourism for the heads of each of the four provinces we would be going through, to advise them what we were doing and request their support. Letters like that, with official stamps, are extremely useful. I returned to the hostel at around 6pm, and before I could sit down, Koa asked where the driver was and started questioning me. 'Well, perhaps you should chase him up,' he said. *Easy there, tiger.*

While I appreciated his interest in ensuring we had a car, having five minutes to breathe after running around all day would have been nice. That night, driver number three came to our hostel, and we loaded up our gear. I was a little apprehensive that the gear was going to be safe and secure. He assured me, however, that where he was staying there was nothing to worry about and he was driving straight there. *Okay. So, this is it, we're ready to go?* I popped a sleeping pill to avoid another sleepless night.

The following morning, I woke after a wonderful sleep to a message from the driver. 'I've been arrested and I'm at the police station with the car.' *You must be kidding me!* I couldn't believe what I was reading. *How on earth did he manage to get arrested?* He was going to drive to his accommodation and sleep. I frantically messaged my fixer Joanna, who'd arranged this car.

'Meet me at the police station,' she said, giving me directions.

We packed our gear that wasn't already in the car and took a taxi to meet her. On our way over, Joanna messaged to say that we'd take the car with all our gear, and she'd arrange another driver, or I'd drive. The flaw in this cunning plan was that the arresting police officer, who had long clocked off his shift, had taken the car keys with him. *What? Why? Why wouldn't you leave them at the station? TIA — This is Africa.*

---

* Boda bodas, generally just referred to as bodas, are motorbike taxis. While motorbike taxis are found throughout Africa, it is in East African that the term boda boda is used.

Joanna was fantastic at relentlessly prodding, prompting and pushing the police to sort this out. The driver had always been reliable, and she was disappointed with him, as well as angry. We finally saw the sheepish-looking driver, and we were told that he'd run a red light, been pulled over by the cops and then tried to deny it all and got lippy with them. *Muppet.*

After three and a half hours, we had the keys, and Joanna had sourced driver number four for us. We were finally off, and I was feeling relieved while at the same time slightly concerned as to what was going to go wrong next.

I was pleasantly distracted by the breathtaking drive through the glorious Rwandan countryside. It's known as 'the land of a thousand hills', and they're not wrong. There was an endless range of undulating, bountiful hills, many etched with terraces filled with crops.

The roads winding their way around these continuous hills were enough to prompt travel sickness in Peter and Koa. *Ah, travelling with kids.* Fortunately I was armed with travel calm pills, which sorted them out.

Just as I was relaxing, letting myself be hypnotised by the movement of the car and scenery, we came to an unexpected stop. The spare tyre under the car had fallen off and then the boot wouldn't shut. I nearly lost the top of my thumb trying to fix the latter. They were both secured with ropes and some ingenuity by the guys.

We continued alongside Lake Kivu, one of the African Great Lakes, which lies on the border of the Democratic Republic of the Congo and Rwanda. At its maximum, it's 85 kilometres long and 45 kilometres wide, making it Africa's sixth largest lake. It is spectacular with the flourishing hills meeting the blue waters as far as the eye could see. I longed to get on the water and paddle on this impressive lake. This was going to be a theme for the trip — glimpses of places that would warrant a holiday on their own.

We pressed on, and after a four-hour drive, we were at the meeting point with our guides to take us into the Nyungwe National Park. This is one of the oldest rainforests in Africa and home to the source of the Nile, or at least the one I had selected.

It's also home to a population of chimpanzees and many other primate species, making it a popular spot for trail walking. It's teaming with fauna and flora — over 1,000 plant species, 300 bird species, 120 butterfly species and 75 known mammal species[3]. The forest was dense; its tall trees blocking out much of the sunlight. It was an enjoyable, easy undulating walk along the narrow path with a simple focus — get to the source, which created a feeling of excited anticipation.

After 45 minutes of walking, we turned a corner and suddenly there it was. A green sign with yellow writing denoted the muddy pool below as being the furthest source of the Nile. A picture of this sign had been central to my vision board during the two years of planning. The tears welled and rolled down my cheeks. It had seemed such a far-off, impossible goal for so long. The tears were quickly replaced with a beaming smile and an enormous sense of happiness and gratitude.

There has been a fair bit of debate around where the source of the Nile is found. Some say Uganda, some Rwanda, and others Burundi. I went for a source in Rwanda, which was discovered by the *Ascend the Nile* expedition in 2006. They determined that the headwaters of the Rukarara River, deep in Nyungwe Forest, are the source of the Nile.

We pulled out our two flags — mine was the Australian flag, Paulo's Ugandan — and took heaps of photos to record this momentous occasion before making our way back to the car, me with a huge smile on my face and filled with a sense of satisfaction. As we approached the car, I had a gut feeling that things weren't going to go to plan. I hoped I was wrong. We said goodbye to our fabulous guides and set off to our lodge for the night.

About 40 minutes into our two-and-a-half-hour journey along a bumpy, narrow dirt road, we got a flat. The guys set to work changing the tyre. This was made testing by a faulty jack. They exercised some creativity by using rocks and wooden blocks to jack the car and finally the tyre was changed.

The light had faded, and we were under the cover of darkness, in the middle of nowhere, with a small crowd huddled close watching this spectacle. I kept hearing the word *'mzungu'* being uttered. This is a word any white person visiting east Africa and beyond will hear repeatedly. Literally translated, it means 'someone who roams around' and was used to describe the eighteenth-century European explorers because, to the locals, they seemed to move around aimlessly. Now the term is used in a friendly way to describe someone with white skin, or more generally, any foreigner. It was a word I heard ringing out constantly as I made my way through Rwanda, Tanzania and Uganda.

Finally, with the stars now out, we were on our way again. Sadly though, not for long. The spare tyre was a dud. *You must be joking!*

I made the call that we'd turn around in the hope that we could slowly limp our way back to Gisovu and the tea plantation there. Or at least get close. But nope — that was wishful thinking. Within ten minutes we were down to the rim. And Koa started to feel sick. *Kids!*

I called Joanna, who spoke to people at the Gisovu Tea Plantation. They were about 40 minutes away by car. Justin, one of the owners of the plantation, was our saviour. He thoughtfully deployed his driver to pick us up while we employed two local guys to act as security for our car for the night. We took some essentials and headed off.

On arrival, Justin gave us a warm welcome and arranged for us to be fed and then shown to some rooms. *What a legend.* I went to bed feeling very grateful, having made it to the source and to have been looked after so charitably. Yes, things hadn't gone to plan once again, but these unexpected turns of events, while at times frustrating, brought a sense of satisfaction at having found a way around them as a team.

The next morning, we were given breakfast, and all was looking positive until the driver rocked up and broke some bad news, 'Sarah, the engine keeps cutting out.' I sighed in dismay. *Really, we don't get one day without car problems?*

'The good news is one of the tyres is now fixed, so we have four good tyres!' he said with a smile. 'These cars sometimes need a long time to warm up. Let's leave it running, and I'm sure it will be fine.' After letting the engine run, it seemed okay, so we decided to chance it and set off, hoping that with no spare we were going to make it.

Koa said, 'Sarah, it's going to be fine.' He seemed to have a strong gut instinct, so his words gave me some comfort.

Joanna, who was worried that we might break down again, sent a backup car to be on standby, just in case. I was blessed to have her support throughout all of this!

All these car issues felt like the final test before hitting the water. They were obstacles to face up to and overcome to prove that I really wanted to reach the start of this expedition. As Marcus Aurelius said, 'The impediment to action advances action. What stands in the way becomes the way.' One thing was for sure, 'the way' was forever changing and never seemed to follow 'the plan'.

Thankfully, Koa's prediction was right, and we reached Kitabi, marking the end of significant car problems.

We got to Kitabi Eco Lodge with time to kill. The lodge sat on Mount Kitabi, which was surrounded by the endless hills and terraced farms. The accommodation was in small, simple thatched huts. Sitting up at 2,400 metres above sea level, it was cold, but the views were a breathtaking distraction. It was wonderful to pause and take it all in.

It was also time to tell the team about Dave.

In May 2017, I undertook Hostile Environment Awareness Training (HEAT). This was a condensed version of the course that involved Dave running through the hostile situations I could face on my journey and how to deal with them. Cheery things like kidnapping and being shot at. He gave a thorough briefing of the countries I was set to travel through, highlighting the key risks. Plus, there was general travel security and safety focused on the relevant countries and cultures.

It helped ensure my risk management plan was thorough. This plan involved identifying what could go wrong and worst case, broken down into five categories of risk.

There were the health risks — the injuries that could occur and all the diseases and illnesses I could get. There were the environmental risks — extreme heat, cold, wind, storms, rapids.

There were the animal risks — the aggressive beasts, such as hippos and crocs, the many venomous creatures, parasites that dig into your skin, and everything in between. Then there were the people risks — such as being refused entry to countries, unlawful arrest through to attacks and kidnapping. Finally, there were equipment risks — identifying the critical equipment.

I estimated the likelihood of each risk eventuating along with the impact. From that, there was an overall 'risk rating'. Basically, most things rated 'significant', meaning a potential unhappy ending. The next step was to see what I could do to either minimise the likelihood or impact of each risk, such as getting vaccinations, having adequate insurance, and/or having an action plan, skills or having backup equipment in place to deal with situations.

However, there were still gaps in the plans, which I wasn't comfortable with. One was not having detailed intelligence on the areas I was travelling through, and the other knowing how to deal with crisis situations. It was going to be nigh on impossible to come up with appropriate protocols for my crisis team back home to follow if, say, I was to get arrested or kidnapped. It would also put unfair responsibility and stress on them.

I therefore decided that I needed professional help, and got in touch with Dave, who I ended up engaging via the company where he worked. I would check in with Dave daily with pre-agreed code names and using a 1 to 5 rating (one being the best, five the worst) to advise on the status of security, health, mental state, communications and supplies. This quick and simple update would be accompanied by my plan for the day, such as the distance we planned to cover. He would provide intel reports on these sections, which were incredibly detailed.

Dave was on hand to manage any crises that came up and direct my crisis team as needed. The team comprised of my friends Sue, Daniel, James and Nina. In addition, Sue and Daniel had shared financial power of attorney. They all had each other's contact details and were ready to leap into action if needed. I was, and still am, indebted to them for stepping up to this role. Dave went far beyond his remit. He was there to discuss key decisions, and having him on my team gave me so much confidence. I couldn't have done the trip without him. We shared a slightly dark sense of humour and he made me laugh when I needed it the most.

With the guys, I didn't go into a lot of detail about Dave and what he was doing; it wasn't necessary. I made sure they would contact him in an emergency and showed them how to use the satellite phone and GPS.

With the briefing done, it was time for dinner.

We checked out the menu, which included rabbit. Peter had never seen that on a menu before. 'Rabbit? As in the animal? No way!' He was shocked. It didn't prompt enough curiosity to order it. It also turned out that Koa was a fussy eater. Apparently, he couldn't have cold drinks because it 'hurt his heart'. *You what?*

This seeming delicateness was at odds with the outward mental and physical strength that he presented. This juxtaposition was compounded by the list of foods he couldn't or wouldn't eat — no dairy, no biscuits or sweets, and little or no chicken. So, when I had asked before leaving if anyone had any dietary restrictions, then would have been the ideal time to let me know!

Getting information and feedback out of the guys was like pulling teeth at times. And too often the answer I got was what they thought I wanted to hear, not necessarily the truth. It was all about learning different cultures, and I'd been warned that Ugandans were known for suffering in silence and not speaking up.

After dinner, we huddled around a big open fire and sipped tea. The drafty huts and our cold beds lacked appeal at that point, but before we knew it, it was time to turn in.

The guys walked into their hut containing three beds. Peter was the first to pull back his blankets and find a hot balloon-type thing. He freaked out, wondering what it was.

Then Koa and Paulo pulled back their blankets to find the same 'surprise' — hot water bottles were something none of the guys had seen before. I was filled with joy when I discovered mine. It was time to try and get some sleep. Tomorrow was set to be a big day with paddles finally hitting the water.

We woke early and had a simple breakfast before the driver came to pick us up. We drove (without issues!) to the put-in site. On the way, I was apprehensive and filled with nagging worries ...

- Was there vital gear I didn't have?

- Did we have enough food?

- Was all the gear going to work?

- Was I going to be able to hack it?

- What was the camping going to be like?
  (I'd never really camped in the wilderness before.)

- What was ahead of us?

With so many risks, it was inevitable that there would be more challenges, and things wouldn't go to plan.

After a couple of hours of driving, I suddenly got a glimpse of the river. Seeing it made me happy, and to my surprise, my concerns dissolved and were smothered by elation. *This is really happening!*

It was time to set up, which involved unloading everything, pumping up the raft, attaching the frame and oars and then loading the gear and tying it down. 'The gear' included three barrels of food, another barrel with all the electrical gear (solar chargers, cameras, powerbanks, laptop), an extensive first aid kit and medical supplies, spare oars and paddles, clothing, water filter, jerry cans and camping gear.

We pulled over next to the river, which was about 20 metres wide with short, steep grassy banks and a metal bridge spanning the muddy water. This wasn't the sort of thing the locals saw here, and a crowd quickly grew around us and across the nearby bridge. It was *Umuganda* day. The word means 'a coming together for a common purpose to achieve an outcome'.

It's why Rwanda is so incredibly clean. On the fourth Saturday morning each month, the traffic stops, stores are closed, and everyone pitches in to clean the streets, dig drainage ditches, build schools and do their part to make Rwanda better.

There wasn't much cleaning up being done here — they said watching us counted for *Umuganda* day. I thought that was a stretch, but it was cool having this audience who was clearly transfixed by the strange spectacle unfolding in front of them. After an hour or so, the raft was set. It was time for us to put our trust in each other and get underway.

At 11.32am on 27 October 2018, paddles finally hit the water. Suddenly, all the stress, the two years of work, reconnaissance trips, slow progress, the problems and obstacles, were behind me. The leap of faith had paid off. I couldn't stop smiling.

I am ACTUALLY here.

This mighty dream that had seemed completely unattainable at times had become a reality — my reality. Strange as it may sound, if we were only on the water for a day, it was enough.

Someone who knew what would be involved once said to me, 'Sarah, just making it to the start will be a huge achievement.'

The sense of achievement of making it to this point was enormous. That was what this trip was all about and what I had been striving for. The journey, the adventure and the challenge had long taken over from the ego-led 'first'. My 'why' had been tested repeatedly, and it felt like I'd had to prove how much I wanted to do this. The path to this point had been filled with ups and downs and detours away from my precious project plans. I'd had to let go of trying to control everything and, like the river, go with the flow.

Despite all the obstacles and detours, it had been a blast. There had been so much satisfaction from overcoming the speed humps to get here. There's a quote from Frank A Clark, 'If you find a path with no obstacles, it probably doesn't lead anywhere.'

And it won't be as exciting or rewarding.

We continued on our way with Koa in the kayak, Paulo on the oars, and Peter and me upfront on either side of the raft, taking photos and filming this auspicious occasion before picking up the paddles.

Many of the locals weren't ready to say goodbye. As we started making our way down the river, we had people running along the river, shouting, laughing and waving. The buzz of excitement continued. The river gave us a gentle introduction, moving smoothly and calmly. It was brown, full of silt and mud, and fairly narrow. Gradually, the banks moved further away as the river slowly widened, and we got into our rhythm.

The river set the pace, and the scene slowly unfolded in front of us. Travelling by river is a special way to see a country, from a perspective few are fortunate to enjoy. On this trip it was going to get us into remote regions.

Saying that, in Rwanda, you feel remote but are never far away from people. The country is about 26,338 square kilometres (a bit smaller than Belgium) with a population of around 13 million[4], making it very densely populated. Everyone was so friendly, warm and kind, while simultaneously fairly bemused by what we were doing.

Rwanda is probably one of the most progressive countries in Africa. They have endeavoured to make it an easy place to do business, improve healthcare (life expectancy increased ten years in the space of a decade). It's been cleaned up (there is no littering, and plastic bags are banned), poverty has been reduced, and gender equality improved. They have the highest representation of women in government at over 60 per cent[5] and are ranked 7th in the 2021 Gender Gap report. Australia ranked a disappointing 50th[6].

The landscapes are varied, and they have worked hard to attract tourism. There's plenty to see. You have the large national parks with walks and treks on offer, including gorilla tracking in the Volcanoes National Park. There's the Akagera National Park with game drives on offer. In the west, there's the beautiful Lake Kivu, which we'd travelled past. Being a relatively small country, it's easy to get around. I recommend it as a destination to pop on your bucket list. With so much to do and see, I'd love to come back here.

It was nearing dark by the time we got off the river, which was not the plan. I wanted to find a spot to camp about an hour before the sunset, to give us time to set up and make dinner.

However, finding a decent spot without heaps of people proved tricky. Eventually we found a suitable location, secured the raft and unloaded what we needed. Tents were put up in the dark, and it was a quick pasta and pesto dinner before retreating into my little tent. *Day one - done!*

CHAPTER FIVE
DAYS 2-7

You gain strength, courage and confidence by every experience in which you really stop to look fear in the face.

Eleanor Roosevelt

We made good progress along the Rukarara River, then the Mwogo before joining the Nyabarongo, three rivers that feed into the Nile. As we made our way further, the river slowly widened, up to 200 metres in some areas. The hills sometimes came all the way down to the river's edge, disappearing into the brown water. Other times, there would be a flat stretch of land at the bottom of the hills that led to the riverbank, which at most was a metre high. The sky was blue, dappled with the odd small cloud. The sun made for warm weather.

There was work to be done. The river was very low in places, resulting in the raft grounding, so I would jump out with the person with me upfront and push the raft back into deeper water.

I also had my first crack on the oars, which was hard work! I had an all-new respect for the guys doing this for up to three hours at a time. When using the heavy wooden oars, you either had to sit or stand facing the direction you were going and forward paddle. If you were standing, you moved the oars in a circular motion with each oar at the opposite point of the circle.

At the same time, you swayed from side to side in a rhythmic way to help move the oars. The guys made it look effortless and rhythmical. How, I do not know. There was nothing effortless or rhythmical about my efforts. We reached a reservoir ahead of the Nyabarongo Hydroelectric Power Station. The water flow slowed as the river turned into a lake, making it laborious work with the sun beating down.

I was still getting used to using the GPS in this environment; there were a few alternative routes as we made our way. With time pressing on us to make it to the dam, and the guys not wanting to row any further than necessary in the dead water, I had to get the directions right. We were all relieved when the wall blocking our path came into view.

This power station and dam wasn't on the GPS or any maps I had. Luckily, I'd had a heads up. Steve Venton of Kingfisher Journeys in Rwanda was one of many people who'd contacted me prior to leaving Australia after hearing my plans. He gave me valuable information and advice. He also introduced me to Dan Folta, who lives in Rwanda and warned me about this dam. If he hadn't, we would have received a nasty surprise reaching it, because you needed a car to get around it. At the dam the river is rerouted through a tunnel under the mountain, and it was approximately a five-kilometre detour to get back to the water.

Not only did Dan give me lots of valuable advice for the section, but he also introduced me to a guy called Jean, who managed the power station. On approaching the dam wall, I called Jean. He graciously sent a car to get us and take us to the rooms used by staff. The kindness of strangers throughout the trip blew me away.

It was a long and painful process to unload the raft, deflate it, carry the gear up an awkward bank, over a wall and to the waiting car. Then, after a short drive, we arrived at our refuge for the night tired and unloaded what we needed. We were all tired and a bit cranky, Koa in particular.

I pulled out some pasta, because it was quick to cook. But no, they wanted rice, which was going to take so much longer and therefore made no sense to me. I was 'hangry' and wanted to minimise the time it took to get food to my stomach. However, the guys had worked hard, and I wasn't about to deny them.

While cooking, I left the pan briefly to grab something. Even though the food didn't burn during this time, this didn't meet Peter's approval. 'As the woman cooking, you don't leave it until it is ready,' he said.

My eyes widened and jaw dropped. I was momentarily speechless and took a deep breath. Now was not the time for a gender equality conversation, so I pointed out that we were a team, and he was welcome to help.

We stayed in one of the spare rooms, with Paulo on a bed, Koa and Peter sharing a double mattress, and me on my sleeping mat on the floor. I wanted to make sure the guys had a good night's sleep. But I don't think any of us slept very well. It was cold. We were all in very unfamiliar territory. I was still getting used to my sleeping mat and sleeping in a room with others. There was a lot I needed to adjust to.

The next day, the mood in the team was still low. The car took us down to the river. The dam was switched off, which meant the water levels were super low, but they 'turned the tap on', so the river filled up enough for us to put-in at the closest and most convenient point. The mood slowly improved as we made our way downriver, chatting as we went. Most of the time the guys talked in Luganda, unless they were talking to me.

Uganda is a multilingual country with over 40 languages grouped into three main language families: Bantu, Central Sudanic, and Nilotic. English is one official language, left over from the colonial days. Another is Swahili, spoken in many eastern and southern African countries[7]. Not understanding what they were saying suited me, most of the time.

During the planning, it dawned on me that I would be with people pretty much 24/7 on this expedition. That filled me with horror, and I wasn't sure how I'd cope. I am someone who needs my own time and space. It's my safe place. When the guys chatted among themselves, I kind of felt like I was on my own, in a good way. It did make it a tiny bit lonely at times, but I happily took that over having to talk all the time or getting dragged into any minor bickering between them.

I asked the guys about Uganda, its politics and what it was like growing up there. One anecdote made me laugh. It used to be the case that kids couldn't go to school until they could reach their hand over the top of their head and touch the opposite ear. The visual of these cute little kids desperately trying to touch their ears cracked me up.

Some aspects of growing up were less humorous, as Peter explained. The boys get circumcised, but not usually until they are teenagers. The circumcision ceremony is a time-honoured rite of passage for all boys. Circumcisions takes place every two years, on the even year. The process starts months before, when the boys are selected. Then during the ceremony, the villagers come together and celebrate for days ahead of the ritual itself.

I arrived in Uganda in the season for circumcisions and would regularly see groups of locals in a procession, singing and chanting as part of this ceremony. Then comes the day for circumcision. The boys line up, naked, in front of the village, and one by one they have their foreskin removed. The implements used vary; usually, it's a knife. They are expected not to flinch, let alone cry, or they will bring shame on themselves and their family. *They breed 'em tough here!*

Far more shocking are the child sacrifices that still take place in Uganda. While not widespread, it continues, driven by the belief that the blood of the young is a powerful ingredient for potions and spells concocted by witch doctors. Witch doctors search for children without marks. To keep their kids safe, many parents pierce their children's ears or get their boys circumcised early to protect them. A friend was considering getting her daughter's ears pierced for this very reason[8].

Locally in Jinja, I was told that when new buildings — particularly schools or churches — are built, a child is sometimes sacrificed and buried below the foundations. It seems hard to believe that this goes on. However, the practice is far less common than it used to be. The Ugandan Government has legislated to protect against child sacrifice, and there are charities, organisations and people trying to protect children and prevent these acts taking place.

A long way from all of this, we continued to make our way along the river, passing under a few old bridges. The guys seemed excited each time a bridge came into view. I didn't get it, but then realised where I lived, bridges were commonplace. London, my hometown for 15 years prior to moving to Australia, is home to 35 bridges across the Thames[9]. By my reckoning, there'd be less than 20 along the entire 6,693 kilometres of the Nile, with only four of them in Uganda.

We approached one, which looked more like a semi-collapsed walkway, with no room for us to pass under. The day was hot, and we'd been constantly dousing ourselves and the boat with water by filling our helmets that we had ready for the white water sections.

Due to the heat, the air in the raft expanded and risked splitting so, on hot days, we had to cool it. This was all well and good until you got to crocodile territory — then reaching over to fill your helmet with water becomes a risky task. Early that afternoon, the weather turned from hot and sunny to cloudy and windy. The skies darkened with a rumble of thunder; the rain started, and the temperature dropped. It was freezing.

We arrived at this bridge and we were going to need portage* around it, so I called it a day. It was 3pm, and the unload, portage and reload was going to take an hour. It wasn't worth getting back on the water, only to have to stop for the night an hour or so later.

We were quickly surrounded again by a curious crowd.

The guys picked a spot to set up camp, and we began unloading the raft, battling against the wind and rain. Once emptied, we carried the raft up and put it on its side leaning against some tall bamboo, to create a barrier against the wind and rain that had me shivering like crazy. I am a sook when it comes to the cold.

We secured the raft and put the tents up. All of this was made difficult by the crowd around us who had zero concept of personal space. Once I started cooking, they edged claustrophobically close. If the strange boat and all the gear bemused them, seeing a *mzungu* cooking on a stove was award-winning entertainment.

A local woman came forward and started chatting with Koa. My shivering concerned her, and I appreciated her looking out for my wellbeing. She was also worried about security as, apparently, there were some untrustworthy people around. She kindly arranged for a couple of guys to act as security, who we paid for their services.

The chief, who was a tall and imposing man with a friendly smile, welcomed us to his village and repeatedly gave me exuberant and awkward hugs. A whiff of his breath suggested his enthusiasm was alcohol-fuelled.

---

* Portaging is the practice of carrying watercraft or cargo over land, either around an obstacle in a river, or between two bodies of water.

Chances were he'd gotten stuck into some 'banana beer', an East African staple known locally as *urwagwa*[10]. The process to make this brew starts by covering the ripe unpeeled bananas with banana leaves and leaving them for a couple of days to ripen further. The bananas are then covered in fresh leaves and placed in a fermentation pit. After a few days, the banana meat is removed from the skin, crushed, juiced and diluted with water and then filtered. Next, sorghum is added, which kicks off the fermentation. A few more days allow it to ferment further, and then, *voila*, you have banana beer.

As darkness started to fall, the novelty of us wore off and everyone slowly went back about their business. It meant I could finally go 'bushy bushy' (what the guys called going to the loo when out in the wilderness). I'd been busting, but the audience had made it impossible to find some privacy. We had rice and pesto for dinner, which Koa and I prepared, and we all cheered up. It had been quite miserable up to this point. However, with food in our stomach, the rain gone, and peace and quiet, we relaxed.

It helped that Koa had cheered up. His moods tended to dictate the mood of Peter and Paulo. If Koa was down or grumpy, Peter and Paulo were quiet. As usual, it was early to bed. Once darkness fell, there wasn't much to do except sleep. Or at least we tried to. Our nearby security guards were a chatty pair.

Waking up, we enjoyed feeling the warmth of the sun on our skin once again and let it fuel us to cover 60 kilometres, which was a good distance. We spotted our first crocodiles, or 'flat dogs' as many refer to them. These behemoth relics from the dinosaur age were sunning themselves on the sandy riverbank, but they rushed into the water as we approached and with a flick of their tails disappeared into the muddy water. These were Nile crocodiles, the species found all along the Nile (the name being a giveaway) and throughout sub-Saharan Africa.

They are the second largest of the crocodile species after Australia's saltwater crocs. They grow up to a terrifying six metres in length, weighing up to 750 kilograms[11]. There was an infamous croc of epic proportions roaming the Ruzizi River in Burundi, which lies to the south of Rwanda. He was named Gustave and was credited with hundreds of deaths, reaching a near-mythical status. A documentary was made about this beast called *Capturing the Killer Croc*.

This species is notorious for being highly aggressive and responsible for hundreds of human deaths every year. Even Michael Phelps couldn't get away from one in the water. I'd heard that these crocs had been recorded reaching up to 35 kilometres per hour. Having heard plenty of horror stories, these crocs terrified me. One tragic incident involved Hendri Coetzee. He was leading a kayaking expedition in the Democratic Republic of the Congo in 2010, when a crocodile launched itself out of the water at him. It dragged him under, never to be seen again. It was a loss felt deeply among the close-knit community in Jinja where he lived and worked.

While the crocs we saw weren't these mammoth ones, the guys assured me that they were in the 'big' category. So, there was no more sitting on the edge of the raft or letting our toes swing in the water. Given we camped so close to the river, there was also no more leaving the tent once we'd turned in.

We found a good spot to camp that night. In the background, since the glue smashing incident, I'd been trying to get some replacement glue. I didn't like the idea of not being able to repair the raft, even if the need to was unlikely. Nicci from Jinja Basecamp had sent a new pot of glue to Kigali for Joanna to then find a way to deliver it to me. We'd been messaging and she arranged for one of her team members to meet us. However, being able to say exactly where we'd be and when was tricky.

To my amazement, just after we'd set up camp, I looked down to see a ferry (in the form of a small wooden boat) carrying Leandre, one of Joanna's team members across the river! As I hugged him enthusiastically (which seemed to totally freak him out), I told him that he should be a detective, having actually found us along our travels.

But then the rains hit big time. Before leaving, Koa had sourced a tent to hire for him, Peter and Paulo, although I wasn't convinced it was watertight. I discovered my cynicism was well founded. The guys endured a sleepless night in a swimming pool. Fortunately, I'd brought a tarp for future use. While we'd only been on the water for five days, it already felt like quite an adventure.

The following day, which was largely uneventful, we finished close to Kigali at an agreed meeting spot to find Susanne, a German journalist who had made contact and arranged for us to meet. She snapped a few photos of our arrival, and we chatted. She asked me questions about the trip and why I was doing it. She also interviewed Peter. I was apprehensive about what he might say. And as I don't understand German, I couldn't read the article. So, to this day, I don't know what she wrote and didn't try to find out. Ignorance can be bliss.

Once Susanne left, we made camp, had dinner, and I was about to turn in when I had my first less than pleasant close encounter with the wildlife.

The moths would often come out at night and on this particular night there were swarms of small ones, about the size of a fly. My headtorch naturally attracted them, and one flew into my ear. Every few seconds it would start flapping and sounded like it was deep inside my head. It was horrible, and I forced myself to breathe deeply to stop myself freaking out.

Paulo checked it out— it was in a fair way, and banging my head into my hand was doing nothing to shift it. Neither was putting a light next to my ear in the hope of encouraging it out. So, I retrieved tweezers from the first aid kit, handed them to Paulo and tried to keep still as he went to work. Thankfully, he managed to remove it. *Eww!*

I woke the next morning to the noise of hippos. Hippos have the fearsome reputation of killing more people than any other animal in Africa, and they scare the hell out of me. They are one of the most aggressive animals on the planet, found throughout sub-Saharan African. These feisty, territorial vegans grow up to a colossal 3,200 kilograms[12]. They may look cumbersome and unwieldy, but they are quick blighters, reaching 30 kilometres per hour on the land and eight kilometres per hour in the water.

There was tension in the air as we got on the river, and it wasn't too long before we met our first pod of hippos. We made our way past them without any issues. The plan, generally, when you're in hippo territory is to slap the surface of the water with a paddle. They spend up to 16 hours each day submerged to keep cool. When you slap the water, they resurface to see what the noise is, so you can then spot where they are and give them a wide berth. That's all fine on a wide river where you have space to manoeuvre, but here it was just 50 to 70 metres wide and twisted and turned with short steep banks, so it was impossible to see what was ahead.

 PADDLE THE NILE

Cruising along, the river was about to bend to the left and then right. As we rounded the left bend, a baby hippo popped up slightly ahead of us in the shallows on the left. We stopped paddling, but the river continued to carry us. I'd barely muttered the words, 'Where's Mum?' and she popped up on our right. We unintentionally drifted between her and bub.

You don't need to be David Attenborough to know this was a gigantic mistake.

The mother lost it and came at us huffing and puffing. Paulo employed all his athleticism to leap to the front of the raft as she gave us a hefty nudge, putting her head under the raft to seemingly try and flip it.

I felt the sensation of pure primal fear spread through my body — there was no space for thinking, just action. We frantically tried to paddle away from her, but she came at us again, determined to inflict damage. Koa was on the oars, and Peter and I were on either side paddling upfront. Looking towards the riverbank we were desperately trying to get to, I felt a sudden tug on our craft. I turned to see the hippo attached to the back of the raft, less than three metres away from me. *Fuck!* She had sunk her enormous teeth in and put a gaping hole in the raft.

Letting go momentarily, the angry mother paused, possibly put off by the pop and rush of air through the hole she'd created. It gave us a short window to get to land and leap to safety onto the riverbank. We stood breathing deeply, hearts racing as we watched nervously to see what she was going to do next. She backed off a little. And then a little more. We breathed a sigh of relief and started unloading the raft, while keeping an eye on the hippo. We were helped by some local men who had been tending the land.

The raft was pulled up out of the water and the damage inspected. The hole was 40 centimetres long and 15 centimetres wide. The raft was made up of separately inflated compartments, so only the one with the hole had deflated. After offloading and deflating the raft, the guys started patching the hole (thank goodness we had the replacement glue). Shaken by our near-death encounter, there wasn't much talking among us.

I was deep in my thoughts, processing what had just happened. We were extremely lucky to have come out unscathed. Had it been a lighter or smaller raft, she would have flipped us. After about an hour and a half, the hole patched, the raft reinflated and reloaded, we gingerly got back on the water, filled with trepidation. I was so scared. I'd walked into this expedition accepting that death was a possibility. Up until today, that had been a theoretical exercise. This incident brought home the reality of what that meant. I didn't want to get back on the water, but at the same time I was determined to continue.

Talking to the locals, we were informed there were plenty more hippos to come. I'd been warned they were going to be a problem before setting off. Peter made the wise call that if we could get off the river in future encounters, we would, and we'd leave the raft in the water and use a rope to tow it past them. While hippos do get out of the water and are fast on land, they tend not to do this during the day. One of the key reasons I'd chosen to do this section in a raft was because of the hippos.

My thinking being that it was safer than a kayak. It was, but it hadn't provided the level of safety I'd hoped. This new plan gave me some confidence. It wasn't long before we had to put Peter's plan into practice, coming across an enormous male hippo. We got to the opposite side of the river upstream of him and climbed up the riverbank. I'm no hippo body language expert, but the opening and closing of his large, powerful jaws, his snorting, jumping up and down and scattering of his excrement with his tail, suggested to me he was deeply unimpressed by our presence and was poised to attack.

We waited for this psychotic display to calm down and then slowly towed the raft past, and, once again, tentatively got back on the water. My heart was pounding. We were set to repeat this routine on multiple occasions. That night, I heard noises outside the tent — it was a hippo. There was no getting away from these belligerent beasts! When the sun goes down, they come out to graze, making it up to ten kilometres inland. So, where we could, we put ropes around our camp to stop them coming close. While a bit of rope won't stop a 3,200-kilogram hippo, they tend to avoid it, as they have surprisingly sensitive skin.

Before we pulled up for the day, we got chased again. Not with the same aggression as before, but enough to have us stop twice, get out and wait and watch. Hippos now top the list of my least favourite animals.

The weather didn't improve things. The lovely warm days had yielded to cold and rain. Peter had sensibly brought a pair of waterproof trousers that I looked at enviously, wishing I'd done the same, along with having more layers to mitigate constantly feeling chilly and damp. And everything was filthy. The raft had holes around the edge of the bottom to allow water out when going through rapids, but it also let some in, resulting in a muddy coating in the raft.

The river here was still brown with mud, and there was no chance to get clean, with only a wet wipe bath each night. This silty river also played havoc with my water filter. I'd chosen a top of the range MSR filter, which did an incredible job of turning this murky soup into sparkling clean and safe drinking water. Despite us running the water through material to try and remove some of the silt before purifying, the filter clogged up and there was no getting water through it.

I had made sure there was a backup to this critical piece of equipment in the form of water purifying tablets. It made the water safe, but not particularly pleasant to drink.

The rain meant we had to put our tents up on muddy ground. Each night, soon after pulling up and unloading what we needed and then setting up camp, we'd be surrounded by curious locals.

Making our food, next to all the expensive gear and while on my search for fulfillment, I was very aware of being amid these locals who were struggling to survive. Most were in tattered clothes, hungry and living a basic hand-to-mouth existence with little hope for the future. I felt guilty and embarrassed. It was why I was raising money for CARE.

Now we were up to day seven and about to find out that hippos weren't the only threat on this section ...

CHAPTER SIX
DAYS 8–10

Only those who will risk going too far can possibly find out how far one can go.

T. S. Eliot

The Nyabarongo River becomes the Akagera River at Rwanda's border with Burundi, on the edge of Lake Rweru. I had the hang of the GPS by now, but there were multiple channels to choose from that were not on the GPS. We asked some local fishermen, in their narrow dugout canoe, the channel for the Akagera River. They were directing us when another pair came and took over from them.

Without us realising it, the directions they then gave nudged us over the unmarked border between Rwanda and Burundi. The guy sitting upfront in the canoe stood out. Unlike the other fishermen in their tattered clothes, this guy wore a black bomber jacket, camouflage shorts and schmick haircut. I was a tad suspicious. He told us to wait while he called his friends, who would show us the way.

His 'friends' turned out to be from the Burundi National Defence Force. So much for being a good Samaritan. Three members of the army arrived in a small metal motorboat, machine gun perched at the front, with its operator at the ready, and the other two men behind him clutching their AK-47s.

With no plans to enter Burundi, we didn't have visas to be there. The man in charge inspected our passports and documents, and I gave him a copy of the letter from the Rwandan Tourism Board. After some deliberating, and even though we had barely crossed the border, we were instructed to row across the lake for questioning.

A cheeky request for a tow was met with a steely look and a curt, 'No.' *It was worth a try.* After 30 tedious minutes of padding across the lake, we reached the other side. There we were ordered out of the raft and questioned by the army.

This was mostly conducted in Swahili, with Peter as our spokesperson and translator. It was a role he stepped into spectacularly well each time English wasn't being used, which was most of the time. He had a natural, friendly way of dealing with the frostiest of receptions and getting people onside. After the initial questioning, I spoke to the man in charge, who spoke English, and he assured me we'd be on our way shortly. *Awesome!* The police were just going to ask a few questions, he advised. *I didn't realise the police were even here.*

Up until this point, we had been surrounded by men in army uniforms and the rest were in rip-off Adidas tracksuits. It turned out that this was the 'weekend get-up' for senior cops. It felt like I was in the middle of an 80s Miami Vice-style drug bust. But we were in the jungle. With no Crockett and Tubbs.

After questioning us, the police decided they wanted to inspect our gear. This was not so awesome. Everything had to be unloaded, and they went through the whole kit and caboodle with a fine-tooth comb, down to taking the food out of the barrels and opening every box of matches.

They were somewhat puzzled by my feminine hygiene products, and it was poor Koa who had to explain what they were, bringing me some brief amusement in an otherwise unamusing and frustrating situation. When they got to my satellite phone, Koa said it was a mobile. This was smart thinking, because in some countries, satellite phones are looked upon with suspicion, fearing the owner might be a spy. The same goes for the GPS, which I had hidden in my PFD. Our GoPros, my USBs, laptop, and memory cards were confiscated.

By this time there was a crowd of at least a hundred villagers quietly watching this spectacle unfold in front of them. It looked like something out of *Apocalypse Now* deep in the jungle. A cordon was set up to keep these curious onlookers back.

Then ... things went from bad to worse.

We were ordered to deflate the raft. With some dissidence, we took our time and made the most of it by cleaning out the filthy vessel. Then they announced we were to be taken two hours deeper into Burundi for more questioning with the head of the police of the Muyinga Province.

Frustrating as it was, these weren't the kind of guys to argue with, so we loaded up their truck for the two-hour ride. The truck was a flatbed utility vehicle (or 'ute', as we say in Australia). It had two bench seats on the back facing out. We sat on these, two on each side, me next to Paulo, with a policeman at each corner clutching their AK-47s, one pointing perilously at my toes.

After 30 minutes, the car pulled over in a village. The policeman in charge got out, and I asked that we be allowed to change. The temperature was dropping as darkness fell, and the guys were cold in damp river gear. He agreed. While we needed to change, it was also a front for my hidden agenda. I needed to get a message out to Dave.

While crossing the lake, I had surreptitiously sent a text to Dave via the GPS to briefly let him know what was happening. While he would be able to see where I was via the tracker on my GPS, I needed to get another message to him that we were being taken deep into Burundi.

I predicted that, being a woman, if we were getting changed, I'd be given a room on my own. I was right, so I quickly changed and punched out another message. It was all very James Bond, and I have to say I found the whole thing wildly exciting. I underestimated the seriousness of the situation.

Burundi has an interesting history. The original inhabitants of Burundi were the Twa, a Pygmy people who now make up just one per cent of the population. The remaining population is a mix of the Hutus (approximately 85 per cent) and the Tutsi (approximately 14 per cent)[13]. Traditionally, the differences were work-related and not ethnic. The Hutus were those in agriculture, and the Tutsis were the cattle-owning elite.

People say they looked different, that the Tutsi were tall and lighter skinned, while Hutu were short and darker skinned. In reality, these differences are not so clear[14]. In 1933, the Belgians, who had colonised the country, created strict separate ethnic groups and required everyone to carry an identity card indicating tribal ethnicity as Tutsi, Hutu or Twa. They created massive inequality between the groups, which aggravated the divide and was set to fuel ethnic violence once colonisation ended[15].

During this colonial period, Burundi was united with Rwanda to form one country, Ruanda-Urundi, until gaining independence from Belgium in 1962, when Rwanda and Burundi returned to being separate countries[16]. Bouts of ethnic cleansing followed in Burundi, along with two civil wars and genocide in the 70s and early 90s, leaving the country underdeveloped and one of the poorest globally.

In 1994, the presidents of both Rwanda (Juvénal Habyarimana) and Burundi (Cyprien Ntaryamira) were killed when their aeroplane was shot down. Both presidents were Hutu, and their deaths were blamed on the Tutsis. As a result, Hutu youth gangs began massacring Tutsis, as happened across the border in Rwanda, triggering the Rwandan genocide. In Burundi, a low-intensity civil war continued that lasted over ten years.

This was all complemented by political strife and attempted coups until eventually, Hutu rebel leader Pierre Nkurunziza was elected president by Parliament in 2005, in a peace deal brokered by Nelson Mandela. Ongoing peace talks had varying levels of success with intermittent violence. A new cease-fire was agreed in 2008.

This progress was undermined by accusations from human rights groups that the government refused to accept. Critics of the president's policies were persecuted. Nkurunziza was re-elected in 2010 and again in the 2015 election, even though the Constitution established a two-term limit for the president. Violence throughout the campaigns and elections created concerns. The elections were also criticised by the international community and largely boycotted by the opposition. The International Criminal Court has since launched a full investigation into alleged crimes against humanity.

To the outside world, it seems there is now peace, but there are reports of killings quietly continuing – people considered to not be supportive enough of the ruling government being targeted.

The Burundian police have a history of using unnecessary and lethal force. Reports of killings, torture, rape, disappearances, degrading treatment and arbitrary arrests are commonplace.

According to a BBC documentary, *Inside Burundi's Killing Machine* there is a hidden but systematic program of torture and killing described by the locals as *'Kamwe Kamwe'*, or 'One by One'.

As a result of the endless turmoil, violence and corruption, Burundi was rated the world's least happy nation in the 2018 World Happiness Report[17].

For us, while things weren't great, there was no immediate threat to our safety. After changing and sending the SOS while the police had a beer or two, we were back on the truck in front of another large audience. I was tipping they didn't see too many blonde female *mzungus* being detained by the police.

We then continued to the next village. As we pulled away after another brief stop, someone in the new crowd that had gathered took a photo on their phone. One of the policemen saw the flash, stopped the car and ordered the driver to reverse. The policeman jumped out and grabbed a man from the crowd. It wasn't the guy who took the photo, but he thought it was. He threw the innocent man to the ground and kicked him so hard in the chest, I thought he cracked a rib or two.

Underway once again, we raced through the countryside at breakneck speed. Knowing the police had been drinking had us hanging on that little bit tighter. We got to our destination intact for more questioning.

We were shown into a small room and told to sit on a wooden bench. With paint flaking off the walls, a thick layer of dust on the old desk and a yellowed computer that I doubt had been powered up for some time, it looked like this room didn't entertain many visitors. There were bags of what looked like sand in one corner, one with a wooden gun on top. *Weird.*

The chief policeman, who had been part of our questioning at the lake, took a seat behind the desk. Two others sat opposite him and joined the conversation. Questions went over what we'd already been asked. What happened? What are you doing here? Our answers were written down to form a statement. They also asked about our marital and family situations. *Really? Relevance?* I was pissed off, tired, hungry and frustrated.

They asked for our phones and passports. While we were talking, I subtly deleted my message history with Dave that would have looked highly suspect with our code words and check-ins. Dave had advised me to keep all phones and laptops 'clean', with no intel reports or other messages that might create suspicion.

After an hour, we were told we were being taken to a hotel for the night and we might be allowed to leave the following day. I couldn't believe that we were being *detained*. We had been tricked across the border. But I knew that arguing or resisting would only inflame the situation. On the upside, we were heading to a hotel and not police cells. From what I'd seen of the station so far, I guessed that would have been an unpleasant experience.

By the time we got outside, the police had unloaded our gear into another room. We were given a minute to grab what we needed. I still had my GPS hidden on me and was able to sneak the satellite phone out, along with some clothes and toiletries.

As we got outside, a man — who turned out to be the local chief prosecutor —wandered up to me.

'I hear you're single and without children.'

'Yes,' I confirmed.

'That's shameful,' he replied. *Oh, get fucked!* At this point I was cranky, but I forced a smile in response.

We were then taken to a hotel and placed under house arrest while our fate was considered. The place was basic but clean. My excitement at seeing an ensuite bathroom and shower was short-lived when I spied the 15-litre jerry can. We were getting a bucket bath only. Mind you, I was happy to take that and be clean for the first time in a while.

With French still being one of the languages spoken here, thanks to colonial Belgian rule, it was time to brush up on my school-girl French and get us some food. There was a small restaurant in the hotel, which was run by some lovely nuns from the church across the road. I ordered us some food and we ate and turned in for the night, all exhausted. Our rooms and the restaurant were on the first floor. I'd picked a room with doors out onto the large veranda running the width of the hotel.

Under the cover of darkness, I decided to risk putting in a call to Dave on the satellite phone. There was an armed policeman outside the hotel, and this risked the phone being confiscated or me being punished for making a call, but it was worth the chance, having had no reply to my previous GPS messages.

Unlocking the door and ducking down, I made my way onto the veranda, hid behind a wall and dialled. The sound of Dave's voice was music to my ears. He'd got my messages. I later found out that I'd forgotten to use my identity word, 'Fox', at the start of each message. He'd gone comms silent on me, not knowing if it was me, or if someone had the GPS, or I was under duress.

He said, 'I got your messages and have followed your progress. Actions are underway to sort out your release.'

I relaxed and was so thankful that Dave was there to help. Goodness knows what I would have done without him. The aim was to get us back across the border into Rwanda asap.

'In the meantime,' he said, 'remain calm and compliant, because things can change very quickly.'

'Yep, sure thing,' I assured him.

'Good. And let me know if there are any developments at your end.' *Thank goodness for Dave. We love Dave.*

I went back to my room and had a cold bucket wash. I had a bed and was clean, so things were by no means all bad. The guys meanwhile were crammed into the room next to me.

During breakfast the next day, the chief prosecutor, Mr 'That's Shameful', came in. Once he'd finished eating, he walked over to us. After some pleasantries, he advised, 'You've been found not guilty.'

I resisted the temptation for any smart arse replies and settled for a more diplomatic, 'That's great news, thank you.' Apparently, we just had to wait for some big boss to approve our release and then should be on our way.

However, it was a long, slow, boring waiting game.

After the Sunday church service across the road, the worshippers climbed the stairs to the veranda and through the double doors into the hotel restaurant. There were about eight tables, a small television in one corner, with the kitchen hidden behind the door at the other end. Outside at the bottom of the stairs was our armed policeman in his dark-blue uniform and beret.

Occasionally, he'd mix it up and stand across the road — the crazy kid. The guard was a tad unnecessary, I felt. How far would a blonde *mzungu*, with no passport, no phone and no local currency get? As people entered the restaurant, a few asked if I was on holiday. My French wasn't good enough for a real explanation, and to be honest, even if I had the words, I couldn't be bothered. So, it went more like, 'Oui, je suis en vacance. C'est tres bien ici!'*

I did explain the situation to one of the nuns, Beatrice, who was curious as to why we were here. She was thoroughly dismayed at the situation and said she was going to pray for us. It was nice to have someone locally in our corner, bringing the 'Big Man' with her too. All help was gratefully accepted.

While there was still uncertainty as to what would happen next, I found the edginess of it all exhilarating. There was zero point in stressing, with little we could do to remedy the situation.

'Control the controllables', the mantra I'd used so often was back. The only thing we could control was our response, so I tried to make the most of the situation.

I used our confinement to get to know the guys better.

First up, I chatted to Koa and listened to his story about his family, the lack of a father growing up, his wife and children and the hopes and dreams he had for them. Once he got going, there was no stopping him.

Next was Peter. He was single but did have a daughter. Unfortunately, he and his partner separated, and she left their daughter with Peter. He was smart and would have gone to university if there'd been enough money, but the accepted practice of polygamy meant his father's income was spread thin.

---

* Yes, I am on holiday. It's great here!

Peter followed in his brother's footsteps and became a rafting guide as well as a white water kayaker and instructor. He regularly travelled to Kenya to teach there, which included training the British army. This explained his skilful and non-stop use of expletives. I thought I had a potty mouth until I met him!

I'd already had a chance to speak to Paulo in the run-up to the trip, so it was just general chit-chat with him. I knew that he too had an unfriendly ex. Unlike Peter, he was only given limited access to his children, but he now had a girlfriend that he referred to as his wife. This is often the case, as marrying is expensive, so girlfriends become wives in name until the money can be saved.

This bonding time was valuable, and it quickly changed the dynamics, with us now having this 'shared suffering'. The conversation flowed easily, interspersed with laughs and jokes. More hours passed, filled with me pacing back and forth on the veranda, just for something to do. We'd held off ordering lunch on the foolish assumption that we'd soon be on our way.

At 5pm, the senior policeman dropped in. We sat outside on the balcony to talk. He now informed me that an additional senior person needed to approve our release, but they were currently flying back from France, so we wouldn't get an answer until tomorrow. This meant another night here. I felt like they were stringing us along, looking for any opportunity to hold us. The question was, how long before we'd be transferred to a jail?

While we were chatting, the lovely nun brought the priest over to question the policeman about the situation. *Bless them.* While the policeman was there (out of his Adidas threads and now in his Sunday best), the governor of the region called to see how we were.

More pointless small talk followed, and then he asked if I would give him my phone number and address when I was released. *You have to be kidding me?* Once again, my internal filter kicked in and translated my instinctive response to, 'Yeah, sure,' with a forced smile.

After breakfast on day three of confinement, we were told we were being taken to the Rwandan border to be released. There was just some final paperwork to be completed, but I wasn't filled with confidence.

To my surprise though, at around 10.30am, they came to get us. One of the guys brought my laptop and our phones. He asked me to turn the laptop on and show him some files. Good job I'd deleted anything that might arouse suspicion. Then the phones were checked. They'd all been switched on, despite being off when we handed them over. Once the checks were done, he was satisfied. And after I settled the bill with Rwandan francs, we were taken back to the police compound.

Once there, we carried all our gear out of the room it had been left in. Some light fingers had put an end to our biscuits. *Arseholes.* To my relief and surprise, all the electricals were still there, including my main camera that hadn't been confiscated in their search.

Over the next few days, we found several other items missing, including my thongs (flipflops), a Shaw and Partners-branded baseball cap, the safety knife and whistle from my PFD, tins of corned beef, and toilet paper. They'd also tried a tin of Heinz Baked Beans. Clearly they were not a fan — the open tin had been left slowly oozing its contents into the dry bag it was in. And they had taken the precious meat given to us by Paul from Jinja Basecamp.

However, there was still no sign of our passports, and the situation continued to feel tense. So, I called Dave again, but this time openly on the satellite phone, now that we were theoretically on our way. He explained that we were going to be driven to the Rwanda border where Joanna would have a car waiting for us to take us to Kigali. There we'd spend a couple of days before moving on again.

Finally, they indicated it was time to get going. They tried to split us into two cars, but I was adamant that we stick together, no matter how squashed we were in the back seat of the ute. My concern was they would take the guys elsewhere if they weren't with me.

Another car followed, and off we went.

A call came through to a policeman sitting in the front — it was the British High Commission in Rwanda checking on my wellbeing. The man passed the phone to me.

'Did they hurt you, torture you or threaten you in any way?' they asked. 'No,' I replied.

This became a regular question from the High Commission — and they usually seemed surprised when I said 'no'. It brought home the seriousness of the situation.

At one point we stopped, and the policeman got out and made some calls, which added to the tension. I was waiting for them to call the release off. Thankfully, we got underway again, and after a couple of hours we reached the border.

When we got out of the car, the head policeman, true to his word, asked for my phone number. I resisted the urge to give a fake number, as we weren't out of the woods yet.

Our passports were finally returned to us, and I was taken into a room. I looked around and spotted a Rwandan flag on the desk. I was in Rwandan immigration, and the man across the desk asked me to sit down, smiled and said, 'You're safe now.'

A sense of relief spread through me, and I let out a sigh and smiled at him, 'Thank you.'

CHAPTER SEVEN
DAYS 10–13

‘I realised that my battle to survive this war would have to be fought inside of me.

Immaculée Ilibagiza (Rwandan genocide survivor)[18]

While taking the Rwandan immigration manager through the details of our recent 'adventure', I received a message from the Burundian policeman who now had my number, simply saying, 'Hi there.' I replied, 'Hi,' wondering if it was sent as a test to check I'd given him my actual number; I made a mental note to block his number once we were safely across the border.

After running through the chain of events, I waited outside while Peter was asked to go through the same process. I think they needed to corroborate our stories. The driver Joanna had sent to pick us up joined us as Koa, Paulo and I waited outside. He'd kindly brought some drinks and snacks. Koa said that the Burundian policeman had commented that Koa was always next to me. Always there. I hadn't picked up on it, but over the next few weeks I noticed it. Koa was always there, in a gently protective way. I appreciated it more than he could ever have imagined.

When the papers were finally signed to allow us back into Rwanda, it was time to put our gear in and on the car that Joanna had sent for us and get the hell out of there. With the car packed, a quick photo and some less than fond farewells to our Burundian 'friends', we were on our way. As we were driven under the sign saying: 'Welcome to Rwanda', we cheered and high-fived each other. *Holy hell, what an episode.*

I then called Dave again. He was thrilled to hear we were safe and told me he'd sent an email to Mum to briefly outline the situation. The cyber team at TCG had found a couple of tweets with pictures of us during our initial questioning at the lake. He was worried a newspaper would pick up on it, run a story, and Mum would have a nervous breakdown on reading it. I learned that Dave had quickly driven from Victoria to Canberra to harness the specialist support of officials in the diplomatic and intelligence communities and worked tirelessly with all his contacts to ensure our release.

Things could have escalated without his help. He had barely slept throughout the whole affair, and it was time for him to return home and have a wee break from *Paddle the Nile*. All the risk plans had kicked in and worked. The key to this is, have a 'Dave'.

There were a lot of people working behind the scenes to ensure our quick return to Rwanda. To all, I will be eternally indebted.

There was a positive from this detour, and that was spending a couple of days back in Kigali to regroup and catch our breath before getting on the river again. It was also a chance to clean clothes and charge up all the electricals. We returned to the hostel we had first stayed at in Kigali. It was good to be back somewhere familiar. Joanna was there to meet us and gave me a big hug. I was thrilled to see her, and she was relieved that we were all okay. I was thankful that the RDB insisted I engage a fixer. Neither of us had expected she'd have so much to fix!

That night, we went out for dinner to celebrate being free individuals again.

The next morning over breakfast, I chatted to the guys to see if there was anything they wanted to do that day. They had no requests, but I was keen to do something together rather than just hang around at the hostel all day.

I suggested we go to the Genocide Memorial. I had read many positive reviews, and I was eager to see it. I remembered hearing about some of the horrors when it happened and had read multiple books about it. The guys had a neutral response to the suggestion, and I took the lack of reluctance as a positive.

On the way, I found a place that sold maps of Rwanda and bought one for each of us as a keepsake.

The Rwandan genocide kicked off after President Juvénal Habyarimana, a Hutu, was assassinated on 6 April 1994 when his plane was shot down with the Burundian president (mentioned earlier). His departure created a power vacuum and ended the peace accord. The result was the start of the killings that many believe had been planned for over a year by the Hutu political elite after decades of resentment and violence against the Tutsis.

The genocide was well organised and practised. In 1990, the army had begun arming civilians with weapons, such as machetes, and training the Hutu youth extremists — the *Interahamwe*.

On 11 January 1994, General Roméo Dallaire, the commander of the UN peacekeeping forces in Rwanda, sent what became known as the 'Genocide Fax' to UN Headquarters. This fax became a symbol of the failure of the international community to prevent the subsequent genocide that took place [19].

Dallaire reported that he had been warned that there was an 'anti-Tutsi extermination' plot. He requested authority to raid suspected arms caches, but his request was rejected.

A few weeks into the genocide, a group of bureaucrats assessed the situation and decided, 'We will recommend to our government not to intervene, as the risks are high and all that is here are humans [20].'

All that is here are humans. That was their response. No strategic or resource value to the world powers, just humans. It makes my blood boil.

Come April 1994, after the plane was shot down, militias were given lists of government opponents to be killed, along with their families [21]. The brutality that followed is impossible to fathom, with Hutu men killing their Tutsi wives, fearing for their own lives if they didn't. Neighbours killed neighbours. The 'cockroaches', as the Tutsis were often referred to, had to be weeded out and killed. More hit lists were handed out, and the names were read out on the radio. The killings were assisted by the *Interahamwe*.

The West stood and watched. Both the UN and Belgium, who colonised Rwanda, did nothing to stop the killings. The United States too, after losing troops in Somalia, were reticent to get involved in another African conflict. President Clinton issued a presidential directive, stating that the United States wouldn't engage in any humanitarian operation unless it was in self-interest.

The French, allies of the Hutu government, sent forces to evacuate their citizens and later created supposed 'safe zones', but they were highly criticised for not doing enough to stop the killings. The feeling of abandonment is deeply felt by surviving Tutsis.

The end came when the RPF, headed by the now President Paul Kagame, with the backing of the Ugandan army, gradually seized more territory, until 4 July 1994, when its forces made their way to the Kigali. It is estimated that 800,000 Tutsi were slaughtered in the 100-day genocide. That equates to more than five people being murdered every minute, 24 hours a day for 100 days. It wasn't just the Tutsis — the Twa people were also targets. On top of those killed, it is estimated that over one hundred thousand women were raped[22].

It is a country still deeply impacted by the events of 1994. The survivors are continuing to deal with the horrors they experienced and saw, many bearing both physical and mental scars. After the end of the war, efforts were undertaken to find and convict killers. There has also been much work done to attempt to reconcile and prevent any such tragedy being repeated.

President Paul Kagame put in place a policy of ethnic reconciliation. Convicted killers are reintegrated into society by publicly apologising for the crimes they committed. Survivors forgive. Kagame has attempted to deal with the underlying cause of the genocide — ethnic differences. There are now no Hutus and Tutsis. They are Rwandans. One tribe.

Back at the Genocide Memorial, we were coming to the end of the tour. There was a room filled with photos of some of the babies who were slaughtered. At the Ntarama church, a small building at the back, became a slaughterhouse for babies. The most heartless *Interahamwe* gathered the kids and newborns here and killed them in a brutal, horrific manner. The photos of the babies were accompanied by descriptions of how they died. This room at the museum is also dotted with boxes of tissues. It would be hard for anyone to leave the room with dry eyes. I certainly didn't.

While this may not have exactly been a 'team rousing' experience, I'm glad we visited it. The guys said they were too. After, we sat outside in stunned silence, trying to process what we had learnt.

I also used the time in the capital to replenish supplies after the Burundian police made light of things such as our biscuits and toilet paper. Plus I managed to find a tent for the guys. We also went to a restaurant that served food with which the guys were more familiar. That made them a bit more chirpy.

After a couple of days regrouping in Kigali, it was time to get back on the water. I decided we would start a fair way from the Burundi border. We cheered when we finally got on the Akagera River. At this point, we were less than two weeks into the trip, and it had already been quite a mission.

Part of me questioned whether I should continue. I wanted to but wondered if it would be considered reckless to keep going, given everything that had happened. While I don't generally pay too much attention to what people think, I have seen and heard the criticism levelled at adventurers who have come a cropper and their decisions deemed rash. I didn't voice my feelings and reasoned that it was all very fresh, and I needed time to form some perspective about it. The ongoing support from Dave gave me confidence too. I knew that if I was being rash, he would let me know.

The Akagera dips into Tanzania, and we had seven days making our way through here before crossing the border back into Uganda.

We hit some rapids on our first day, including a nice Grade V, which made things more interesting. And, of course, there were also hippos to keep us on our toes. But when we came across a pod, we weren't met with an overly aggressive response. I secretly hoped the Tanzanian hippos were a friendlier bunch.

The next pod we met towards the end of the following day needed careful negotiating. There was a mother and a new baby and at least another four hippos, including a large male. We got off the river on the opposite bank to observe and make a plan. The waterway narrowed where we were, and given the baby's presence, we were reluctant to make any hasty moves.

A portage was out of the question, as the terrain made it too hard to get the gear off, and, with the sun setting, we were running out of time.

Peter, however, spotted a window of opportunity. 'Those two are shagging. Mum's looking upstream, and the baby is on the opposite bank. Koa and I are going to float the raft past. Sarah, you and Paulo meet us around the corner.'

He wasn't getting any arguments from me — I was delighted to not to be in the raft close to these river monsters. The guys made it past, and Paulo and I jumped in, and we paddled about 200 metres downstream where we found a spot to get out. As much as I'd liked to have put a bigger distance between us and the hippos, it was nearly dark.

We found some cow pens, which were partially fenced areas, and quickly set up camp, using the rope from my throw bag* to make a barrier across the front of the pen to keep the hippos away from us during their nocturnal grazing.

I'm not sure any of us slept well. We knew we were potentially going to have to contend with them in the morning. Luckily, they turned out to not be an issue, which was an unexpected relief.

In this area of Tanzania, the river and scenery had gradually changed from what we'd seen through Rwanda. The water was less muddy, and the consistent short, steep riverbanks with fields of planted crops at the top had gone. Now there was more variety, which included low, gentle hills, often obscured by trees and thick foliage.

Here were the classic Acacia trees that grow tall with their flat canopy making them look like giant umbrellas. In some areas there were tall reeds and grasses coming down to the river, along with sections of papyrus.

Papyrus are tall leafless plants generally growing two to three metres high that look like giant dandelions with the thick stem topped by a cluster of thin green shoots. These reed-like aquatic plants, native to Africa, grow along the Nile in dense stands.

Humans have a long history of using papyrus, dating back to ancient Egyptian times when it was used to make one of the first types of paper. The English word 'paper' comes from the word 'papyrus'. Papyrus is used to make roofs and handicrafts such as baskets and mats. While it has its uses, for us it was at times a hazard and an inconvenience, because the thick foliage created an impenetrable barrier to being able to get off the river.

---

* A throw bag is a long rope in and attached to a bag. We all had one, clipped around our waist. They are primarily used for rescues. For example, when someone has fallen in the water, you throw the bag to them (remembering to hang onto the other end!).

There were also cattle, with long horns. They would come down to the river in large herds to drink. In Rwanda, I had seen very little animal farming, only agriculture.

The river was 100 metres wide or more, with a reasonable flow, and we came across sections of small rapids. Each time, I wondered if they were going to give way to much larger and more dangerous sections of white water. While I had enjoyed my scoot down the rapids before we set off, I was still afraid of big water.

And before I knew it, my fears were realised when I heard thundering water — there were massive rapids ahead of us now.

Koa, acting as our safety kayaker, went to look at the different channels to see if there was one we could run. He came back and advised that we were going to have to portage. We had pulled up below a steep bank. As we approached the bank, I could see there was a large site of either building work or excavation happening at the top.

Peter and Koa climbed the bank to see if there was a way around and perhaps some muscle or a vehicle to help us. They came back to report that the response was a resounding, and unfriendly 'no', and they'd been told to move on. As we paddled across the river to try to find a spot between the deep papyrus to portage, I felt nervous. While I completely trusted the guys when it came to the white water, to me it looked like we were going straight into larger rapids. It was a complicated narrow channel between islands in the fast-moving water to get to the exit point, and it took us perilously close to being sucked down the whopping rapids.

I was incredibly relieved when we made it. Now it was time to untie and unload everything between the trees that graced the riverbanks. We exchanged some Tanzanian shillings for strong hands from local boys to help us carry the gear around the rapids. The unload and reload took well over an hour, and it was hard work, but well worth the effort to avoid taking on potentially lethal white water. Everything had to be tied down before we could get back on the river.

As the guys finished packing the raft, I made breakfast. It had been a hectic and stressful start to the day, and I was ready for some sustenance. Not knowing what lay ahead of us, I wanted to have us fed and ready for what was next. It was a chance to regroup, and for me to distract myself. After coming close to those treacherous rapids, my anxiety levels were well up!

CHAPTER EIGHT
DAYS 13–19

*The fear of facing your fears is harder to
overcome than the fear itself.*

Anonymous

We were back on the water, and after a short rapid, we were able to
have the breakfast I had prepared. I secretly hoped that that was the
last of the big white water. Unfortunately, my ears — now a highly
sensitive radar for the sound of rapids — picked up the noise of white
water ahead. It wasn't long before the bubble and spray of water came
into sight once again.

We made it into an eddy, which is a calm current of water running
in the opposite direction to the main current. You find them behind
obstacles in the rapids, like rocks or where the riverbank is uneven
and creates an obstacle to the flowing water.

They can be used to get out of rapids, like those we had here. This
section was dotted with large and small islands. The larger ones had
trees, reeds and papyrus, obscuring a view of the rapids. We were in
the middle of the river, behind one island and in front of another large
one that we were able to get out onto.

As we looked around, we noticed that we had come too far into
the rapids to be able to portage, but our exit was blocked by thick
papyrus. There were three channels between two main islands, one
of which we were on.

Koa went off to check our options. As we waited, a hippo popped up in front of us. *Not again!* They don't usually hang out in rapids. *Great, it's not like my heart isn't already pounding.* We stayed put and hoped the hippo would do the same. Thankfully, it did.

Koa returned to report that we couldn't run the middle and right channels. The channel on the left looked okay until the corner, but beyond that was anyone's guess. Out of options, we set off, with Peter on the oars and Paulo and me upfront paddling.

I wasn't optimistic. If there were huge rapids on the other two sections, I reckoned it was unlikely this was going to an easy, safe run. The initial section was fine, with rapids that would have been fun if I hadn't been filled with dread of what might lay ahead of us.

It turned out to be my worst nightmare.

We rounded the right-hand corner, and to my horror there was a massive drop to our right with water gushing over it. My stomach did an almighty flip. Once again, as my adrenaline levels spiked, the sensation of pure primal fear spread through my body.

Calmly and confidently, Peter told us to turn around and forward paddle, to try to get us into an eddy close to the left riverbank and avoid being sucked over this monstrous rapid. Koa, in his manoeuvrable kayak, had been able to make it to an eddy, so he could only sit and watch our desperate attempts to get to safety. We made it to the river's edge, but the current was too strong, and we were being sucked towards the edge of the waterfall. Paulo, in his panic, tried unsuccessfully to grab onto branches.

During the rafting trip in Jinja, I'd managed to switch my mindset from feeling threatened by a large rapid to seeing it as a challenge, and as a result, love it. Here I was totally in threat mentality! I was on the back foot and didn't want to be here. My decision-making skills took a total dive to those of a two-year-old as my amygdala* took control — I went into flight mode.

I stood up, looking for options to jump off the back of the raft onto the bank. I wanted out. There wasn't a hope in hell that I would have made it. My deeply flawed plan was cut short by Koa yelling, 'Sarah, GET DOWN!'

---

* The amygdala is part of the brain and plays a role in how we assess and respond to environmental threats, including the fight, flight or freeze response.

I promptly obeyed, turned around, got into the bottom of the raft and hung on as we plunged over the falls. The power of the water coming over the drop would have created a strong current travelling deep towards the bottom of the river before reversing back on itself. This kind of hydraulic, a hole, can flip a raft or trap a person in this constant spinning current.

We hit the water, went under, and I felt the pressure of one of the food barrels on my head as the raft buckled and bent in half on impact. When we popped up, we started careering down the rapids with no idea what was ahead.

That waterfall was the warm-up, for all we knew. And unfortunately, there was nothing to do but hang on and hope.

Looking ahead, to my horror, I spotted Peter floating in the rapids. He'd been thrown out of the raft. 'I need to get a throw bag to Peter.' I yelled, beginning to stand up.

'Get down!' Paulo shouted, just in time, as we careered under some low-hanging branches that would have taken my head off.

I felt helpless watching Peter disappear under the forceful rapids before popping up again. Fortunately, we made it through the rapids into calmer waters. Peter finally caught up, and we pulled him into the raft. I then paddled us to the riverbank.

Paulo, however, had lost his paddle and was clutching his elbow that had taken a knock. The fear I'd felt just moments earlier was replaced with pure relief washing over me. We got off the river, pulled the raft up and laughed and shared our own versions of the events. Having gone from 'facing death' (at least that's how it felt to me), we were now enjoying the dopamine and endorphin high! Fear had become fun. This was your classic Type Two fun.

Koa couldn't believe his eyes when he came around the corner and saw us and the raft all in one piece.

During this latest incident, we lost one plastic food box, two paddles and the Ugandan flag. The flag was never seen again, but the plastic box was picked up after 30 minutes, one paddle after an hour, and then, to our utter amazement, we found the other paddle floating ahead of us four days later!

That afternoon, we pulled up early after a few more decent-sized but enjoyable rapids. It had been a big day. The spot we found was, to me, the epitome of the African savannah — rolling grasslands with clumps of bushes and the iconic umbrella-shaped Acacia trees. It was the type of landscape I'd been lucky to see on a couple of safaris in South Africa. Today, it was so much more special — we'd earnt the beautiful view.

The early finish meant there was time to build a fire, enjoy a relaxed evening and watch GoPro footage of the day's events. As we sat by the fire, feeling its warmth on our skin, I couldn't remember feeling happier. There was probably still some of those feel-good chemicals flowing through my veins, intermingled with immense contentment, and a feeling of accomplishment having seemingly defied the odds and survived another terrifying incident.

As we sat there, a couple of locals approached. There was an older man dressed in a black lightweight raincoat, jeans and gumboots (Wellington boots). I estimated the other man was a young adult. He too had gumboots, but with royal-blue soccer shorts, a brightly coloured purple and yellow t-shirt with a suit-style brown jacket.

They came and shared the warmth of the fire and chatted with the guys in Swahili. They asked what we were doing, where we'd come from, where we were going, and wanted a photo with me. The photos were taken, and then they went to head off. Before leaving, they pointed to the path leading to the river. 'The elephants use that as a watering hole,' the older man advised. *Great.* So now we were going to be trampled by elephants in the night. The drama was never-ending.

Thankfully, we were spared from being trampled in our sleeping bags and, in the morning, we were back on our way. By now we had settled into a good routine. We would get up at sunrise, which in Rwanda was about 5.15am and here in Tanzania and Uganda, an hour later.

We would take the tents down and pack everything up before loading the raft and tying everything down. At some point, when weren't dealing with hippos, rapids or the Burundian army, I would make breakfast. This consisted of oats, raisins, ground peanuts, a scoop of protein powder all mixed with some water with a liberal tablespoon of Nutella and peanut butter. This fuelled us for the day. Bowls and cutlery were washed in the river as we went. I did feel I was playing Russian roulette with a stomach upset, but so far, I had managed to stay healthy.

The food was fine, but what I did miss was my morning coffee. The guys were always keen to get going, and I didn't want to slow things down just to feed my caffeine addiction. Usually, that would have to wait until after our evening meal.

Snacks were mostly biscuits, raisins or fruit and nut bars. Koa had the bars because he wouldn't eat biscuits, for fear of rotting his teeth. Most days we didn't have lunch unless there were leftovers, which was a rare event. In the evening, dinner was prepared as soon as the tents were up. We had rice, pasta or couscous with either pesto, peanut butter or Nutella. It turns out spaghetti and Nutella is a dream combination. *Who knew!* It's possible you need a day of paddling behind you to fully appreciate it.

Paulo was satisfied with the food, but Peter and Koa were less enthusiastic. Peter didn't like couscous. *What's there to not like about it?* Neither were big fans of the breakfast either. I was surprised at how picky they were, but I guessed this was foreign food to them and not what they usually had.

Back home, their day would start with something like a *chapati* or *rolex* — no, not a high-end Swiss watch. *Rolex* is a popular street food item in Uganda, generally made up of an egg omelette and veggies wrapped in a *chapati*. Another popular choice is *katogo* — a mixture of diced cassava and beans. Both were delicious options, but it was tough, as there was none of that here, no other options, and no supermarkets to get any alternatives.

Back in Uganda, I'd studied the route carefully and loaded it into my GPS. I had a general idea of where the exit points were if, for example, someone got seriously hurt and we needed an evacuation. Each day, I would look at the route in more detail to see what lay ahead. Where we were now, the river regularly had long sections of deep papyrus on one side with steep white and cream cliffs on the other. This made me nervous, as there was no getting off the river in the case of an emergency.

As we made our way past an island, a hippo popped up in the shallows and started following us. We had to get off the river before we angered him. There was a small gap in the papyrus, so we pulled in, got out of the raft and quietly waited and watched as the hippo put on one of those psychotic displays we'd seen before.

He jumped up and down, scattered excrement with his tail, while aggressively opening and closing his giant jaws. The messaged seemed clear, 'This is MY river, and I will rip you to pieces if you get back on it.'

I was shitting myself. There was nowhere to go and no way of towing the raft like we had before. If something happened, we couldn't get medical help, and we'd used up all the glue to patch the raft. So, we had no choice but to nervously wait it out. I'm sure the guys would have been able to hear my heart pounding in my chest.

After a while, the hippo gradually started making his way back to his favoured spot behind the island. He would go underwater for 30 seconds or so, move up stream a little, pop back up and look at us.

Peter very wisely called it. 'Next time he goes under, we get in the raft and wait until he comes up. Then when he goes under again, we quietly paddle away.'

It was a genius plan.

We quietly climbed into the raft as he submerged and then paddled away in stealth mode the next time he disappeared. Koa said when he came up and saw we'd gone, he went about his way back upstream. *Fucking hippos.*

This encounter put me back on edge, but I tried to reason with myself. There was no point in stressing constantly about these beasts. This wouldn't make them disappear or make them more friendly. 'Control the controllables', I reminded myself. I had accepted the risk of hippos on the river and the worst case. Continuing to worry would suck the joy out of the trip and waste energy.

The internal chat helped. I let it go and enjoyed the days, confident that we'd be able to deal with whatever came up. Peter helped reassure me. He was gifted at calmly evaluating the situation and coming up with solutions to deal with the bigger problems. He never seemed to stress or worry. I wanted to be more like him.

Letting go of the stress created the space to be in the moment and take it all in. There was so much to appreciate, drifting along this magnificent river with the ever-changing scenery, deeply immersed in nature. As it shifted back to deep jungle running along the banks of the river, we spotted monkeys swinging through the treetops. It felt very *Heart of Darkness.*

I began to savour the relative monotony of getting up, paddling, eating, sleeping, repeating. It was a gift to have the time to think and reflect. This was a stark contrast to life back home, always on the go, always feeling the need to fill the days to the brim, to be constantly 'doing'. I listened to a podcast by Rich Roll where someone questioned this kind of behaviour — are we in the 'do more to be more' trap? Why can't we just 'be'? Can that ever be enough? For me, the answer is no, but I probably spend too much time at one end of the scale.

While it was still early days in this adventure, I knew my life had now taken a turn and I wouldn't want to go back to my old career. Prior to this expedition, I had worked in financial services. My desire to break into the fast-paced world of international banking was mostly inspired by films and TV shows depicting dealing rooms as adrenaline-filled, boisterous, blokey yet kind of glamorous environments. All of that appealed to me. The money-making opportunities were also there.

However, my degree in physiology, not brilliant A-level results, and the recession of the early 1990s was going to make it challenging to get my foot on the ladder. So, I borrowed books from the library about banking and economics, pulled together my resume, lied about my A-level results, and got creative. I'd done an introductory secretarial course and eventually got a job in a Japanese bank as an administrative assistant working in the dealing room. This was it.

I then launched myself into a baptism of fire that I loved. This was *Wolf of Wall Street* days. People shouted at each other, drank heavily, gave you endless shit, and you gave it back with interest. It was fierce. It was fun. Among the chaos of fast-moving markets, there'd be paper-ball cricket played, practical jokes and golf putting practice between the desks.

Traders spent their hour-and-a-half lunchbreaks in the pub and would have blown every breath test on return. We had a direct phone line to the pub downstairs, used to drag a dealer back mid-pint if a client called. This was back in the 'dark ages' before mobiles. I then got a job as one of the foreign exchange trader's assistant – a stressful role that involved being shouted at frequently. While I was fond of the environment, being a trader wasn't my skillset. That was when I moved into risk management.

However, the environment was comparatively dull. There was no banter, no fielding office cricket, but the work suited me and my analytical mind. This was a job for life, with this industry being wrapped in more rules and regulations. The result was a successful (yet dry) career, moving through a variety of roles. The work was okay, at times enjoyable, but it wasn't something that made me come *alive* or brought meaning. It did, however, facilitate my move to Australia, for which I'll be forever grateful, but it was my life outside of work that I lived for.

In 2008, I had a timeout from banking when I took voluntary redundancy and went backpacking solo around the world. I returned and followed my love and passion for sport and fitness by becoming an outdoor personal trainer in Bondi.

After four years, the novelty of spending my time telling people to squat, lunge, push, pull and run had dwindled.

I returned to the familiarity and nice pay cheque that comes with working in investment banking, landing a job at Macquarie Bank. It was the best company I'd worked at. I thrived on the high-performance environment, being surrounded by smart people, and I found the work rewarding — but again, I can't say it made me come alive. It was while I was there that my plans for this expedition came together. I knew now, that on my return, it would be time to work out what was next for me. With months of paddling ahead of me, I had time to ponder what that might be.

For now, I focused on just being and enjoying the present. I hoped that I would hang onto this long after the expedition finished. There were no texts, emails, social media, or other distractions. There were no logistics to arrange. It was a simple life, yet this pleasing monotony was countered by getting up each day and heading into the unknown. And I thrived on it.

The dense forest and papyrus made it hard to find a camp spot. That night, I made the call to camp next to a pumphouse, which took water from the river to an extensive sugarcane plantation. It was noisy, but we were short on options. Up until then, the only suitable spot had already been taken by a troop of baboons.

We pulled up at the pumphouse, got out and found a woman and a security guard. We asked if it would be all right for us to camp there. She said it 'should' be fine but advised us to take our passports and go with the security guard to check with the main security office.

I optimistically assumed this office would be at the top of the long flight of steps close to where we'd pulled up. But no — two kilometres later, we arrived. Security at the office said that we could camp there, but we needed to check in with the local police. This was not good, as our passports and documents hadn't been stamped coming into Tanzania. Effectively we'd entered the country illegally, but there wasn't much in the way of passport control on the river. Without ground support to take us to an official border crossing, I worked on the theory that we'd be in and out of Tanzania before anyone noticed.

When we arrived at the police station, another two kilometres away, my heart was beating that bit faster once again.

The police officer asked, 'Where are your entry stamps?'

My stomach turned, and images of being arrested again flashed before my eyes. Stupidly, I didn't have the GPS with me, or any communication equipment to get a message to Dave. *Muppet.*

We explained the situation, and there were more questions. Then the officer said, 'So, your passports will be stamped when you leave Tanzania?'

'Absolutely,' I lied, knowing it would be the same level of immigration leaving Tanzania. Amazingly, he said, 'That's okay then.' *Really? No spending a night in a Tanzanian jail?* There were relieved smiles all round, and off we went ... before he changed his mind. We reached camp exhausted, having completed a round trip of about eight kilometres walking after a long day on the river.

I hoped that by the time we got back to camp, Peter would have taken the initiative and set up their tent and started preparing dinner. No such luck; he was just sitting there playing with his phone. I was pissed off. He then turned his nose up at the couscous I cooked.

'Don't you like it?' I asked.

'No,' was his simple reply. Yet he had eaten it without complaint the other day. Tired, hungry, and annoyed at this lengthy, stressful round trip, I resisted the urge to verbally slap him. It was Koa's birthday, so there was no time for Miss Cranky Pants.

Once dinner was cooked, I presented Koa with a somewhat crumpled birthday hat and a Bondi Beach baseball cap that I'd brought from Australia as a potential goodwill incentive if needed — or in this case, a birthday present.

The woman looking after the pumphouse was a sweetie. She got me a chair, seeing as I was a 'Mama' (what anyone who looks old enough to have kids is called). She then proceeded to pour used pump oil on the ground around my tent to keep the ants away. She also lent Peter her phone to make calls. He was always on his phone, and his SIM didn't work here. I tried to give her some money in thanks, but she refused, only accepting some biscuits and sweet tea — oh, and a few photos. *Bless her!*

Back on the river, we sporadically spied smuggling routes. There'd be bags of contraband ready to be taken across the river. Dave accurately warned of these in his daily intel reports. The only risk was that the smugglers, who would be armed, might be concerned that we would report them or steal their goods, and they might be tempted to eliminate the risk. We took care not to camp anywhere near them.

Day 16 was blissfully uneventful with no hippos, no police and no rapids. However, we did have a challenge finding a good camping spot again. With the sun edging close to the horizon, there was nothing but papyrus on both sides.

Eventually, Peter stopped the raft and made his way up a steep bank through a gap in the foliage. 'This is good!' he shouted down. I had my reservations, but on climbing, we were treated to a breathtaking view. It was the best penthouse.

The routine was the same each time. We'd secure the raft and unload what we needed for the night. Then we'd pick our spots to put up the tents, with the guys always making sure they were close to me for my safety. I'd put up my tent, pop my bags inside, have a quick wet wipe wash, put talc on my feet to help keep trench foot at bay and get changed into dry, warm gear. That was heaven, feeling dry and warm. Then it was time to put the GPS on to charge using one of the powerbanks. Then I would work with the guys to make some culinary delight.

I loved that moment when dinner was made, beds were ready for us, and it was time to briefly relax and reflect on the day. Breathe deep and take it all in. And this night it was spectacular watching the sky glow in reds and yellows before the sun finally disappeared and it was time to retreat to my little tent for the night.

On day 18, we awoke to hear the guffaw and snort of a hippo in the river. I hadn't slept well because I'd take the Malerone (anti-malaria) pills too close to sleeping, which had given me bad dreams and a restless night. Once again, we got on the water apprehensive of what creature might be lying in wait.

A few hours later, after some easy going paddling, I was jolted out of my tranquil demeanour by another hippo. We heard the animal snorting before we saw it. We quickly became motionless and silent. Then we heard it again and caught a glimpse of it on the opposite side of the river ahead of us, before it ducked back under the water.

We paddled in stealthily once again, hoping we could creep by before it resurfaced, and we almost made it, but then the hippo started following us. *Oh no, here we go again!*

For once though, it seemed like more of an inquisitive follow than an attack, and after following us for 100 metres or so, the hippo gave up and returned to its spot in the river.

Later that afternoon, we nearly ran over another hippo! It popped up in front of us, prompting some frantic evasive back-paddling by us. To our surprise, it let us on our way, only following us briefly. The hippos did seem a bit more chilled in this section, but I wasn't about to completely relax in their presence. I was desperate to make it to Lake Victoria without more drama, and we were so close now, with just over a day to go.

Our final hippo encounter for this section came soon after. As we rounded a corner, a hippo came crashing down into the river and gave us another short chase. A little further on we spotted a big croc sunning itself on a narrow sandy patch on the river's edge. On seeing us, it rushed into the water. I'd been told that hippos and crocs don't tend to hang out together. I took this croc sighting as good news and that there were no hippos in the vicinity; I think the term is, 'clutching at straws'. Fortunately though, we would be hippo-free from here until we made it back to Jinja.

As we progressed that day, we came across fishermen out in their tiny dugout wooden canoes. Some of them displayed incredible balance, standing in these unstable narrow vessels, propelling themselves along with a long paddle. The presence of these fishermen, like the crocs, gave me hope that we had passed hippo hell.

Once again, we struggled to find somewhere to camp, thanks to the thick papyrus. So, we asked some fishermen if there were any spots coming up. 'Just around the corner,' was the reply.

Twenty corners later, with the sun setting, we were worried because there was nowhere to get off the river. I think they meant it was around 'a' corner, not 'the' corner. To our relief, a small landing site finally came into view, with five huts on it. The resident fishermen let us camp and gave us some dried fish for dinner. I chose to have some couscous and pesto, a cup of coffee and an early night. I was exhausted from the stress of all the hippo encounters and was ready for a good sleep.

I left the guys to prepare the fish with ground peanuts made into a sauce and served with rice. They were pleased to eat local food. My desire for a good night's sleep was cut short at about 1.30am rather uniquely by a catfish in a jerry can. For some reason, a fish that had been caught was being kept alive, and it wasn't happy about its residence.

It was the final day of this section, and before we set off, we thanked the fishermen for their generosity and for letting us stay. I was ready to be out of the raft. The paddling was awkward and uncomfortable, and I was filthy. I'm pretty sure my leggings could have remained standing unassisted. I was excited at the prospect of being able to unpack once again and get clean. Through this section in Tanzania, I had no mobile reception. And while the break from emails and social media had been good, I missed being able to contact my friends and was looking forward to being back online and sharing some stories.

After a few hours, we reached a customs office next to the river. We got out and spoke to the men in charge. We thought they might want to check everything, but after a few questions, they let us carry on. We were now back in Uganda and edging ever closer to the end of this first section.

Come lunchtime that day, the river slowly widened and then there was water as far as the eye could see. This was Lake Victoria. I captured this auspicious moment on my GoPro as we made our way onto this huge lake. 'We made it!' I shouted.

'We didn't die!' exclaimed Peter jubilantly, and we cheered and whooped and hollered.

We all felt relief, with an element of surprise; given everything that happened, we had in fact survived. This was a tremendous milestone!

Day 1: Paulo, Peter, Koa & Sarah (L-R) at the source of the Nile in Nyungwe Forest, Rwanda

Day 1: Sarah & Paulo (L-R) in Rwanda

Day 2: Koa in Rwanda

Day 14: Paulo, Peter & Koa (L-R) in Tanzania

PART 3

Lake Victoria and Uganda

Experiencing the culture and avoiding kidnap

CHAPTER NINE
DAYS 19–24

*I determined never to stop until I came to
the end and achieved my purpose.*

David Livingstone

We made our way to the nearby Kasensero landing site* where we were met by the driver. He was to take the gear we didn't need back to Jinja and swap the raft for two tandem kayaks for us to use to cross the lake. In theory, it was a great idea. In practice, less so.

My initial plan had been to use a single kayak and engage a local fisherman to guide me across the lake. Since I arrived in Africa, I had been trying to take delivery of the folding kayak sent to me by one of my kind sponsors. Unfortunately, they had not been able to get it to me before leaving Australia and it had proved incredibly frustrating and expensive getting it through customs and to me in Uganda. It hadn't arrived by the time I was ready to cross Lake Victoria, so Plan B was needed. The guys were keen to keep going, and I was keen to continue as a team. I liked them — we'd been through a lot together, and they made me feel safe — so Peter arranged to get kayaks for the crossing.

---

* A landing site is an area next to the water where the fishermen land and launch their craft from.

Lake Victoria is Africa's largest lake and the second-largest freshwater lake in the world. It has a shoreline spanning 7,142 kilometres, which is shared by Kenya, Uganda and Tanzania. It was named Lake Nyanza until the great explorer John Hanning Speke renamed it Lake Victoria after Queen Victoria during his expedition with Richard Francis Burton in their search for the source of the Nile.

This source had eluded explorers and geographers since ancient Egypt. By the 1850s, the secret had yet to be uncovered. It had fascinated many people, going back millennia, with Alexander the Great, Julius Caesar, and Nero dispatching men to locate the source. Uncovering the source became a goal set to bring together some of history's greatest explorers: David Livingstone, Richard Burton, John Hanning Speke, James Grant, Samuel Baker and Henry Morton Stanley, creating some of the most fascinating stories of exploration of our time[23].

For many years, Lake Victoria was considered the source, with Speke the first to make this claim during his expedition with Burton. It had been a challenging expedition, with them both getting ill. Speke made the speedier recovery, and on arrival at Lake Victoria, claimed that it was the source. That led to a falling out between them. Speke returned to Africa to confirm his claims, yet without conclusive proof, doubts remained.

Next up was David Livingstone. He too had a challenging time of it, with his team deserting him, illness, and he went missing. Henry Morton Stanley was sent to find him, and on 10 November 1871, he succeeded, supposedly greeting him with the iconic words, 'Dr Livingstone, I presume?' Stanley's expedition confirmed Speke's claim that Lake Victoria was indeed the source.

Since then, there have been many more expeditions in search of the source of the Nile. Generally, there are two accepted sources, one in Rwanda and one in Burundi. However, the search and the controversy has continued with no exact agreed point of the source.

For us now, our search was far simpler. First, we needed somewhere to store the kayaks. A local guy showed us to a building nearby that we could put them in, and it was locked after us. Next, we needed somewhere to rest our heads for the night before starting the crossing of this famous lake. The same guy showed us to a guesthouse for the night.

Dave had warned me that this town was a hotspot of drugs, alcohol, prostitution, and also home of the first recorded case of HIV in Uganda and where HIV prevalence remains high.

It certainly didn't have a great vibe. It wasn't helped by a couple of extremely drunken men trying to make me their new best friend in the large crowd that surrounded us as we packed up the gear to be taken back to Jinja.

As we were going to be in kayaks on this next part of the journey, we needed to considerably reduce what we were taking.

We were shown to the guesthouse, and my spider senses were triggered when I saw metal bars across the bar, a lock on the outside of the shared bathroom and UV lights illuminating the corridor. My suspicions were confirmed on entering my room and seeing three condoms and a small bar of soap by the bed. The guesthouse doubled as a brothel. *I kid you not!*

When we returned after dinner, there were several women dancing intimately with clients, and the noises emanating from the toilets suggested business was booming. It wasn't the only thing booming — the music was cranking until the early hours. My plans for a good night's sleep before a humongous day of paddling were scuppered.

The next morning, with all of us sleep-deprived, we prepared ourselves for the 60-kilometre crossing to the Ssese Islands. We ate a *rolex* each, and then retrieved our kayaks and carried them down to the shore. It wasn't long before a curious crowd surrounded us as we loaded the gear before launching onto the lake with no sign of the island we were aiming for. Looking out at the horizon, I felt uneasy having to rely solely on the GPS to guide us, with no marine flares and only a high-level weather forecast. This went against everything this risk manager would consider optimal.

We set off into a strong headwind, and after four hours, while the GPS assured me that we were heading in the right direction, there was still no sight of the island we needed to get to. Sitting upfront, I was soaked by the constant chop created by the strong winds whipping up the water.

After five hours of paddling, it was clear we weren't going to make it in daylight. It was time for a team meeting.

'Guys, we have a choice. We either carry on and paddle in the dark or possibly see if we can get a fisherman to help us. Or we turn around and go back.'

The guys didn't want to turn back, so we pressed on.

Two hours later, while land was in sight, my predictions were that it would be 10pm by the time we'd make it there. The tandem kayaks we were using were very heavy, making it slow going. Paulo and Koa were finding it tough and running out of juice. So, I made the call to get a ride from some fishermen in their big wooden boats. It was that or sleep in the kayaks, and the guys voted against that option.

We signalled the first fishermen who came within shouting distance. They came over but were keen to stick with their plan to fish, rather than earn some shillings taking us to land.

The next fishermen were ready to help us. They called over another boat, a price was agreed, and we were split between the two boats. Peter, myself and our kayak and gear in one, with Koa and Paulo in the other. There were two men in each of these large wooden boats. They were about 7-metres long, with a v-shaped hull, and very pointed bow. Inside were wooden struts across the width of the boat at regular intervals to help maintain the structure and doubling as a seat. In the bottom of the boat was all the fishing equipment and an anchor. We flew across the water, propelled by a powerful engine.

It was dark by the time we made land. Peter then went to meet the chairman. Every time we arrived at a village, as is protocol in Uganda, we had to notify the chairman. We would explain what we were doing and ask for their permission to stay in the village before signing the visitors' book. Often, we also had to report to the local police and show our identification documents.

The chairman is the elected head of the village executive committee, which is a set-up like the board of a company. They are expected to assist in the maintenance of law, order and security. The role includes implementing policies, communicating to government and other authorities. They also initiate, support and participate in self-help projects, as well as monitor government projects [24].

We went to the police station, which was a couple of wooden shack buildings, signed the visitors' book and stored our kayaks there. We were then shown to a guesthouse, which was more like a motel. The rooms, around a central courtyard and garden, each had a big metal door with heavy bolts.

Tired and hungry, we went to a local restaurant. It was another simple wooden shack with mud floors. There were two low tables with benches either side. Dinner was Nile perch, and it was scrumptious.

We had come out onto the lake on the west side about halfway up, and we needed to get to Jinja — approximately in the middle of the northern shores. Across the lake are a few islands.

My plan was to go from island to island to make for a more direct crossing rather than sticking to the shores of the lake. It was going to require some long paddling days to make it from one island to the next — nothing as long as day one — but clearly it wasn't going to work.

If we had been in smaller, lighter kayaks, or if I'd been on my own, it was doable, but these guys weren't used to long days of paddling. Therefore, I suggested, 'We need to have more flexibility in how far we paddle each day, so how about we make our way to the north-east of this island and then head back to the mainland? From there we can hug the shore and make our way to Jinja. What do you think?' They agreed.

'I do have some concerns though,' I continued. 'One is the wildlife. It's likely that we'll have more hippos and crocs closer to shore. The only way to reduce that risk is that we paddle out a long way each day from shore. On the way, I also need to get some money and food for long days in the kayaks, as I have no idea how remote these sections will be.' The guys shrugged unenthusiastically, but the new plan was agreed upon.

I put a call into Dave to let him know the change of plans. He was positive about the approach and gave me some good feedback. The reassurance was appreciated. Making these decisions, when it's something I've never done, wasn't easy. Having someone highly experienced who I trusted implicitly made all the difference.

We set off further around this island closer to the main town where I could get money and supplies. It was another long day in the kayaks, and again Koa and Paulo struggled.

Being a tandem white water guide, Koa joked, 'My client isn't very happy!' Paulo sat there grimly.

'What Tripadvisor rating would you give this, Paulo? I asked.

'No comment,' he replied. He finally threw in the towel. 'I can't go on,' he said gloomily.

While part of me had been internally high-fiving myself for repeatedly out-paddling the guys, it was a massive pain in the arse.

We made our way to shore, and Peter and I jumped on a *boda* and headed into town to get some money and sort out Plan D, or wherever we were up to now. The ATM was empty, so we had to wait a couple of hours for someone to come off their lunch break and fill it. *TIA. This is Africa.* (I said this numerous times, and usually with a large sigh.)

While waiting, I spotted a ferry linking this island to the mainland. I made the call that we'd get that ferry to Entebbe and then hire a boat to take us part of the way back to Jinja, before spending a day in the kayaks to bring us home. As much as I wanted to paddle all of it, I knew the team weren't going to hack it.

While this was moving away from my plan to paddle the length of the Nile, my priorities had changed. And so, I came back to my 'why', which I was still unpacking. I had come to realise that this trip was all about the journey, the adventure, and the search for personal achievement and fulfillment. The 'how' was less relevant. To be honest, all the problem-solving and changes added to the whole adventure. On top of that, we had become a close team, and I wanted us to finish this section together.

I am so used to racing in the many competitions I enter, trying to get from start to finish as fast as possible. And in a way, I'd been doing that here — focused on getting from the source to the Mediterranean as planned. This, however, created restrictions and parameters that blinkered me to different experiences and encounters. I was now learning to let go of the control, and by removing the constraints, I was having more fun while simultaneously taking some pressure off. There was already plenty of that.

Peter and I then found someone with a truck. We arranged with the driver to take us back to Koa and Paulo, pick up the kayaks and gear and drive us to where the ferry would depart. Peter decided to wind Koa up. 'We couldn't get money out of the ATM and we're going to have to camp here.' Koa's face dropped, not being a fan of camping and more of my *mzungu* food. I couldn't help but laugh. He eventually realised it was a joke, and we loaded up the kayaks and our gear.

Sitting in the back of that truck, bumping through a palm tree plantation with the stars gradually coming out, I'd never felt so overjoyed. I was awash with this incredible sense of freedom and intense love of this adventure. This trip was making me come alive in a way I never had before.

That night, after some fish and chips in one of the small local restaurants, we stayed at a guesthouse close to where the ferry was to depart early the following morning. While it was heavenly having a 'real' wash, albeit a cold shower, and be in a bed, we had to double up because there were only two rooms. Koa and Paulo shared one room and Peter and I the other. I hardly slept, not being used to sharing a bed with someone.

After barely three hours sleep, it was an early start for the ferry, having been instructed to be there at 6am to load our kayaks. I should have known better – it ended up being closer to 7am, with me inwardly groaning while we waited, craving the warm bed I had unnecessarily left.

We enjoyed the three-hour crossing to Entebbe. I forked out the extra for first class, which meant we had a padded seat — worth it, even if we were squished in.

On reaching the other side, close to Entebbe on the northern shores of the lake, we found a fabulous bed and breakfast, the Blue Monkey. It was pure luxury — large, newly renovated rooms with views of the lake — and best of all, they all had hot water and comfortable queen-size beds. *Oh, the joy!*

The next day, the guys went to ask about boats heading to Jinja. If I wasn't going to paddle, I wanted to make sure we still went by water. I gave them some money to get to the landing site and was left behind to avoid the *mzungu* surcharge. While I was waiting, I called Mum. It had been a while since I'd spoken to her, and it was so good to hear her familiar voice. I was glad to update her of our travels and incidents and hopefully put her mind at rest, at least temporarily. I worried about the stress this trip was putting on her, so I tried to message and call her regularly.

The guys returned and said that it was expensive to get boats at the landing site they had gone to, so the plan was to head to a different site the next day where they were told there should be cheaper boats. So that's what we did.

The landing site was hectic, a hive of activity, with people and goods arriving and departing in brightly coloured wooden boats next to a busy market filled with booths and people selling all manner of fish, food and other items. I stayed out of sight while lengthy negotiations and bargaining took place to secure the 100-kilometre ride towards Jinja. Eventually, at 2.45pm, we were off again. To begin with, it was heavenly — speeding across this spectacular lake, passing verdant palm-inhabited islands, listening to music until finally the sunset over the horizon and darkness fell.

And then it went to shit.

The boat drivers had gone the long way, which was neither fuel nor time-efficient. The boat owner the guys had made the deal with started calling because it was taking so long for us to arrive.

He wanted more money and tried to bribe Peter, encouraging him to get more money from me and they'd split it. Peter refused, so this 'boss man' instructed his guys to take us to the nearest landing site and dump us if I didn't hand over more cash. *Nice.*

Come 11.30pm, a massive storm hit as we arrived at the landing site where, without handing over cash, we were to be offloaded. There was no one around; it was dark, pouring with rain, the wind was howling, and flashes of lightning lit up the sky. Peter cracked it and said he was off to find the police.

Before I could stop him, he was gone. I didn't have an entry stamp to Uganda, or an exit stamp from Rwanda, and I didn't relish the idea of difficult conversations with the police if they rocked up, who were guaranteed to ask for passports. When the fisherman tried to persuade me off the boat, I said, 'No, I'm staying here.' *Nice try, sunshine.* There was no way I was disembarking, confident he would use it as an opportunity to do a runner.

Peter finally came back, minus the police, and I paid the extra money, which had reduced considerably since this saga had kicked off. The threat of the police had helped.

Around 2.30am, we finally reached our destination. With no nearby guesthouses, we set up camp on a patch of grass a couple of hundred metres from shore. I finally crawled into my sleeping bag at 3.15am and passed out with exhaustion.

I was reluctantly woken at 6.15am— this was a busy landing site, with the fishermen returning with their catches from night-time trawling. It was the last day though, so we didn't have to rush. We enjoyed some coffee and *mandazi*, which are square donuts and so tasty, particularly when you dip them in the coffee — too good! The guys were in high spirits, as they were nearly home. I also shared some biscuits that we hadn't eaten, with the local kids. It was a relatively short paddle and on home ground for the guys. *What could possibly go wrong?*

Despite our driver having cleared the pick-up point with the authorities for a long portage around the dam, it wasn't with the right people.

As soon as we landed at the agreed meeting point, we were quickly approached by some police who appeared from nowhere. They were two water police and one regular policeman. I'd taken a photo of the bridge as we approached, which is a big no-no. While the guys were answering questions, I surreptitiously deleted the images, coughing to cover up the beeps of the GoPro as I did.

I stayed out of the way, trying to make myself invisible.

Peter then came over. 'They want to see our documents.'

With no stamp in my passport, I was bricking it. This wasn't helped by the sinister looks one of the policemen gave me. He made me feel extremely uncomfortable, and I had a strong sense that being in prison, under his guard, was to be avoided. I was expecting to have to pay a bribe at the very least.

A long discussion took place between the water police and regular policeman. The former, chomping at the bit to lock us up; the latter, wanting to send us on our way with a warning. The latter, to our enormous relief and my surprise, won and we were sent on our way with no bribes having to be paid.

After the portage, it really was back on the water for the homestretch. At around 5.30pm on 19 November, we pulled into the Nile River Explorers (NRE) camp and walked up the steps towards the bar. Billy, the manger of NRE, and his wife Minette gave me a massive hug. It was so good to see them and be back. The bar was busy, filled with lots of familiar faces. After unloading the gear, the story sharing began.

 PADDLE THE NILE

This first big section was now completed. *Halleluiah!*

This had been a steep learning curve, not just about how to execute an expedition, but about myself — what I enjoy, who I am, what I'm capable of, the things that drive me, what scares me and how I react when faced with terrifying experiences.

I didn't have any expectations going into this expedition. Strange as it may sound, I hadn't anticipated relishing it anywhere near as much as I had. It had been the most incredible adventure, awakening something in me that had been lying dormant. As I fell asleep that night, smiling, that sense of fulfillment that prompted this whole trip was there. If the expedition finished here, it was enough.

CHAPTER TEN
DAYS 25–43

A mind that is stretched by a new experience can never go back to its old dimensions.

Oliver Wendell Holmes Jr.

During this break to prepare for the next section, I repeated an assessment, called the Judgement Index, with Peak Dynamics. This was to assess how I was holding up across several indicators as the stress and tiredness built up through the trip. The indicators included problem-solving, self-criticism, coping, attitude, focus and more. Generally, as fatigue increases, both physically and mentally, with the stress of extreme conditions, decision-making skills and the other indicators can start to be adversely impacted. There are examples of this resulting in tragic consequences on expeditions.

I'd completed a baseline assessment before kicking off on my travels and the results I got from Sandy Loder, founder and chief executive of Peak Dynamics, were good news — I was in a better state of mind now than before I left Australia (when I was off-the-scale stressed), and everything rated good or strong.

It would seem the adventure lifestyle suited me.

I wrote detailed personalised thank you notes to the guys for all they had done. These were accompanied by a small soapstone hippo each, as a light-hearted reminder. Paulo very sweetly sent me a text thanking me for looking after them and being such a good 'mother' to them. I'm sure it had been challenging for them in many ways — being away from home for an extended period, and in constantly demanding situations.

It was also Koa's first trip out of the country. Another challenge would have been having a female leader and regularly having to rely on me. Women in Uganda are second fiddle, something pointed out to me before embarking on the trip.

Leadership had been challenging for me, being in an alien environment and doing something I'd never done before. It meant I was always handing the mantle to the guys and taking it back when needed. I had the utmost respect for their experience and skills, and I trusted them and tried to empower them to make the necessary decisions, cutting in only when needed.

At the same time, I felt the weight of my duty of care to them and wanted to look out for them and their needs. I felt, as a team, while things may have not been smooth sailing, we had worked well together through the never-ending trials.

The lack of gender equality was clear and is embedded in the culture in Uganda. One custom shocked me the first time I witnessed it. We were at a restaurant, outside with the four of us sitting on some benches while pots of food bubbled away next to us. The woman who owned the restaurant came over to find out what we wanted. She knelt in front of Peter before getting up and speaking to him. At first, I wasn't sure what I'd witnessed, so I guessed maybe she'd knelt to pick something up. The truth didn't cross my mind.

Then it happened again, and I asked the guys why the women did this.

I was told that women and girls kneel in deference to men and their elders, which is common for many African ethnic groups. It is a sign of respect, and if not done, the woman risks being considered poorly brought up, disrespectful and elitist.

When it happened to me and a young girl dropped to her knees in front of me, I had to resist my instinctive urge to grab her by the hand, pull her up and tell her she never has to kneel for anyone — being a staunch feminist and all.

But I had to respect their customs. This custom is debated, however, and it's rarely seen in the cities and towns. It was only in the remote areas that it seemed prevalent. Here in Africa, traditional ways are frequently still the way, and women are treated very differently.

One evening during dinner with Rob and some of his friends, I gained another insight into how differently women are treated. Rob's girlfriend's brother-in-law, John, was joining us. He was an officer in the Ugandan army.

When I arrived, Rob introduced me to the people around the table, and John asked Rob, 'Where is she from?' *Why doesn't he ask me directly?*

I was gobsmacked. Then he asked Rob, 'How does Australia make money?' expecting him to speak for me. Having never been to Australia, Rob suggested, 'Ask Sarah, as I don't know.' But this guy continued to direct all the questions to Rob. And for each question, Rob stayed silent and let me answer. It was a bizarre conversation.

Women have it tough in Uganda. They do all the domestic duties, which is common around the world. However, without washing machines, ovens, vacuum cleaners, running water and all the other household time-saving devices we have in the West, it's hard and time-consuming work.

Many women have jobs as well as carrying out the chores, cooking and looking after the children. The guys in my team acknowledged that women work much harder than the men. While they may work harder, the men tend to take control of the money and rule the roost while contributing less to the household chores, particularly in rural areas. Work is underway to empower women, but it has a long way to go.

Learning all of this, I could see how it would be strange for the guys to be led by me. It was something I was acutely aware of throughout our time together.

Back in Jinja, I had moved into a place affectionately known as 'the elephant's arse'. It is called this because of the large model elephant's backside on one side of the building and head on the other side. I was in a small self-contained first floor room, with a shower and toilet reached by going down the stairs outside to the ground floor. Above was a large roof terrace with stunning views of the Nile. It was attached to a crazy golf course dotted with other large model safari animals and part of the All Terrain Quad Biking that Rob was now managing. The owner, Shirray, a fellow Aussie, kindly let me stay there for free.

I cherished having alone time and space. There was a lot of washing to be done, of me, my clothes and my kit, which was all tinged with the muddy water we'd travelled through. It was a joy to be clean again and in fresh clothes.

Away from everything, it was the perfect place to reflect, chill and then sort everything out for the next section, as well as catch up on emails, update social media and get a newsletter out.

I had been commissioned by World Nomads to provide a series of articles on my trip. There had been one before departure, and now it was time for the next one; there was no shortage of stories to share.

It was great to finally speak to close friends, particularly my female friends. As much as I loved the male company, I welcomed some feminine energy around me.

The day after our return, I climbed the ladder to the roof terrace just before sunrise, my favourite time of day. I sat loosely hugging my knees, watching the glow of orange and red grow in the sky and monkeys skylarking about, all while sipping a coffee with the Nile gently flowing in the background.

A smile started from within. It was like a transcendent moment of pure joy and complete happiness. Africa is my 'happy place'. It had been my go-to destination for many years, inspired by my mother who'd lived in South Africa in her mid-twenties. I never bored of hearing her stories and would pour over her photo albums. It held such mystery — a place of beauty and danger, of history, and a kind of romance.

Growing up, I was deeply envious of friends going on holiday there. Other than a short holiday to Tunisia when I was a toddler, it wasn't until I was 21 when I set foot on Africa 'properly' with a trip to Kenya. My boyfriend through my twenties never had much interest in the continent, so it wasn't until we broke up when I was in my early thirties that I came back, again and again.

There was a horseback safari in South Africa, trips to Cape Town, and driving the stunning Garden Route. There was Mozambique, Zambia, with a short trip to Zimbabwe, horseriding across the desert in Namibia, and then the reconnaissance trips to Uganda, Sudan and Egypt. During these various trips, I bungee-jumped, skydived, scuba-dived, saw the 'Big Five', white water kayaked, and rafted.

Now I'd added a couple more countries, had a mad adventure and was far from being bored with this continent. Instead, it fuelled my desire to spend more time here. Africa has a way of seeping into your bones and drawing you in, so you never want to leave. To me there is this incredible rawness, such beauty in the landscapes and the people; it is tough and harsh, filled with rich and diverse cultures.

Another lure is getting to experience a freedom here that I don't enjoy in the nanny state I live in back home in Australia where so much is controlled and sanitised. One small example was being forced to put locks on my windows of the unit I own to restrict how much they could be opened to stop accidents happening.

In contrast in Africa, away from a litigious society, I'm free to fly around on the back of a *boda*. If I choose not to wear a helmet, so be it. If I want to ride around in the back of a truck, climb a roof, do dumb shit, I can. If it goes tits up, I'm the one responsible. Not everyone will agree that this type of freedom is good, but I like it, and I hope Africa will be a big part of my future.

Here now I was filled with a contentment I hadn't felt for a long time. The only downside was indulging in bad habits. Out of my Bondi routine of super healthy eating and training, it had been a slippery slope to poor diet choices while being lazy. Without my usual structure, it was frighteningly easy to let the bad habits get the better of me. I even had the odd cigarette, something I hadn't done since my early twenties. The sooner we were back on the river the better!

To my relief, Paulo, Peter and Koa agreed to come on this next section — once their pay was settled. So, after a couple of weeks, we were on the water again.

I was itching to get back there, but still a little apprehensive, knowing the potential perils awaiting us. *Time to armour up, get tough and get going.* Nothing to do but get on with it. As Robin Sharma says, 'Being scared is part of being alive. Accept it. Walk through it.'

As soon as we were on the water, the uneasiness melted away. This was day thirty-seven.

We kicked things off with a super fun start running the same rapids I'd done on the rafting trip with NRE before heading to Rwanda. We ran the raft empty, meeting the driver with all our gear, ready to take us around the newly built Isimba Hydroelectric Power Station, and the dam. This dam was a source of anger for the locals. Its completion took out some of the rapids on the river, creating uncertainty to those relying directly and indirectly on the people who came to visit these rapids. There is still plenty of white water and joy to be had, so I hope that it continues to be on people's bucket list. It certainly should be.

However, it proved to be the last bit of white water for us. The other side of the dam was flat and often slow water all the way. This section was a chance to see more of Uganda and experience the culture.

We camped for the first few nights on our way to Lake Kyoga. This section up to the lake was wonderfully free from wildlife ready to rip us limb from limb. We made the most of it with regular swims. It also meant I could jump out if I needed a pee. Away from this comparative safety, I was going 'bushy bushy' in the boat, as finding a spot to pull up was often impossible, and the wildlife posed too much of a risk. I didn't relish the idea of being taken by a hulking croc with my pants round my ankles.

In preparation, I had brought with me a round plastic pot with a screw on lid. If I needed to pee, I'd tell the guys and swap places with whoever was lounging at the back (prime position in the boat). I could squat down, hidden by the kayak across the back of the raft and its high sides. Needless to say, even though the pot got a thorough washing, the guys wouldn't go near it with a barge pole.

One day towards the end of this section, I went to pee ... but there was no pot. Some light fingers had made off with it in the night. It was the only thing that got stolen on the whole trip (other than what the Burundian police took). There was a certain karma to it.

The menu had changed for this section, following the lack of enthusiasm for what had been served up before. I took Peter to the market in town before setting off to get things they would rather eat. I was content with anything, having become a fan of the local food, but drew a line at the small, dried silverfish – they could enjoy that and leave me out.

We swapped the spaghetti for *posho*, and Nutella for dried silverfish. Then any time we were in a village or town, we'd sniff out some local food. *Posho* is a firm dough-like mashed potato made from maize flour and is a staple that is given various names across Africa and beyond. Another favourite of mine is *matoke*, a traditional and popular food in Uganda. It's a starchy banana, not sweet, and is usually served mashed, often with ground nut (g-nut) sauce. This is a thick, creamy sauce made from peanuts. The only thing is, delectable as *matoke* and g-nut sauce are, it's guaranteed to put some extra junk in your trunk, so I needed to minimise how much I consumed.

Sweet potato is also popular. These foods are served with beans, fish or meat. There were plenty of fishermen along our route. In the afternoon of our second day back on the water, we met one who had a large catch. It was perfect timing, and I bought a tilapia from him.

That night, we camped next to a small village. The guys poached the fish, adding some ground peanuts and tomatoes to make a sauce. Peter was on '*posho* duty' and mixed the flour with water, using the mingling stick. This is the name given to the wooden spoon used to mix the posho. It's a bit of a workout, as the flour and water become a cement-like texture that you must keep moving to stop it burning and ensure there are no lumps.

Once prepared, we sat overlooking the Nile with the sun setting behind it. It was moments like this that brought a feeling of calm satisfaction. Happiness from a day exploring new places, progressing on our journey, and the beauty of the river and the surrounds unfolding before us with each stroke we took. And there was a certain element of relief that we'd survived another day. The guys were now good friends, and we shared many laughs. As I watched the sun dipping behind the horizon, eating the feast the guys had prepared, there was nowhere I would rather have been.

We reached Lake Kyoga the following day. The river entered the lake from the south and exited to the west. It is a long, narrow lake with two smaller lakes adjoined to its norther shores. On reaching the lake, we struggled to find a spot to land. The banks were thick with our nemesis — impenetrable papyrus — and it looked like we might be sleeping on the raft.

Eventually, with directions from some fishermen and a long, hard paddle, we got to a landing site as the stars started to come out. It was frantic there with the fishermen going in and out from a large flat piece of land littered with plastic bags, bottles and more. Behind this sprawling rubbish tip was an expansive village. We decided to hit up a guesthouse, rather than pitch our tents among the rubbish.

Peter quickly went to check in with the chairman, as well as with the police, and arranged for someone to act as security for the raft and the gear we didn't take with us, in exchange for some Ugandan shillings.

The guesthouse was like the others we'd stayed in. Each room had big metal doors with heavy bolts. People were coming and going all night, banging the doors as they went about their business. Outside, not far away, there was music blaring, and just as I'd got to sleep ... the local stray dogs started howling in unison.

If I achieved three hours of sleep, I'd be surprised. On its own, I'd have been fine, but this was stacked on a few weeks of sleeping badly, and this was the final straw. I was borderline hallucinating the next day.

We returned to the raft, buying some *mandazi* and *chapatis* on the way. Once underway, I nestled down into the bottom of the raft and pulled my buff (tubular neck scarf) over my eyes and tried to sleep. As much as I tried, sleep evaded me, so I gave up, picked up a paddle and got to it.

We made our way to the north side of the lake, where it seemed there were more places to stop. I then got sacked from paddling. Koa came to the front and suggested I take photos at the back. It was a polite way of saying my paddling sucked. I was disappointed with myself for letting tiredness get the better of me.

With no moving water, paddling across the lake was a long, hard slog; clumps of water hyacinth kept getting wedged under the raft, and we were battling headwinds. Rafts aren't aerodynamic at the best of times, and these other issues slowed things down considerably more.

We reached the north side to be met by more deep papyrus all the way, again making camping impossible. We had to find landing sites, but these were hard to unearth, as they were hidden down narrow channels through the papyrus. And the areas weren't on the GPS; however, Google Maps worked a treat with the slightest of shadows on the satellite images giving away these narrow channels to dry land.

As we approached, fishermen almost magically appeared through the wall of foliage, revealing where we needed to head. Making our way down the channel, passing fishermen on their way out, we came to a bustling landing site and vast village. There were people, young and old, along the water's edge, which was packed with wooden fishing boats. Catches were being unloaded, while other craft were being prepared for night-time fishing.

Making our way along the row of boats, we found a spot for our unwieldy raft and pulled up. While Peter went to find the chairman, we waited, with people coming up, curious as to who we were and what we were doing. On his return, Peter arranged for security, and we took what we needed and made our way to a guesthouse.

On our way, we were stopped and questioned. It turned out that there were two villages close together, and we were staying at a different one to where we had landed and checked in with the chairman.

It was the chairman of this new village who was questioning us. 'Why have you not come to me?' he asked, clearly unimpressed. Addressing Koa, he asked, 'Are you seven? Do you not know that you have to sign in?' The guys looked like naughty kids, staring down at their feet. Koa explained what had happened and apologised. The chairman's tone then lightened, and he wished me well on my journey.

After a quick bucket bath at the guesthouse, we went out to eat. Fish was in abundance, so we bought one and took it to a restaurant to be cooked. Served with rice, it was delicious and was washed down with an ice-cold Coca-Cola. After a hot day on the water, it was liquid heaven. We chatted about our plans and agreed we needed an early start because it was such slow going.

We were up and on the water by 6.30am. With no camp to pack up, it was much quicker. However, with the sun beating down on us from a cloudless sky, and the never-ending clumps of water hyacinth accumulating under the raft, we moved again at a snail's pace. Whoever was on the oars would have to jump up and down in an attempt to push the dreaded plant away from beneath us.

If the guys weren't on the oars or upfront paddling with me, they took prime spot up the back, either sitting on the back of the raft or in the kayak. The kayak, which was balanced across the back of the boat, made an ideal napping spot. They would lie on it, bum on the seat, using their PFD as a pillow. Peter was the king of napping — if he wasn't working, he was sleeping, and I envied his ability to cat nap so easily.

Two days later, at the end of another long slog on the water, we were hunting for places to sleep. The satellite view on Google Maps suggested there might be one ahead. It was only when a fisherman popped out, that we realised where it was. If he hadn't come out when he did, we would have missed the channel because it was so small. It was too narrow, however, for the raft.

So, Peter, always being proactive and problem-solving, took the kayak and made his way down the channel, while the rest of us sat and waited. After about 20 minutes, Peter returned with a local man in his small fishing boat behind him. Peter had spoken to the chairman and arranged for this guy to act as security. He was going to spend the night on the raft, which we secured to the papyrus. There was another fisherman with him. This man was going to ferry us from the raft to the landing site and village. I was thankful to Peter for arranging all of this.

We grabbed what we needed for the night — clothes, sleeping bags and toiletries — and got in the fishing boat. The fisherman sat at the back, and using a single paddle, he took us down the narrow passage between the papyrus. I felt like we were making our way to Narnia, a secret magical world.

As we approached the village, the channel widened into the landing site, crammed with fishing boats and people coming and going. Behind was the village, consisting of round mud huts with dried grass-thatched roofs dotted between the trees and shrubs.

After storing the kayak in a secure concrete room, we were taken through the shrub to the chairman's house. Peter explained that he had invited us to stay. In a clearing in the bush was his concrete house, which had a small veranda on one side. It was surrounded by a few mud huts housing the chickens and a rooster, and further away was another building with the drop toilet.

We were given chairs while the house was prepared, and we sat and chatted as some of the chairman's family gathered at a safe distance. One of his grandchildren looked scared. She would have been maybe seven years old. The chairman took her by the arm and guided her over to us.

Terrified, she covered her eyes with her little hands, in an 'if I can't see you, then you can't see me' way. When they stood a metre or so in front of me, the chairman gently pried her hands from her face. Her eyes widened in terror, she took in a deep breath and screamed! The poor kid. I'm tipping they don't get too many *mzungus* visiting. She quickly extracted herself from her grandfather's grip and ran away as fast as her little legs could take her and then made sure she kept a safe distance from this strange, ghostly figure.

Once the chairman's wife was satisfied the house was ready, she came out to invite us in. She was wearing the traditional *gomesi* attire — a floor-length dress with a square neckline and short puffed sleeves. The dress was tied by a sash over the hips. In rural areas, it's often seen as the daily dress, while in more urban places, it is only used for specials occasions, such as weddings.

She asked if I'd like my water warmed up, which was very kind of her, but not necessary. I was allowed to bathe first, which did surprise me. I expected the guys to get first dibs. The bathroom was a narrow room about two metres long, all concrete with a drainage point at the end. Ready for me was a large washing-up bowl filled with water and a small bar of soap next to it.

I undressed, quickly washed, dried and popped on my off-water clothes. Then I was shown into the living room while the guys washed. The room was about three metres square with a sofa and a couple of armchairs and a small TV and coffee table.

We sat and chatted to the chairman until dinner, which consisted of sweet potato and beans followed by some mango. After chatting some more, we were shown to our room. It contained two single beds, along with a mattress and mat on the floor, which took up all the floor space. Paulo and I took the beds, Peter the mattress, and Koa the mat. It was like a big sleepover. Our host family had given up these beds for us and put their best linen on them.

The kindness and generosity they showed us was extraordinary. While they didn't ask for money, when we left, I insisted. It was such a privilege to witness, up close and personal, how they lived. I believe that because I was with local guys and the only foreigner, I was gifted with a far richer cultural experience on this journey. It was one of the key reasons why I wanted local paddlers with me all the way. So far, it was paying off, and I was so appreciative for this unique insight.

Following our night at the chairman's house, we were back on the water. As we slowly made our way across the lake, Koa started voicing concerns both he and Paulo had. They had listened to some fisherman's tales of aggressive crocodiles and hippos ahead, and they were scared. They didn't want to do the section.

Experience to date suggested that unless a story had been corroborated by a few people, then the likelihood was that it was embellished. A true fisherman's story. Someone may have once seen a crocodile, but after a few more retellings of the incident, it morphed into a colossal, vicious maneater.

Peter and I wanted to continue. Nervous … yes … but I wanted to press on. So, what was I to do? If I made them carry on and something happened, I couldn't live with it, and I had a duty of care to them.

I didn't really have a choice and reluctantly made the call that we would get out early and do the short section by car. I was disappointed and kind of surprised that they were so tentative. I can't say I was excited about doing this section, but I was willing to give it a shot.

CHAPTER ELEVEN
DAYS 44–49

*I am grateful for all my problems. After each one was overcome,
I became stronger and more able to meet those
that were still to come. I grew in all my difficulties.*

James Cash Penney

TCG, the company Dave worked for, had a cyber team. They did sweeps of my social media to see if there were any untoward people following me or commenting. I was posting mostly on an Instagram account set up for this trip, and also to my Facebook page for *Paddle the Nile.* While I didn't have a huge following, it was growing.

The team from TCG also searched chat rooms and various online places for talk about me or my expedition. In my daily intelligence report from Dave, he said the cyber team had come across a man with a history of kidnapping talking about me. Not in any threatening way, but the fact that this man knew about me was a red flag. He was based in Masindi Port, exactly where we were going to have to get off the river. It was the only decent exit point for some distance.

We got off the river, and Peter made some calls to arrange a car — once again finding solutions. We had to hang around for a couple of hours, and it was impossible not to stand out with all our gear and me being the only *mzungu* in the vicinity. I didn't tell the guys of the threat, just stayed super observant, tried to stay out of view and kept

Dave updated. I made sure my grab bag was always with me — as the name suggests — to grab as needed. And during the day, I wore my escape pouch at all times.

The escape pouch was a waterproof bum bag containing copies of my passports, basic survival equipment, first aid and medical supplies, a small powerbank, mini torch, water purifying tablets, money and a credit card. Plus, my GPS was on me.

The grab bag was a waterproof backpack containing my passports, permits and travel documents, a small solar charger, small multitool, password-protected USB, water bottle, more first aid gear and medical supplies, satellite phone, notebook and pen, tissues, wet wipes, headtorch, small radio and scanner, light waterproof jacket, an energy bar and a thin thermal top.

I got the guys lunch in a nearby shack restaurant, but I held off eating, knowing we were heading to a stunning hotel and great *mzungu* food. Koa came over after he'd eaten and offered me some corn on the cob and was super chatty. I think he sensed I was disappointed to be missing the section and was trying to cheer me up.

We sat around for a couple of hours waiting. While there was the very slight threat of kidnap, I was relaxed, reasoning it would be highly unlikely that this man would know I was here or make a move to grab me.

The car eventually arrived, driven by the lovely Achilles who ran tours in Murchison River National Park. We loaded up and were off to Murchison River Lodge for a couple of nights of pure luxury. The lodge is set on the southern bank of the Nile, opposite Murchison Falls National Park. It is off the grid, treading softly on the environment, but without compromise to the guests. They focus on sustainability, working with and empowering the local community and have created an oasis that is a pure joy to experience.

We sat in the large open-sided thatch-covered restaurant with stunning panoramic views, watching the Nile slowly drift past as the sun began to set. We were given two twin safari tents. They were large and luxurious; we're talking mega glamping here! After a shower, we returned to the restaurant for dinner, and *mzungu* food, which I devoured. It was all such a treat! The guys, however, were quiet and didn't seem comfortable in the surrounds. After dinner, we chatted to Chris and Georgie, the owners who had generously put us up.

Making the most of our day off, I took the guys on a game drive in the park. They had never been on one. There were giraffe, various types of antelope, buffalo, elephants and more. Achilles drove us in his people carrier, with Koa, Peter and I sitting on the roof as we made our way around the park. Once again, the joy of being able to do potentially dumb shit was fun. Although, Paulo seemed more risk averse, so he took the safer option and stayed inside the car.

In the afternoon, we went on a cruise up to see Murchison Falls.

The top of Murchison Falls is the narrowest part of the river, at just seven metres wide, so as you can imagine, the water passes through this rocky gap with incredible force, before tumbling and thundering 43 metres into the crocodile-infested waters below known as *The Devil's Cauldron*.

In the 1860s the falls were named by Samuel and Florence Baker, the first Europeans to see them. They were named after Roderick Murchison — the then president of the Royal Geographic Society[25].

It is here in 1954 that American journalist and award-winning novelist, Ernest Hemingway, and his wife, were in a plane crash as they flew over the falls. Hemingway had an unlucky time of it, when, the next day he boarded another plane, which crashed on take-off. Hemingway was injured but survived. However, news of his survival failed to make it to the world press, and during his recovery, Hemingway had the chance to read his obituaries in newspapers from around the world[26]. He loved Africa and is quoted as saying, 'I never knew of a morning in Africa when I woke up that I was not happy'. This was a sentiment I could relate to.

It was a chilled boat ride as we watched elephants bathing in the river, giraffe wandering past and crocodiles basking at the water's edge before swiftly entering with a flick of their tail. There were plenty of hippos too, and during the ride, one chased the boat. This was a big double-decker craft, which just goes to show how ridiculously aggressive these beasts are.

It was nice to be on the water, enjoying the views and tranquillity and not fearing for our lives, as we observed these animals around us. We were taken as close to *The Devil's Cauldron* as was safe. Close enough to feel the spray of the falls on our skin.

Koa continued to make an effort to chat to me, still clearly trying to make up for my having to miss the section the day before, and I appreciated the effort, but he didn't need to. The disappointment was behind me then. It was done, we were safe, and I was loving this afternoon cruise.

Back at the lodge, it was heavenly to relax a little more, catch up on my diary and chill. Making the most of the wi-fi, I put some social media posts up. After dinner, we had to have an escort back to our rooms, as the hippos would often come through the grounds when they grazed at night.

The next day, Chris kindly gave us a ride in his boat through the delta up to where we could put-in. There were so many hippos in this area. It had lots of hippo-favoured shallow areas, even in the middle of the river, making it hard to navigate and avoid them. I was relieved that I'd made the call to go by boat for this short section.

Once dropped off, it was time to inflate and load the raft again. We'd lost count of how many times we'd done this. It was going to be the last time. The river was wide and relatively slow moving, with the hippo threat never far away. We'd been told there were plenty on the stretch ahead. *Oh joy!*

The guys were scared, and so was I.

For the next couple of days, we didn't see any hippos, which was a relief, and I began to relax. Perversely, I started to miss the fear, which surprised me, as I'm no adrenaline junkie. What I appreciated over the course of this journey was my 'addiction' to stress hormones, because I actively put myself in pressure situations, sometime unnecessarily. That could be putting myself into an environment in which I wasn't comfortable or that stretched me, like leaving assignments to the last minute. It might be taking on more projects than I could handle, partly because I liked to have lots on the go and got bored easily, but it created that tension within. Then, there was the rush of getting through whatever situation it was.

Stress has been a part of my life for as long as I can remember. In my younger years, it wasn't out of choice. As a child, I was painfully shy, to the point I would cry if someone in the same room laughed, because I thought they were laughing at me. When Mum took me to kid's parties, she'd have to get one of the adults to distract me so she could make a speedy exit before I noticed and beg her not to leave me.

As I grew older, while there was no more crying, I remained shy and anxious until my late teens. There were also periods of increased stress during this time. The draconian primary school I went to had very strict teachers. We would be smacked for minor things. Once, I was smacked for having sweaty hands in needlework.

I was a fussy eater as a kid and another time at lunch I regurgitated the boiled turnip we'd been served that I couldn't stomach. The headmistress demanded I eat everything on my plate. Fortunately one of the older girls saved me and took my plate away.

We were also rarely allowed to play, and I was bullied. I was eventually diagnosed with stress headaches aged just seven years old. Thankfully, Mum then enrolled me in another school, which was 'friendlier'.

However, there was a positive from all of this. These negative experiences ... the stress, the shyness, along with positives like Mum encouraging me to try different sports, pushing myself in sport, taking on new challenges, and all the travelling I'd done ... meant that feeling of being out of my comfort zone and leaving that cosy place of familiarity, safety and certainty, was strangely familiar.

There was almost a feeling of comfort in the discomfort. This helped me cultivate an openness and confidence to let curiosity be my compass, taking me to new places and experiences and to explore myself and my limits. It had brought me to this expedition.

We continued our way towards the border with South Sudan. While we didn't see many hippos, the threat was there, and I always looked to minimise the risk.

One day, we reached a point where the river split as it made its way either side of a long narrow island. I checked satellite images to decide which route to take. The choice was a shorter, narrow channel, or a longer, wider one. The short one had no exit points and was away from any roads. The longer one did have exit points. I made the call that we'd go the longer way, much to Koa's dismay. He wanted to take the short cut and was clearly annoyed with my decision and tried to change my mind. I overruled him.

By this point, I had more confidence in making on-water decisions. It was the right call. When the channels rejoined, we saw a pod of hippos near the end of the shorter, narrower route.

With only a few days left on this section, we encountered only one real nasty. It was a swarm of small flies that hit us one afternoon and stuck around until after we'd eaten. While not dangerous, it was deeply unpleasant, as they were EVERYWHERE. They stuck to us, the boat, and dived into the food we were cooking.

We also proceeded to get ripped off by the locals. All up, it wasn't the best of days.

Generally one, or all, of us would sign the visitors' book at each village. These were supplied by the local government and looked official. At this stop, however, the visitors' book was an exercise book that looked like it had just been purchased. And in it, the locals had written a 'declaration' that I was an Australian staying there on my path to Ethiopia. No other visitors' book had such a declaration. Instead, things like your name, address, ID document details and phone number were listed.

After filling out this dubious visitors' book, I was asked if I would like to make a contribution ... to what? I had no idea — the village? Not a charge, but a contribution. One, it seemed, where I didn't have a choice. About UGX60,000 (Ugandan shillings) was going to be an acceptable donation. In context, this is what the previous night's accommodation, food and security collectively cost. In the big scheme of things, it wasn't much, only about US$17. The problem was that I was running out of cash, and this was clearly a ruse. The guys were far more annoyed about it than I was. We settled on UGX50,000.

It was worth it though, as this was a stunning spot to camp. I was content to be back camping, and before going to sleep we were treated to a breathtaking sunset across the Nile.

While the papyrus continued, there were more trees along the banks, and in the distance, rolling hills, making a change from the relatively flat landscape from Jinja to here. Watching the clumps of water hyacinth float by was almost hypnotic. I had such a sense of calm. The villagers here, as always, were curious, kind, and full of smiles. I was tinged with sadness that this section was drawing to a close.

There were a few mosquitos, so I covered myself with repellent. I'd given up with the malaria tablets. If I didn't take them with food, I felt nauseous. If I took them at night, I had nightmares. Then I'd forget. It got to the point that I wasn't taking them regularly, so stopped completely. I'd never intended to take them for the entire trip. Instead, I covered up and had malaria treatment with us.

Peter joked, 'You are like the Red Cross for the mosquitos. Come and get your blood here!' He made me laugh.

The last night was spent camping again. We had finished early, finding a good spot to stop, and I made the most of it by recording some video. Turning the camera on myself, I was horrified by what I saw! There were enormous bags under my eyes, and I looked exhausted from the sleep deprivation. As much as I was sad that the section was nearly over, I was looking forward to catching up on sleep.

The last day, we made it to the 'takeout', which was as close to the South Sudan border as we could safely get to.

We pulled up, got off the water and quite literally jumped for joy! There was relief that once again we had survived. We waited a little while for our driver to arrive. It was hot, so I took cover under the shade of a tree 100 metres or so away. Koa came and sat with me, not to chat, just to be there, as he always did. These gentle, thoughtful actions always made me smile in appreciation.

The car finally arrived, and we loaded up for the last time. On our way back to Jinja, we stopped in Gulu for some food. This area is the home of the Acholi people and a man who rose to prominence in the mid-1990s. His name is Joseph Kony. He became a household name in many countries with the social media campaign #Kony2012 that was instigated to raise awareness about the atrocities he was carrying out.

He has been described as a terrorist, prophet and murderer, wanted for war crimes, yet for decades had avoided capture[27]. He created the Lord's Resistance Army (LRA) to fight against government oppression, abducting thousands of children and forcing them to become soldiers, and women and girls were forced into sexual slavery. He brutalised people of Uganda with many mutilated by the LRA, having their limbs, ears, noses and lips hacked off. It is estimated that more than tens of thousands were killed and extensive numbers were internally displaced throughout his reign of terror.

For us though, it was home time.

It was a long drive back to Jinja, and the driver stopped to fill up with petrol; however, he didn't keep an eye on the petrol pump attendant, who fake filled it. Come 2am, we were down to fumes and stuck on the side of the road. We were tired and wanted to be home. Luckily we were near Jinja, so after a short *boda* ride, the driver was able to fill a jerry can at a petrol station and we finally arrived back.

And there it was, Jinja!

We had made it from Rwanda to the border with South Sudan; the toughest sections, logistically, were done. This had been the section I feared the most and now it was behind me. I had jumped into the deep end and learnt to swim.

From the day I had set foot in Africa for this trip, I had felt so far out of my comfort zone. This invisible barrier had been broken many times, and my world had expanded and felt a bigger place. My fears relating to this expedition were losing their power, because I'd learnt to trust my abilities, and my belief that I might complete my mission had grown.

When I finally crawled into bed that night, I felt intensely grateful for all that had happened, and I was excited knowing that there was so much more still to come.

CHAPTER TWELVE
DAYS 50–71

Very little is needed to make a happy life;
it is all within yourself,
in your way of thinking.

Marcus Aurelius

Jinja was beginning to feel like home. It was the familiarity, the friends I'd made, the sense of belonging and the meaning it held for me. For me, home isn't just a place, it's a feeling, and over the years there are many places that have felt like home. Some I've been in for weeks, others for years. Now I had another.

Jinja, sitting at 1,140 metres above sea level, is a bustling town set on the shores of Lake Victoria and the banks of the river Nile, surrounded by villages. Nile River Explorers was in one of these villages, Bujagali, which was about a 15-minute *boda* ride into town.

Jinja has one main street, aptly named Main Street, which is about two kilometres long and lined with colonial-styled buildings and shops. The ground has a reddish-brown hue from the dusty earth on which the town is built. The side streets have more shops, many spilling onto the narrow pavements. The centre buzzes with people, *bodas*, *matatus* (minibuses) and cars.

There is Central Market in a building filling an entire block, and it extends over a couple of floors. It is home to thousands of vendors selling everything from fruit and vegetables to meat and fish, arts and crafts, clothes, homewares and furniture. It is a feast for the senses.

Main Street is home to plenty of restaurants and cafés serving local food, Indian food and other delights for the many tourists coming through. It included The Deli, which was my favourite. It's a classic hangout for *mzungus* looking for a taste of home. After my time on the river, it was so satisfying to get my fill of veggies while sitting out in the quiet garden.

The most significant economic activity is tourism. With all the white water activities, boat trips on the lake, the site of the original source of the Nile, horse riding, quad biking and more, it has much to offer and is only 80 kilometres from the capital, Kampala. I loved being there.

It is where Mahatma Ghandi's ashes were brought, and it has had its fair share of well-known visitors, including Queen Elizabeth II who visited in 1954, and King Faisal of Saudi Arabia, who came to see the source of the Nile nearly 50 years ago, with his host Idi Amin[28]. In fact, Jinja is where Idi Amin, the man considered one of the cruellest despots in world history, accelerated his ascension to leadership.

Uganda, like many African countries, has a turbulent and violent history. It was colonised by Britain until the 1960s when power was transferred back to the people. However, it was left with an almost non-existent political system before its independence in October 1962. Milton Obote was elected prime minister, and the King of Buganda, Sir Edward Mutesa, became the first president in 1963[29].

In January 1964, there was a mutiny at the military barracks in Jinja. The result of the subsequent negotiations included the rapid promotion of many officers, including the infamous Idi Amin. Obote ousted Sir Edward Mutesa with the help of Amin and made himself president. Obote and Amin became close associates, and Obote promoted Amin.

While on the outside, Amin appeared to be a close supporter of Obote, the reality was he had other ideas. He strengthened his position within the army until 25 January 1971, when Amin took the opportunity while Obote was overseas to stage a successful military coup. Amin became the new president, and what followed was a bloody eight-year reign of terror that led to the death of tens if not hundreds of thousands of Ugandans and the economic destruction of the country. Amin was cruel and sadistic, considered to be 'one of the most brutal military dictators … in post-independence Africa'. He was finally ousted from power in 1979[30].

Amin was replaced by a succession of presidents until 29 January 1986, when Museveni became president and has remained in power since.

For me, there were no murdering dictators to evade while here — life was easy. It was once again time to unwind in Jinja. There was a pause on organising and logistics. Instead, I enjoyed having the space to reflect once again and catch up with everyone there and speak to friends and family back home.

With the successful completion of this initial section, I felt lighter with the weight of worry and fear lifted.

One day I got a *boda* from town to where I was staying. Within 60 seconds, the driver asked if I was married. My earlier trips to Africa taught me to go against my policy of honesty and, instead say, 'Yes,' to avoid a potentially awkward conversation on how we weren't meant for each other.

'Can you find me a *mzungu* wife then?' the driver asked. *Nothing like cutting straight to the point.*

'It's not just because they're good in bed,' he added. Nice to see he had depth.

'You clearly know what you want,' I replied. 'How old are you?'

'Twenty-four,' he answered.

'Well, I do have quite a few single friends, but they're all in their thirties or forties.'

'Not a problem.' I saw that response coming.

'Okay, so if I get you a wife, what do I get? A cow, maybe?'

'Absolutely. You find me a *mzungu* wife, and I'll give you a cow.' A pretty good deal.

'But will you be a good husband?' I checked.

'Of course!' We were laughing through the conversation, but he was serious.

He explained that, in his view, Uganda was not a good place to find work. There were no opportunities. He'd been to school, got his O-Levels and A-Levels, but university was too expensive.

While it had been a funny conversation, it was a sad story and one that was all too common here. It is incredibly hard to find good jobs. Those aged between 12 and 35 form 78 per cent of the country's population and between 64 and 70 percent of those old enough to work are unemployed[31]. Sadly, from what I could see, those at the top seemed more interested in power and lining their own pockets than helping their people.

Smiling, I gave my new friend some parting advice. 'If you want a *mzungu* wife, you're going to have to charm them a little, okay? Try and win them over before asking if they're married.'

I went to Kampala to do some Christmas shopping, buy a few things I needed and to fix a big issue, some serious roots. Yes, I am (unapologetically) that vain. My hairdresser back in Sydney had suggested I embrace the grey.

That was plain crazy talk. No. Instead, I found a fabulous Serbian-born hairdresser called Mira in Kampala, and I left her salon a very content blonde.

It was then time to experience my first African Christmas. I had been going to one of the local shack restaurants in Bujagali run by the gorgeous Esther. She graciously invited me to her home for Christmas Day, an invitation I jumped at. She has two kids, one with special needs, and she was raising them alone after her husband left her. Making ends meet was hard. She worked seven days a week, and was understandably stressed about money, health and her children. You'd never know though. She was one of the most positive people I had met, always smiling and laughing.

I went to her house around midday. She lived in the village up one of the narrow dirt tracks. Her basic brick house with corrugated roof consisted of two rooms — one had a sofa, table and chair; the other the beds for her and her boys. There were no windows, just metal shutters. Outside in a covered recess next to the front door she cooked up a feast on two small charcoal stoves.

On advice of what would be appropriate to bring, I'd taken a slab of fizzy drinks. I'd also bought Esther a necklace and gave her some money as a thank you. She had so little and was kind to me, it was the least I could do.

It was the best day, full of talking, laughing, hugging and eating until I was ready to pop. I tucked into my favourite *matoke* with chicken, cabbage, ground peanut sauce, spaghetti, and potatoes. Her kids and other kids from the village came and went as we ate and talked. The strong community spirit was evident. People looked to each other for support. Families tended to live close by. Everyone looked out for each other's children, from feeding them to even dishing out discipline.

It ended up being a bit of a 'Christmas crawl'.

Next was a visit to Minette and Billy (who managed Nile River Explorers), for some yummy dessert shared with them, their daughter and Minette's mum. It was lovely to join a family Christmas, and I appreciated how hospitable they were.

The last stop was Rob, Marj (Rob's girlfriend) and Lucky (the puppy) back at All Terrain Adventures, for more food.

It was a wonderful Christmas, one I'll never forget.

In the background, I'd been following updates on the situation in South Sudan, discussing it with Dave, as well as talking to as many people as possible on the ground there. The unfortunate situation was that even with visas, approvals and private security, the risks in this area were still incredibly high.

Added to it was new intel Dave had.

It seemed that NISS (National Intelligence and Security Services) were suspicious of what I was doing and were going to detain me. I understood this. In a country suffering one of the worst humanitarian crises on the planet, it would be hard to comprehend why someone would paddle down the Nile for fun. The likely assumption was that I was a spy or a journalist.

Being detained was something to avoid. It could have been a few hours to just check what I was up to, or it may have stretched to weeks, even months. There was no predicting it, and without NISS's support, it was going to be hard to get through this area.

Sadly, it meant I would have to come back and do South Sudan another time. I was disappointed to not do any part of this country, but it was always a long shot. All accounts are that it is beautiful, but deeply troubled. The people of South Sudan have suffered for decades. They were at war with the North for 22 years until they achieved independence from Sudan in 2011. Two years later, civil war took hold again, mostly thanks to political and ethnic clashes, and other than a brief lull in 2015, it had continued ever since.

As at 2019, there was a significant humanitarian crisis. More than seven million of the population of nearly twelve million were in desperate need of some form of humanitarian aid[32]. There was hunger, malnutrition, and constant violence towards, and among, civilians and the economy was in crisis.

Since the beginning of the conflict, one in three South Sudanese had been displaced internally and to neighbouring countries. South Sudan had the third largest refugee crisis behind Syria and Afghanistan[33].

I desperately hope they can rebuild their country soon, and experience real, lasting peace and an end to their humanitarian crisis.

All this meant going straight to Sudan.

I planned to be on my way on Boxing Day, but this got delayed until 5 January, as there were issues sorting out my visa, which meant a daytrip to Kampala, to the Sudanese Embassy to sort it out.

Before packing my bags and heading off again, there were some mini-adventures to be had.

First was getting back on the water for some white water kayaking with Peter, which included some hairy rapids that involved me flipping in a Grade IV that was way above my skill level. This was balanced with more relaxing times spent swimming and cruising down the flatwater, taking it all in. And the last treat was horse riding. To me there is nothing better than galloping through fields. Even just hanging with horses is a joy. As a kid, I was very fortunate and had my own pony. It also gave me my first taste of competing and the rush of winning at the local gymkhanas.

This ride with Nile Horseback Safaris took me through the local villages and cantering across the cane fields, with the red earth rushing beneath me in a blur. The ride came to an end overlooking the Nile for some final photos before heading home.

My New Year's Eve was relatively subdued. I went to NRE for dinner with Rob and Marj. After dinner, I called it a night and was asleep before the new year began. Instead, I was up early to watch the sunrise for the first time in 2019. Much better.

This one was extra special being here in Africa, enjoying a brief pause in my expedition. I made a coffee and took it and my sleeping bag up onto the terrace. Sitting there, with the cool morning air on my skin, I looked out over the Nile, watching the sky slowly lighten with red and golden hues.

The monkeys were awake and cavorting in the trees once again, and I was joined briefly by a toucan who landed on the opposite end of the terrace. The spot of light came up off the hills, and I smiled.

In this spectacular place, I allowed myself to reflect on the year that had just passed — from setting the date for this expedition, to all the preparation and stress, and also how worthwhile the relentless persistence had been to get here. I concluded that as years go, 2018 was the best yet.

In the days leading up to my departure for Sudan, I had started to get a slight burning sensation at night in my second smallest toe on my left foot. I initially went into denial and not so sensibly ignored it and hoped it would go away. However, the burning sensation got worse, and the toe was inflamed.

On my final night in Uganda, I saw Peter and asked his opinion. 'Look, see that, do you think it's a jigger?' I asked.

One look and he replied, 'Yes.'

This was not the reply I was hoping for. Jiggers, or *tunga penetrans*[34], are a sand flea found in sandy terrain and warm, dry climates and are common in Uganda. The female flea feeds by burrowing into the skin. The abdomen becomes massively enlarged as it fills with eggs and forms a round sac the shape and size of a pea. The idea of some creepy crawly growing under my skin made me shudder. I knew they were a high risk, and it was something I dreaded.

It had to be removed. Leave it and there was a risk of severe infection, gangrene, and the worst case — a limb being lopped off. *Definitely sub-optimal.*

I asked Peter, 'Do you know how to remove them?'

'Yes,' he replied confidently.

'When was the last time you removed one?' I queried.

'Seven years ago.'

This did not fill me with confidence. *I hope jigger removal is like riding a bike.* Reluctantly, I put my 'big girl pants on' and let him do his thing.

At his request, I got out a needle, Stanley knife blade and a cocktail stick, your standard surgeon's implements. I doused them with antiseptic liquid, internally added a hopeful dose of Aussie 'she'll be right mate', and he set to work. Peter began delicately digging around this pesky parasite. The jigger was in its sac, which he had to avoid bursting because then the eggs would be released. *Eeeww!*

Peter was amazing, slowing working away until finally this white pea-size thing emerged from my toe. I was simultaneously engrossed and grossed out. He cleaned up the wound. The whole thing wasn't as bad as I'd expected, thanks to surgeon Peter.

Now jigger free and 71 days since paddles hit the water, it was time to say goodbye to Uganda and sub-Saharan Africa and switch to a completely different culture and embrace new challenges. Having had such an incredible time thus far, and making many new friends, I was sad to be leaving.

However, a piece of my heart stayed. Uganda had drawn me in and gently wrapped its arms around me, and I knew it wasn't going to be the last time I'd be there.

Day 21: Peter & Sarah (L-R) on Lake Victoria, Uganda

Day 42: Peter & Koa (L-R) on Lake Kyoga, Uganda

Day 44: Sarah & Chairman (L-R) in Uganda

Day 49: Sarah, Peter, Koa & Paulo (L-R) at the end in Uganda

PART 4

Sudan

Kayaking, the Sahara, and civil unrest

CHAPTER THIRTEEN
DAYS 72–81

*It's better to see something once,
than hear about it a thousand times.*

Asian proverb

The plane touched down in Khartoum, the capital of Sudan, in the early hours of the morning. It's a large, chaotic city, sitting at the confluence of the Blue Nile and White Nile. The airport was equally chaotic, filled with people despite the ungodly time. In the arrivals hall, I met the woman sent by the hotel I'd booked to help arriving guests. I was happy to have someone assist in navigating my way through the madness.

I had been warned that satellite phones and GPS devices were usually confiscated without the required, but difficult to obtain, permits. I hadn't even bothered trying to get permits. It had been hard enough just arranging my visa. So, I'd taken them out of the dry box and buried them at the bottom of my grab bag.

When it was my turn to put my bags through the x-ray machine, I felt nervous. And, of course, they wanted to inspect the dry box that held all my other electricals, but they eventually gave me the nod to continue.

However, when I placed my grab bag through, the alarm went off.

'Do you have a camera in there?' an officious-looking officer asked.

'Yes,' I replied, the worry building.

'Get it out,' the officer ordered.

It took some careful manoeuvring to get my camera out without revealing the contraband. The officer looked at my camera and handed it back. 'You can go.'

I breathed a sigh of relief and joined the others in the minibus waiting to take us to the hotel.

Arriving at the Acropole Hotel, we were met by one of the owners, George, who is a tall, slim, white-haired man with a warm smile and calm manner. He's an adept fixer who'd arranged my visa. Once the required government paperwork was done, and I was checked in and shown my room, I fell exhausted and relieved into bed.

The Acropole, Khartoum's oldest hotel, is the choice of journalists and many foreigners. One of the attractions, beyond the lovely rooms and staff, was the awesome wi-fi.

After breakfast, I jumped online to make the most of the connection. Checking Facebook, a post came up that I had to read multiple times — I couldn't believe what I was reading. My heart broke and tears started falling down my cheeks.

My great mate, Brad Deeth, who had been such a support for *Paddle the Nile*, had passed away suddenly while on holiday in Canada. The news hit me like a ton of bricks.

Brad and Dan (Brad's husband) were on holiday in Lake Louise in Canada, and Brad had collapsed at dinner. Despite valiant attempts to resuscitate him, he never regained consciousness. He was just 46 years old. We'd been messaging on Instagram just a few days earlier. Now he was no longer with us. I couldn't believe I was never going to see him again. I, like everyone who knew him, was devastated. My heart went out to Dan. They were an incredible couple, recently married, and loved each other intensely.

Brad was one of the most wonderful humans I had met, so kind and thoughtful, with an infectious smile that could light up a room. He also had a wicked sense of humour and always made me laugh. Once, when it was my birthday, and I kept it quiet at work, he had found out and decorated my desk with a bunch of flowers and a gorgeous card.

He had a way of lifting everyone up. We'd met at work, quickly connected and became close friends. It's rare to find people who really have your back. Brad was one of those gems.

His sudden passing reminded me how precious every day is. We never know when our time will come. We must live every single day wholly and fully. It also reminded me to make the most of every moment we have with those we hold dearest.

Rest in peace, my friend.

My grief made me feel lonely sitting there on the bed, alone in my hotel room, my heart aching with the loss. Numb from the crying, I was staring at the TV but not taking in what was on. I didn't feel like getting back to my to-do list. I just wanted to crawl into bed, pull the covers over me and try and sleep reality away. I wished there was someone to talk to, someone to take the load for a while, someone to pick me up.

However, this trip wasn't going to organise itself. I had no choice; it was time to get on with things.

To me, Khartoum always sounded an exotic location, shrouded in mystery, and it held an almost romantic fascination. A place where the Middle East meets Africa, rich in culture descended from ancient civilisations.

Sudan is home to a diverse population of 45 million made up of close to 600 sub-ethnic groups or tribes, speaking more than 400 dialects and languages. The majority practise Islam, with the remainder following indigenous beliefs or Christianity[35].

It was an interesting time to be here in Sudan. There were regular demonstrations taking place, as the people attempted to overthrow the regime that had been in place for nearly 30 years. They'd had enough of the president and his cronies who had bled the country dry to fill their and their allies' pockets[36].

Sudan had experienced several significant turning points in modern history. In 1956, it gained independence after 56 years under joint British and Egyptian rule. At the time, there was an excellent university, a highly professional army, and proficient civil service. It was a cultural and intellectual hotspot on the continent with good infrastructure and an agricultural industry, including a massive cotton-growing industry.

     PADDLE THE NILE

Things changed abruptly in 1983, when the then president, Gaafa al-Nimeiri, introduced Sharia Law, Islam's legal system derived from the Qur'an, the Hadith (the sayings and conduct of the Prophet Muhammad and fatwas (the rulings of Islamic scholars). Life in Sudan changed overnight.

In the same year Sharia Law was introduced, the second civil war started between the government and the Sudan People's Liberation Army, composed mostly by non-Muslims in the south, who opposed the introduction of Sharia Law. This conflict continued for 22 years, making it one of the longest civil wars on record. Over two million people died because of this bloody war, along with the famine and disease it brought. Additionally, more than four million people had been displaced.

Omar al-Bashir took power following a coup in 1989, but under his watch, Sudan faced the worst humanitarian crises of its time, according to the United Nations, due to the conflict with Dafour that started in 2003. As a result, the International Crime Court issued arrest warrants with charges of crimes against humanity, war crimes and genocide.

Al-Bashir and his oppressive regime oversaw the economic downfall, along with declining education and healthcare standards, to the point that daily life became a struggle for most.

The lifting of US trade sanctions did little to help. Inflation sky-rocketed and the value of the Sudanese pound plummeted.

In late 2018, Al-Bashir imposed austerity measures to stave off economic collapse, increasing economic hardship by increasing fuel prices and having limits on bank withdrawals, which equated to US$10 per day. The final straw for the people was the cutting of bread subsidies, leading to the price of a loaf tripling overnight.

This all sparked mass protests in multiple cities across Sudan that began a few weeks before I arrived. It was a collective 'enough is enough'. The people wanted al-Bashir removed. Despite the protests being peaceful, attempts to break them up turned violent. Protesters were hurt and killed. I heard of many horror stories of atrocities and couldn't help but be struck by the bravery of these demonstrators turning up again and again, constantly lifting their united voice.

The other thing that surprised me was the lack of support from the international community. Throughout my time in Sudan, I was appalled and embarrassed at their continued silence. No wonder the people of Sudan felt alone in their crusade to remove this violent dictator. In the streets around Khartoum, the demonstrations were continuing.

Like so many things in this county, the powers at play were complex, with the potential to blow up. The risk of civil war was high, and some embassies, sensing the climax on the horizon, had started to quietly evacuate non-essential staff. It had the potential to be an extremely volatile situation that could escalate quickly. It meant having a loose evacuation plan in case things did kick off. Expectations were that airports would be shut, and land borders closed.

While what I wanted most was to see a peaceful end and a positive change for the people, I liked the edginess it created.

The protests meant instigating extra levels of caution. Before going anywhere, I'd check in with Dave to see where the protests were and either stay put or plan to avoid them.

After a few days in Khartoum, I met up with Adil, who was involved in the Khartoum Rowing and Canoe Club. He introduced me to Fahed, a wonderful and generous Syrian who'd moved to Sudan some 15 years earlier and had become a Sudanese citizen.

Over the years, he has helped countless fellow Syrians flee the conflict and set up a new life in Sudan away from the violence at home. Now he helped this adventurer, even giving me a place to stay while plans to begin paddling came together. I moved out of the hotel into his sprawling home, which he shared with his housekeeper, the lovely Aster from Ethiopia, and Nicky, the Alsatian guard dog. It was the ideal base to prepare for the next section.

As well as giving me a place to stay, Fahed took me to some of the many restaurants here. I loved the food, particularly one of the Syrian restaurants a group of us went to. It was big and bustling, set with low plastic tables and chairs in a covered outdoor area with fans everywhere. We were served what seemed like a never-ending array of grilled meats, hummus, bread and salads to share. The food was divine. I could have burst by the time we left.

My downtime in Uganda and Sudan, combined with endless hospitality, had resulted in my clothes getting tighter.

Over the years, I've battled with disordered eating and have unhealthy body-image issues. Living in Bondi, surrounded by 'body beautiful', created a distorted image of 'normal'.

I know you don't need to live among the slim and toned to battle your own eating demons. For me, it manifested into obsessive calorie counting, to feel like I had control, which ultimately made me feel good.

The reality was, though, it was controlling me.

I'd avoid going out with friends if it involved eating. And if we did go to restaurants, I'd check the menu first, make my choices and work out the calories. I didn't like eating in front of other people, feeling I'd be judged for what I ate.

The obsession with keeping the calories in check and healthy food choices was countered with binges that took me to depths of shame and self-hatred. I'd feel like a failure. Then I'd be forever weighing myself, taking measurements, and constantly absentmindedly touching protruding bones like my hipbones to make sure a layer of fat hadn't begun to cover them. I loved my training, but my dedication was also spurned by the calories it burnt and a 'train to eat mentality'.

Over the years, I'd tried every diet fad and never reached my goal. And even when I got to less than 15 per cent body fat, I didn't look how I wanted. The sixpack I craved hadn't revealed itself. My eating issues had been around for decades. As a 21-year-old, my then boyfriend was convinced I was anorexic.

I wasn't anorexic (not for want of trying, mind you), but I had dieted and exercised my way to 53 kilograms (117lbs), which is on the low side for my 168-centimetre (5'6") frame and build.

The years that followed saw me gain and lose weight constantly.

In the run-up to the Ocean Surf Ski World Championships in 2017, I saw a dietician, knowing the difference nutrition can make to performance. I'd been told to bring a food diary. *All over it!*

I rocked up with my food intake broken not only into the food items consumed each day, but also the calories and macronutrients for each morsel that had passed my lips. Not only was I obsessed with calories, but I was also fanatical about eating healthily (when I wasn't bingeing on ice-cream). As a bonus, I brought along the last few years' worth of DEXA scans (which show muscle, fat, water and bone mass and percentages). She gave me some great advice, but it was clear I had issues. During the session, I joked about how nutty I was about my food. She did the skin-pinch test to get my body fat percentage, but she wouldn't share the results. She just said, 'Your fat levels are those of an elite athlete.'

While that should have been comforting, I assumed she didn't want to tell me because I wouldn't like the results. She gently suggested I should see a psychologist specialising in eating disorders and recommended one. As I was already seeing one psychologist, I felt another was excessive, but I took her message on board.

Over time, I slowly have become less obsessive, and my relationship with food is healthier, but my body image issues are never far away.

The tight clothes triggered me while I was in Sudan and sparked that unpleasant feeling of shame and self-loathing. The work needed to organise this trip distracted me. I was also working on the theory that the thousands of kilometres of paddling ahead of me would melt away the excess load. I had images of an emaciated me arriving in Egypt. *Like I say, issues.*

Adil arranged a meeting with members from the Khartoum Rowing and Canoe Club, who I'd met during my reconnaissance trip. It was wonderful to see them again. This included the head of the Sudan Rowing and Canoe Federation, Mr Abdelrahim. He was also the head of the Khartoum Rowing and Canoe Club. He was a quiet man, deeply respected and esteemed, who conducted himself with a calm authority. He had worked hard to build the Federation, as well as the Khartoum Rowing and Canoe Club, promoting these sports in Sudan and Central and Eastern Africa. His support was invaluable.

While many others in the Club helped with my preparations for the trip and getting approvals, I worked closely with Mugahid Obaid and Hamza Abdalla, or Captain Hamza, as he was referred to. Mugahid was tall and slim with a beautiful broad smile, kind eyes and a chilled and relaxed air. He spoke excellent English, and I conversed directly with him mostly. He would always positively reassure me, 'Sarah, everything is going to be fine.' Mugahid was married and had a young son, Mohamed.

Captain Hamza had a slightly heavier build and a confident nature, with an air that radiated an intensity and strength. He was, unusually for Sudan and his age, still single and apparently in no rush to wed, claiming, 'The Nile is my wife.'

Preparations were focused on the first section here in Sudan, which led from Kosti in the southern White Nile state back to Khartoum, 320 kilometres later. Mr Abdelrahim and the other men spent hours with the authorities to ensure things went smoothly and approvals were given. Mugahid gave me brief updates, and whenever I tried to thank him, he would always say, 'It's okay, it is our duty to help'.

It was the start of a level of kindness I could never have imagined.

Things took their time to get organised, but I didn't push my agenda like I would at home. It was more like gently nudging it along. And besides, things were done differently here, and these people already had busy lives. It was also a difficult time in Sudan. Everything they were doing was in their limited spare time, and I appreciated the lengths they were going to. They were also trying to get a police escort for me, but the unrest meant their resources were spread thin.

They arranged for one of their elite paddlers, Abdelrahman Mubarak, better known as Busati, to accompany me. It was going to be such a plus having him on my team for this part of the journey.

Mr Abdelrahim wrote official stamped letters explaining what I was doing and that I had their support. These were for me to give to the authorities on the way. They also arranged for me to meet particular people as I travelled. I was humbled by the level of support they provided.

An introduction arranged with the Minister of Tourism, resulted in a letter declaring his support of my trip through Sudan.

Most afternoons, Fahed and I would head down to the Club, which was situated on the banks of the Blue Nile. They had a couple of portacabins and a selection of rowing skiffs and kayaks.

In the water, at the bottom of the steep riverbank, were a couple of small engine boats secured to the pontoon. We would sit at one of the many white chairs and tables and drink teas and coffees prepared by a small vendor, while looking over the water.

Approximately 500 metres upstream was a bridge linking mainland Khartoum to Tuti Island, which sits in the confluence.

About 500 metres to the left and downstream was the confluence and the White Nile. Members of the Club would come down and train, mostly youngsters, often with Captain Hamza whizzing up and down in one of the boats correcting their technique and giving them drills to do.

Prior to my departure to Africa, I had been contacted by Nile Swimmers, who'd seen my posts on Twitter. Nile Swimmers is a UK charity and Sudanese NGO (non-government organisation) focused on drowning prevention. They teach people in Sudan and other countries on how to keep their communities safe around water.

Drowning is an issue along the Nile. Swimming is not taught as widely as it is in many western countries. Resuscitation skills are even more infrequently taught. Yet the Nile is used for everything — to wash in, it's a source of water for drinking and cooking, clothes are cleaned in it, as are vehicles and even animals. It is a means of getting from place to place, and it is a source of food.

On top of the swift currents, there are areas prone to flooding. Collectively, these are a recipe for disaster.

While in Khartoum, I met their country director of Nile Swimmers, the lovely Hind, and heard first-hand the programs they were running. As a lifesaver and former swim teacher, I was fascinated to learn about the lifesaving work done by Hind and her team in Sudan and the challenges they faced.

Returning to Fahed's one afternoon, a man from the neighbourhood was sitting outside on a chair watching the world go by. He was one of al-Bashir's advisors. Fahed introduced me and left us to chat. This man was from the 'golden age' when Sudan was thriving. He held modern-day views in contrast to the regime in place.

He said that the traditional ways alone were not the solution for the needs in this modern world. He felt the country required a mix of traditional and new ways. It was surprising to hear these viewpoints, seemingly at odds to the regime he was advising.

It was fascinating to listen to him, his views and his wisdom, and I would happily have sat talking with him all day. I felt honoured that he took the time to chat with me and share his personal views.

I was thankful to Fahed for introducing me to his network and for sharing insights into Sudanese life. And his involvement was going to continue, because he offered to join me on the first section. He was keen to provide ground support and swap in with Busati for some kayaking. I was thrilled that he was going to be coming along. I enjoyed his company and looked forward to him joining us.

The luxury of having back-up on the ground was appreciated too. This meant not having to carry all the kit in the kayak or trying to balance the weight and volume of food over macronutrients and other preferences. Plus, he would be a huge help with the logistics as well, finding camp spots, and keeping in touch with the Club back in Khartoum.

We were now getting closer to being on our way; however, final police approval was needed. With everything going on in the city, it was an understandably low priority for the police, which meant things took a few days longer.

Nine days after arriving in Sudan, I had the green light. We went to Mr Abdelrahim's house to pick up the letter of support from him, picked up Busati, and we made our way south. I was excited. Soon I'd be back on the water.

CHAPTER FOURTEEN
DAYS 81–88

*Kindness is the light that dissolves all walls
between souls, families and nations.*

Paramahansa Yogananda

It was a five-hour drive to the put-in at Kosti, which was south of Sudan in the White Nile state, with a few police stops on the way. The letter from Mr Abdelrahim, along with copies of my passport were handed over at each stop, and we were quickly on our way again. We stayed the night in Kosti, and the next morning we went to meet with the Minister of Youth and Sport for the White Nile state and his colleagues.

We were shown into a big office with large comfortable chairs in front of an impressive mahogany desk. The officials and their colleagues sat with us, and they were interested to find out more about my trip to date and my plans. They also asked about how Australia differs from Sudan in the sport of kayaking.

'The passion for the sport is the same,' 1 said, 'but it is the available money at both a personal and government level that differs enormously.'

There was minimal investment in the sport here, and the people didn't have the disposal income to spend on brand-new kayaks and paddles, like those in the affluent eastern suburbs of Sydney, where

        PADDLE THE NILE

I lived. Here there were many sharing one kayak and one paddle, and most of the equipment is old. Prior to this trip, I'd collected a bunch of unneeded paddles and PFDs from my local paddling community and sent them here. It wasn't much, but I was keen to do anything I could to help and support their passion.

After some tea and discussions, it was time to launch onto the White Nile. This was what I'd been hanging out for. I craved to be back on the water and to undertake the physical challenge that lay ahead. We made our way to the starting point, and I put my kayak together. With a few observers, Busati and I launched our craft and waved goodbye.

It was brilliant to finally be back placing my paddle in the water, and get into a rhythm, taking one stroke after another. The strong headwind made it tough going, but it didn't take away from how elated I was.

We began with a relatively short day of about four hours on the water. Not having kayaked for three months, there was some physical adjustment needed. We had to paddle through some thick rushes to get to the camping spot for the night where we met Fahed and set up camp. He had gone ahead to find a spot and then directed us to where he was. Some fishermen graciously gave their shack up to the guys. However, I loved getting back in my little tent again.

Usually, each night I'd take a cup of tea with me into my space, my home. Solitude is something I always crave, but it was in short supply on this trip. The moment I got into my tent and zipped myself in, I had that solitude. It was a two-person, super-lightweight tent given to me by Kathmandu. I could sit up in it, and it had space for me and the kit I needed, which always included my escape pouch, grab bag, dry bag containing a few toiletries, some clothes and my dry box of electrical gear — plus, my sleeping mat and sleeping bag.

Once in my tent, I'd pop on my head torch, inflate my sleeping mat, then get out my journal and pen. I wrote about the goings on during the day, how I was feeling, all while enjoying my tea. Diary writing has been something I've done since I was a kid, and it's been one of my best friends and a tool for dealing with challenging times. It was essential here because I have a shocking memory, and I wanted to make sure I captured everything that might fail to get saved in the space between my ears. After writing my diary, there'd be social media updates or just some mindless scrolling, if I had mobile coverage.

If I couldn't wash in the river, it would be a wet wipe bath and cleaning my teeth. The electricals would be put onto charge using powerbanks. Then it would be time to wriggle into my sleeping bag, turn the light off and quickly fall asleep.

The next day, we encountered more headwinds. These were set to plague me nearly all the way to the end. It meant that we weren't covering the kilometres Mugahid had planned for me, which had been my concern. We plugged away, and that afternoon we pulled up in a village to find a spot for the night. A crowd quickly gathered at the riverbank, looking curiously at us and our kayaks, asking Busati what we were doing.

One man invited us to stay. People had told me to be prepared for Sudanese generosity and hospitality. These are core virtues of the Sudanese, linked to people's honour. They feel a sense of duty to offer hospitality, not just to friends and family, but to strangers too. It is second nature to them.

I was eager and curious to experience a homestay, so we accepted the man's charitable offer. We directed Fahed to where we were before loading our gear in his car and making our way to our host's home, which consisted of four cube-like, single-storey buildings split into two rooms each. Some rooms were for sleeping, others for relaxing and one for preparing food. In between, there were empty courtyards, split by walls.

Four metal beds with thin mattresses were brought out to one of these courtyards for us, along with thick blankets. We met the family, and I was invited into the room where one of his daughters was resting with her four-day old baby. Her sister, nieces and nephews were there too. The new mother's sister, Huwaida, spoke some English, so I learnt about their lives there.

And then dinner was served. It consisted of a meat casserole with bread that was almost like a thin pancake. It was yummy.

Eventually, it was time to turn in. It was amazing to snuggle deep in my sleeping bag with the blanket over me and feel the cool night air on my face as I gazed up at the canopy of stars in the African night sky.

The following morning, I was told that we had to go by car for a short section — the team at the Club wanted me to make up some time. After all the time and effort I'd invested into this trip; I was bitterly disappointed. It felt like I was constantly having to compromise. It was like going through the five stages of grief each time one of these setbacks happened. At this point, I was in the 'anger' stage. However, I quickly reached acceptance and pulled out one of my mantras, 'things happen for us, not to us'. I also realised that the anger was at myself for accepting daily kilometres that I didn't think were achievable.

I hadn't wanted to make life difficult for all those assisting me, given they were already doing so much, and I was so grateful to them for all their help. The reality was that other sections had been missed, and this new section was only going to be 30 kilometres. I don't know why this triggered me as it wasn't a big deal.

This, and having to miss some sections in Uganda when the guys didn't want to or couldn't continue, combined to make a valuable lesson. People will not risk as much or be as determined and uncompromising as you to reach your goal. It was suddenly staggeringly obvious.

What might have helped, before setting off, would have been for me to get better at 'selling the goal', to make it a collective goal with each team, rather than just *my* goal. Each individual 'why' for wanting to achieve it might be different, and that's okay. I'd had discussions with teams around decision-making and how we'd do that, but not on getting others to equally invest in the goal itself.

The next step would have been being clear on the execution of the goal. Understanding the importance of that was ahead of me. Another step, potentially trickier to bring about, would have been to try and establish people's tipping points. How much effort would they put in? How hard would they push themselves? What risks they would or would not take?

Armed with the self-doubt I'd had coming into this trip, I'd assumed everyone would be ahead of me on all this.

While all these revelations were surfacing, I needed to be kind to myself. This was the first time I'd ever organised or done anything like this. Dave gave me a boost and told me I was doing incredibly well, even compared with more seasoned explorers who had more money to burn.

Once I regained perspective, my emotions settled down, and I made space for compassion and gratitude to those helping me. I refocused and agreed to do a small section by car.

We were soon back on the river and on our way to Ad Douiem. Being in Sudan, I was conscious of my clothing. Women here had to dress modestly, including covering their hair. The national costume is the *thawb* (*thobe*, *toub*), which is a long piece of cloth wrapped around the body over a top and skirt, covering the body entirely. The hair is covered with a hijab or a scarf. Other than the *thawb*, women will wear a burqa, others a loose-fitting dress that covered the arms and legs down to the ankles.

Foreigners are not expected to comply with the conservative dress code and don't have to cover their hair. However, it is expected that you dress modestly. I paddled in long-sleeve tops, sometimes with another loose-fitting short-sleeve top over and then lycra paddling leggings, plus a baseball cap. The leggings were skin-tight, so I kept a sarong close at hand to wrap around as needed.

We pulled up in Ad Douiem to a warm round of applause. Mr Abdelrahim had been in touch with Colonel (Ret) Assam Abdoulla, who had arranged the greeting. Since his retirement, he had become deeply involved in youth sport and sat on the Sudanese Olympic Committee. It was such an honour to meet him and those who had joined him. They had expected me the day before, and I now felt bad to have kept them waiting. A couple of their young paddlers put on a short display in their kayaks.

They invited me to chat with them before being taken to a hotel. The hotel had seen better days. The entrance looked like it had been blown open by a bomb. What would have been the reception had a dust-covered desk and a few chairs. It looked like the place had been abandoned. The motel-style rooms were basic, but comfortable and they had electricity and a fan, so I was stoked. There were showers in a shared bathroom too — luxury!

The colonel invited me for coffee. I met him outside and we went to one of the local cafés and started chatting. It wasn't long before he mentioned the protests. I always let other people bring up the protests. It was on everyone's mind, but it did surprise me how openly most spoke about it. The colonel was no exception, talking about the situation and how some of the protestors had been tragically killed.

Later, he took us all for dinner where we were joined by his son. He shared some of the challenges people faced, with many having left the villages for Khartoum. There is nothing for them here, so they go to the city in the hope of finding work. The sad thing is that it is a resource-rich country. They could have a thriving agriculture with just a little government investment. There is endless frustration at the government's greed and short-sightedness.

After dinner, the colonel took us to the local Youth Club. It was full of people working out in the gym, playing five-a-side soccer, and sinking baskets on the basketball court. Three musicians came along to play and sing for us. I felt like travelling royalty and was so appreciative of the effort they went to, not only to make me feel welcome and accommodated, but to share their culture.

The next day, we were back on the water after some *legemats* and coffee with the colonel and his son. *Legemats* are bite-sized donuts. Not as dense as the *mandazi* in Uganda, and much smaller, but the same idea. It wasn't exactly the food of champions, but I tucked in enthusiastically.

Arriving at the river, we were again greeted by a strong headwind.

Fahed started on the water with me. Soon after getting going, we passed under a bridge guarded by the army. I tried to paddle away, knowing that they would stop and question us, but I wasn't fast enough. Pretending not to hear their calls was fruitless. They shouted louder, and given they had a fair amount of gun power, we paddled over.

Fahed spoke to them in Arabic, and they told us to get off the water. *Ugh.* So, Fahed put a call into the colonel, who came down with a new official letter. This, along with his presence and explanation, pacified the officials and we were allowed to continue.

The river here was super wide, up to three kilometres, so the wind whipped up some serious chop to paddle into. It was difficult, but each night our efforts were rewarded with some spectacular camping spots.

While we could have been hosted by locals all the way, Fahed and I were keen to sleep under canvas. Either Fahed or his driver, if Fahed was paddling, would find a spot. We'd pull up, set up camp, get a fire going, cook and enjoy our food while chatting and watching breathtaking sunsets across the Nile. It was a special time.

We knew we were approaching the Jebel Aulia Dam when the water flow slowed. On its completion in 1937, it became the largest dam in the world. The stagnant, algae-filled water gave it away too. It was like paddling through a green soup, and it clearly showed one of the negative impacts of dams. Yes, they supply vital electricity, but at an immense environmental cost. For one, dams block the migration of fish, stopping the moving sediment critical for habitations downstream.

Having less free-flowing water results in a lack of oxygen in the water and increases water temperature. This, along with non-native plants and animals, such as snails, taking up residence, kills off many of the native flora and fauna. Dams also generate significant greenhouse gases. All up, large dams have led to the extinction of fish and aquatic species, as well as the disappearance of birds in flood plains, loss of forest, wetland and farmland, erosion of coastal deltas and many other unmitigable impacts.

Then there's the human impact — tens of millions have been displaced, and there are disasters that follow when dams collapse. Sadly, we continue to build more of these environmental disasters when there are numerous alternatives available.

The slow water wasn't the only challenge I was facing. Another was my kayak. It was a folding type ideal for short trips, but not for long distances, at least not for me. As it hadn't been possible for my sponsor to get it to Australia, I couldn't trial it before leaving which had really concerned me. All I'd been able to do was a short test before leaving Uganda. I found it uncomfortable to sit in, and I had to paddle extra hard to keep it straight, given I didn't have the rudder. I had left it behind because it was heavy and extra luggage, and I'd been advised that I wouldn't need it. But I did, especially in these windy conditions, and I was used to paddling kayaks with a rudder.

There was little I could do for now except keep paddling. After a couple of hours of slow going, we reached the takeout and were approaching the end of this section.

Come the last day of this section, the blisters on my hands were brutal, and my body was feeling the fatigue. However, an amazing lift greeted me as we made our final approach into Khartoum. The plan was to paddle up to the confluence and then veer right and paddle briefly upstream on the Blue Nile to return to the Khartoum Rowing and Canoe Club.

As we approached the bridges ahead of the confluence, I could see a few boats and wondered what they were doing. As I got closer, I saw Mr Abdelrahim on one of them.

It turned out that he had arranged for a welcoming party. These boats were waiting for us! On one was the president of the Olympic Committee for Sudan, as well as the chief of water police for Khartoum. Another boat was skippered by Mugahid and yet another by Captain Hamza, and finally there was Adil on his boat.

All these boats had people on board coming to see *our* arrival.

When the president awarded us medals for our effort, I nearly took an unexpected swim when I tried to stand in my kayak while hanging onto the boat so the medal could be placed around my neck. I was completely blown away by it all and felt incredibly honoured that these people had not just given up their valuable time but had made the effort to come out and greet us. It was a highlight of the trip.

I was so grateful to Captain Hamza Abdalla, Mugahid Obaid and Mr Abdelrahim for all the work they did to make this first section a success and for this tremendous reception.

It was good to be in Khartoum again. That section had been a warm-up and trial for what came next —1,500 kilometres of paddling up to the border with Egypt.

This was a point where things would get more remote and the weather, both heat and cold, was likely to play a bigger role.

Before that, I was going to have some rest and a little rejuvenation.

CHAPTER FIFTEEN
DAYS 89–103

There is an emanation from the heart in genuine hospitality which cannot be described, but is immediately felt and puts the stranger at once at his ease.

Washington Irving

It was also a time to catch up on emails, send out my newsletter and write another piece for World Nomads. I spoke to some friends and my mum before ramping up preparations for the next section.

One of the challenges in Sudan was access to money. Thanks to US sanctions, getting cash out of an ATM, via Western Union or using credit cards, was out of the question. You had to bring in all the money you were going to need in cash, in either euros or US dollars. I had brought some, but it wasn't going to be enough.

For the next section, the Club were keen for me to have an escort boat, and this was going to cost me. Luckily, a friend, who'll remain nameless because what he did is illegal, helped me out. I just needed to transfer money to one of his accounts in Europe and then he would give me cash in Sudan. Sounds simple, right? No — even that was problematic.

It was impossible to initiate a transfer using internet banking because my bank required a code sent to my Australian mobile number. As I was in Sudan, using a local SIM card, and not my

Australian mobile number, meant the code wouldn't come through. Even changing the mobile number on my account to my Sudanese number didn't help, neither did using a VPN. Despite hours on the phone to my bank, there was no progress.

So, I had to rely on my great mate Sue, who loaned me the money and made the transfer. Sue was part of my crisis team. We met through work at my first job in London. After we both left the company, we didn't see much of each other. She moved to the United States, and I would hear news through other ex-colleagues.

One of these ex-colleagues, like me, ended up in Sydney. He was having birthday drinks one day and invited me along. When I arrived, to my surprise and joy, Sue was there, and we resumed our friendship. She quickly became one of my closest friends.

She is the wisest, kindest and most thoughtful woman I know, and it was comforting to have her on the team. Someone who I knew always had my back and would be there for me. It was also such a joy to chat to her during my time off the river, share stories and hear what was going on back home. She didn't just stay in touch with me, she also messaged my mum regularly to see how she was doing, knowing how stressful it would be for her. I felt very blessed to have her friendship.

As well as catching up with friends, I needed a different kayak. I chatted to Mugahid about the problems I had and asked if he had any ideas. The Club benevolently lent me one of theirs for the next section. This was a plastic touring kayak with good storage and a rudder. It was perfect! This new one would get me through Sudan.

For Egypt, I found an outlet for kayaks that had what I needed in stock. It was another plastic touring model with a rudder. So, I bought that and arranged to get it sent down to Aswan.

One afternoon, Fahed and I were joined by Adil and Mr Abdelrahim. After some initial chit-chat, Mr Abdelrahim said that he'd arranged for me to do a TV interview the following day. I was surprised, and when I heard it was going to be an hour long and live, I was a tad apprehensive!

Mr Abdelrahim explained that the interviewer was going to meet me the following afternoon to find out a little more about my story ahead of the interview, which I appreciated.

The evening of the interview, Fahed drove me and Adil to the studio. With my Arabic being limited to 'hello' and 'thank you', I needed a translator, and Adil good-naturedly stepped into the role. The studio was at the top of an old building, and I made my way up the stairs hesitantly. The interviewer was there with two guys on sound and camera. I was glad to see such a small crew.

We took our seats and after a short chat we were live on air. I was asked various questions about my trip and my time so far in Sudan. The good thing was that because everything I said had to be translated, the hour-long interview was only about 30 minutes of talking. The time flew by, and before I knew it, we were done and on our way home.

I loved these random, unexpected experiences. It was Hemingway who said, 'It's good to have an end to journey towards; but it is the journey that matters, in the end.' This whole expedition was about accepting that plans would change, going with the flow and saying yes when things like this came up. I was learning to have a lighter grip on my plans and use them more as a guide than 'the rule'.

As well as this interview, there were posts on Facebook by the Club and an article in one of the papers. In theory, this was great, but the reality was it was better for me to have a low profile, from a security perspective.

One day, while I was sitting at a set of traffic lights with Fahed, the man in the car next to us started pointing and talking excitedly. Fahed translated, 'He recognises you as the paddler.' *So much for a low profile.* This was not great when the kidnap risk was never far away.

While in Khartoum, I saw the extraordinary spectacle that is Sufi dancing. With Fahed and some of his friends, we drove out to Omdurman, the largest city in Sudan on the edge of Khartoum. Sufi whirling is a form of dancing and physical meditation, which originated among some Sufi groups and is still practised by the Sufi Dervishes (hence the term 'whirling dervishes')[37]. Sufism is a branch of Islam, and each Friday, worshippers come together as the sun sets to pray and dance in a large cemetery outside the Sheikh Hamed Al Nil Mosque, which houses the tomb of their nineteenth-century Sufi leader.

Most men were dressed in long white robes, *jalabiya*, and wore white brimless caps. The Sufi elders stood out in their brightly coloured green and red robes. Some were in technicoloured dress. Many wore garlands of wooden *misbaha* beads. Green is a popular choice because it symbolises the simplicity and calm of Sufism. Many of the elders had long dreadlocks, which was not what I expected. Seeing them in their attire created an incredible display and feast for the eyes, even before the dancing began.

With the sun setting, the music began. The air became thick with incense as the drumming, music and chanting gradually reached a crescendo, the beat getting faster and faster. The crowd clapped, their energy filling the air, and the dancing continued with increased fervour until it reached a sudden stop — the goal being the inner path to God through *dhikr*: the absolute absorption in worship during prayers, dances, and spinning fervently to induce a trance.

Once the dancing finished, we were surrounded by locals keen to talk, find out where we came from and what we were doing here in Sudan. When I said I was from Australia, one man exclaimed, 'Nicole Kidman, kangaroos, koalas, rugby!' It was interesting to hear what 'from Australia' meant to him! We were invited for coffee and more chatting. It was another unforgettable experience.

On another day, Mugahid suggested a kayak race down at the Club. Being ever so slightly competitive, the only female and looking at the young opposition, I proposed some additions to skew the race in my favour. I suggested making it a triathlon of sorts, which they agreed to.

So, we swam across the Nile, ran along the riverbank, jumped in our kayaks and paddled back to the Club. My cunning plan worked, and I came in a respectable third. It was fun hanging out with everyone from the Club. They were passionate about their sport, embraced fun for the sake of fun, worked hard, and loved to share their culture and make everyone feel at home.

Sport is amazing at bringing people together. As Nelson Mandela so eloquently said, 'Sport has the power to change the world. It has the power to inspire. It has the power to unite people in a way that little else does.'

Sport for me has always played an integral part in my life and brought me so much value, for which I have Mum to thank. She had me trying a variety of sporting activities, on top of those I took part in at school. Involving myself in a plethora of sports gave me the confidence and curiosity to continue to try new sports and not fear sucking at something as a beginner.

It has regularly taken me out of my comfort zone, whether trying something different, pushing myself to new limits or getting out into more challenging environments. It allowed me to also get comfortable with being physically and mentally uncomfortable.

It also provides endless goals for me to work towards, and I love the challenge it brings, which has had ripple effects across my whole life. I've learnt to appreciate the dedication needed to become fitter, stronger and faster. I relish the process. It was never just about the finish line and whether I made it onto the podium.

It was the same with this trip. If it was all about the finish line, then there would have been so much I wouldn't have appreciated, valued, or even noticed along the way.

Beyond that, it's the people I've met and experiences I've been lucky to enjoy. I've made so many of my friends through sport, including my friends here in the Club.

Away from the river, I was privileged to enjoy another new cultural experience. Sudanese weddings have a reputation for being incredible spectacles, steeped in tradition, customs and rituals. Captain Hamza thoughtfully invited me to his cousin's wedding.

I walked into this event where there were close to 1,000 people. Despite being advised I didn't need to cover my hair, entering this huge venue as the only non-Sudanese and with my blonde hair uncovered, I felt very self-conscious.

There was no opportunity to hide in the corner — Mugahid dragged me up to dance. Between him, Hamza and Mr Abdelrahim, my attempts to leave the dance floor were thwarted.

I gave in and danced incredibly badly with everyone to the traditional music being played by the band. I danced with the women, the bride, the groom and many more.

Hamza even thrust a sword into my hand at one point (part of his traditional clothing and dancing). After waving it around briefly, with no clue as to what I was supposed to do with it, I returned it to its owner before I did some damage. I really didn't want to inadvertently kill the bride, which would have been a downer for everyone.

Plates of food were served, washed down with cans of soft drink. This was the first time I'd been to a 'dry' wedding. It suited me, having given up drinking seven years earlier. My relationship with alcohol wasn't healthy, and I didn't need it. While I wasn't smashing a bottle of vodka every night, it felt like something trying to control me. I'd have a glass of wine or two most nights during the week, then more at the weekend and a big night out every so often. It did a wonderful job of numbing and suppressing stress and unwanted emotions.

It became the friend that was always there whether celebrating, happy, sad, stressed or bored. Over time, however, I realised it wasn't my friend. The big nights out had me waking up heavy with shame and guilt.

After one particularly big night, waking up feeling like shit and full of regret, I decided enough was enough. It was time to take back control, so I stopped drinking. I read Allen Carr's book, *The Easy Way to Stop Drinking*[38], and haven't touched a drop since. And I haven't missed it.

Yes, to begin with I felt like a bit of a social outcast, living in a society where drinking alcohol is such a norm. For me, the positives of not drinking totally outweighed any negatives. In fact, I struggled to find any downside. It gave me hours of my life back, and the slow mornings and foggy head syndrome were gone. Instead, I'd wake up alert and ready for action, guilt-and shame-free.

I also gradually began to like and appreciate myself. It challenged me too. Suddenly, there was nothing to numb emotions with. I had to deal with every emotion that came up — stress, anxiety, depression, sadness. There was no more avoidance. Giving up the booze took me on a journey of self-discovery and growth. I saved a fortune, my skin looked better, and I was happier. Best of all, I felt free. That's more than a win-win.

So here I was at this wedding, happily surrounded by non-drinkers and having a blast. The women looked stunning in their brightly coloured dresses. They all smiled at me and encouraged me to dance some more. Those who could speak English chatted to me. I felt so accepted, and my initial feeling of self-consciousness evaporated.

Saying that, I'm pretty sure the bride and groom will look at their wedding video and ask, 'Who on earth was that blonde woman?'

It was a fantastic night and a privilege to be there.

Fun as all this was, I was itching to get back on the water. This was also a good thing from a safety perspective, as the risks were going up …

Dave was becoming increasingly worried that I would be kidnapped and was pushing me to get going as soon as possible. The Club had been creating more publicity, and Dave said the cyber team from TCG were struggling to keep up with the online chat. While I was delaying my social media posts, so people wouldn't know where I was, the risks were increasing the longer I stayed in the one place. This was not specific to Sudan and was a risk throughout the entire trip.

At this point there was at least one questionable man talking about me online, and Dave and his team were keeping an eye on him. They also sent me some names to be on the lookout for.

One day, someone messaged my *Paddle the Nile* Facebook page, 'Hi'. The name was similar to one on the list, but when I told Dave, he advised that this man wasn't one of them. That was the good news.

The bad news was, however, that this new 'friend' was a militia rebel with the Sudan Liberation Movement/Army (SLM/A), a Sudanese rebel group. He also had many connections to the Libyan militia, along with extremist pals in Sudan and Egypt. He had been in Khartoum around the same time as me, so this put me on edge a little.

Prior to departure, I'd been recommended to have a kidnap negotiator back home in readiness, just in case. Better to have someone in place before the shit hit the fan. They'd be helped by Dave, but it needed to be a friend or family member. So, I picked one of my close mates, Daniel. It was a huge ask, and I was incredibly grateful that he agreed without hesitation, saying, 'Sarah, you would have thought long and hard about who to ask. If you think I'm the right person, then yes, of course I'll do it.' That reaction said it all and was why I chose him.

For now, there wasn't much I could do other than stay super vigilant and be smart and try to avoid getting nabbed. I was still staying at Fahed's home, and while part of me very much wanted to get back on the river, I was getting comfortable there. Khartoum now felt like another home, surrounded by my new friends and endless kindness and hospitality.

The protests were continuing, and the government was doing their best to make things difficult. Electricity blackouts started, which people thought might be the government's attempts to make life problematic for the protestors. They also released sewage onto some of the streets to stop the protests. The government was running out of money, and the banking system was on the verge of collapse. There were concerns the Rapid Support Forces (RSF), who were fiercely loyal to al-Bashir, might get violent.

The discussions and planning to get me back on the water were progressing slowly. While I was now more accustomed to the way of doing things here, at times it did test my patience. Fahed understood my frustration, but also appreciated the Sudanese way of doing things and helped me navigate my way and gain a better understanding of how things were done here. I also knew the guys from the Club were working hard to get things organised for me, including continued discussions with the authorities to ensure I had a smooth passage.

One afternoon, while waiting for Mugahid at the Club, a song came on from one of my Spotify playlists. It was Coldplay's *Up and Up*.

Standing there watching the Blue Nile flowing past, listening to the lyrics, the words spoke to me, and my mood instantly lifted; I smiled. It's amazing how it changed my mood and mindset. To this day, that song takes me back to the expedition. For the remainder of the trip, whenever I felt low, I'd play it and smile.

My mindset changed, and I let go. I would set off when I was supposed to. Like I said, I knew the guys from the Club were doing their best against a backdrop of challenging circumstances. To make sure I had everything ready to go, Fahed even drove me to the shops to get the food and other supplies. I also got my visa extended.

The plan was that I would have a support boat with me as well as a paddler, Coach Aimun, from the Club. Initially, the police were going to escort me, but they were a tad preoccupied with the goings on in Khartoum. I would have happily gone without a support boat, as a part of me wanted to be unsupported, but it was a battle not worth fighting, and there were the obvious benefits of having support - no fully laden kayaks, the ability to have more supplies with us plus the increased security it created. The Club gave me another letter to take for the authorities and informed all the key ones of our plan, to ensure we had support and would encounter no hold-ups. This was all so much work, and this trip wouldn't have been possible without them.

The Club's support continued to blow me away. They had embraced me — in their words — into their family. To this day, I still feel part of that family. It wasn't just because I spent time with them organising my trip, it was getting to spend *quality* time with them. And thanks to them, I was getting closer to setting off.

While I was daunted at the length of this next section, 1,500 kilometres, I was excited to start and eager to see what it would be like to kayak this distance.

Prior to Sudan, it had been mostly adventure. This part of the journey would involve more physical and mental challenges, due to the long-distance remote paddling, and I was keen to see how I handled it.

After 16 days in Khartoum, I was back on the water again — one happy paddler.

That morning, Fahed took me, my gear, the food supplies in newly sourced plastic drums, and fuel for the boat to the Club. There, ready and waiting, was our support boat with Captain Salih at the helm and Assam, his co-driver and companion. The purple and white boat was about eight metres long with a fixed canopy and open sides. Inside was a carpeted floor and bench seats around the edge. It was more flash than I was expecting!

We loaded all the gear, food and fuel onto the boat, and I said my farewells to the Club and to Fahed. Coach Aimun and I launched our kayaks, and then, with a final wave goodbye, we turned and began our journey to the Egyptian border.

CHAPTER SIXTEEN
DAYS 103–119

Character cannot be developed in ease and quiet. Only through experience of trial and suffering can the soul be strengthened, vision cleared, ambition inspired, and success achieved.

Helen Keller

We got off to a great start that first day, covering about 35 kilometres. We didn't get on the water until after 10am and called it a day at 5pm, with a lunch break in between. Lunch was prepared by Captain Salih and Assam. It felt more like a luxury holiday than an expedition. This five-star treatment didn't last long, however. I think they were trying to set a good impression, and I appreciated their efforts.

That evening, we pulled up on a small sandy island, made camp and then enjoyed dinner. It was tinned sardines, tomatoes, onions and bread — a simple meal I loved.

Aimun's only comment was, 'Do you cook?'

'Ah … yes, why?'

'You cut the tomatoes too small.' *Now that was a tad harsh!* I had been introduced to Coach Aimun once before we set off, and my initial take was he was a lovely guy with a very direct approach. He was a swim coach, hence being called 'Coach' Aimun, and was set to keep me sane on this section.

Captain Salih was proud of his boat. Aimun told me I was lucky not to speak Arabic, and for Captain Salih's English to be limited, because it saved me from the countless explanations of how wonderful his boat was, and the engine. Assam, who was there to help Captain, was tall, quiet, with a stunning smile and protective aura. From the get-go, both Captain Salih and Assam called me 'Mama Sarah'. Mama is used when 'Madam' would be used back home. It had been the same in Uganda and Rwanda. I was a bit taken aback the first time I was referred to as 'Mama', much like the first time someone, to my horror, called me 'Madam'. It made me feel old.

After the initial surprise, I decided I much preferred 'Mama' to 'Madam'.

At first, these guys were keen to do as much as possible to make me comfortable and keep me happy. It was not entirely surprising though that this enthusiasm did diminish as we clocked up the kilometres. They meant well, and I was glad to have them with us. It was cute how they would always say, 'Anything, Mama Sarah.' They were continually looking out for me.

That night, thanks to a nearby wedding where the music was blaring, along with donkeys braying and a strong wind making my tent flap, I didn't get much sleep. Regardless, I was awake early, but in for a disappointing start. I had images of us getting up and on the water bright and early, but NO!

I had been warned that the Sudanese weren't morning people. I'm the opposite. I like to get up early and not hang around. We had a limited number of daylight hours, and I wanted to make the most of it. So, my mission was to think of something to get them up and going each day.

For the 'warm-up' from Kosti to Khartoum, there had been near continual headwinds. The current was good, but our unwanted friend — the headwind — stuck around. It wasn't long before the sprawling city was behind us, and we were in arid, mountainous regions. The river gently wound its way through the rolling rocky hills on each side. There wasn't much in the way of greenery, just a few hardy shrubs and small trees along the banks. As harsh as the landscape looked, it was stunning. It felt remote, which appealed to my yearning for adventure.

We stopped at a village just before the first set of cataracts, which are small rapids. We took the opportunity to enjoy a coffee.

My hands had blistered quickly, and a local man, seeing the state of my hands, disappeared and returned a few minutes later with plasters. I tried to explain that I had some, but he seemed eager to help, so I took them and thanked him. I tried to give him money, but he refused to accept it.

It was only day two back on the water, but my body was starting to ache, unaccustomed to the activity. In addition to the blisters, my lats were crying out in pain. Luckily, the discomfort didn't put a dent in how upbeat I felt. I loved being on the water, going into remote areas, away from everything and everyone, feeling like I was back on an expedition.

We covered 55 kilometres that day, which was an improvement on the previous day's effort. The island we pulled onto that evening was tiny. Three of us slept on the floor of the boat, and Aimun slept on the island on one of the camp beds I had brought for the guys to use if they wanted.

Captain Salih had bought some fish from the local fishermen, which he wrapped in foil with lime and vegetables and cooked on the campfire for us. This feast was served with more bread and limes and was a delicious reward for our day's paddle.

The next morning, things started looking up when we got on the river at a better time. Regrettably, this was countered with a two-hour stop at 10am. The Sudanese tend to have two meals a day — one late morning and one in the evening. If they have anything earlier, it's often some bread and a flour-based *halva* with jam. *Halva* is generally made from sesame seeds and a lot of sugar — a Sudanese staple. It was pale off-white with a flaky crumbly texture. I tried it, but I wasn't a fan.

For my breakfast, I stuck with oats, the local version of Nutella, which tasted great, and peanut butter. I'd make it before getting on the water and pop it in a Tupperware box ready for the first break. With the slower starts, there was time to make a coffee to fire me up before getting on the water, and I packed myself some biscuits and dates to snack on between meals.

After a few days, the rocky hills were behind us and we were making our way through the Sahara Desert. Our first main stop was Shendi, where we were due to meet Fahed, Captain Hamza and Mugahid. We had a short day on the river and waited for them to arrive. I lay on the floor of the boat, which had been anchored on a sandbank. It was warm and peaceful, and I nearly drifted off to sleep. My body appreciated the extra rest.

The guys arrived after their three-hour drive from Khartoum to take us out to the Meroe Pyramids, a UNESCO World Heritage Site. It turns out that Egypt doesn't have exclusivity when it comes to pyramids. There are some 200 in Sudan.

We arrived at a car park where there was a small museum. You could have driven past and not known what was here. We made our way to the sand-coloured pyramids which were almost camouflaged by the surrounding desert. The sand was rich ochre in colour and contrasted beautifully with the blue sky. Around us there was nothing but sand shaped into rolling dunes as the Sahara stretched further than we could see. The pyramids were much smaller than their Egyptian equivalents. They stood up to about 30 metres in height and had steep sides. Many had a temple-like entrance attached to the base, or what was left of it. These magnificent edifices, made of granite and sandstone, were slowly being eroded by the wind and sand.

They had also taken a beating in the 1830s, when Italian, Guiseppe Ferline made his way through Sudan, blowing the tops off them in search of reported gold and silver.

Some modern replicas had been built to show what they would have looked like in their heyday. These pyramids were built as tombs by the rulers of the Kushite kingdoms over 2,000 years ago[39]. Over 40 Nubian queens and kings had been entombed here. The royal occupants were mummified and buried with jewellery, and Giuseppe helped himself to much of it during his 'explosive' exploration. He returned home and sold what he had pillaged, which is now on display in German museums.

Amazingly, we had the whole place to ourselves.

After looking through the museum and reading about the history, we headed up the steep sand dunes to check out the pyramids. We ventured inside the pyramids that we could and walked around those we couldn't. Then we ran down the sand dunes like kids, smiling, laughing and falling over. The guys loved to enjoy themselves, and it was brilliant to see them all again. It was so lovely of them to do this sizeable trip out of Khartoum to come and see us.

On top of that, Fahed brought more fuel. The crisis in Khartoum meant there were still queues, and in many places, you weren't allowed to fill jerry cans, as they wanted to avoid stockpiling. After unloading the fuel, it was sadly time to say goodbye once again.

The short day on the river did nothing to allow my body to recover. It was still adjusting to the long days of kayaking and it would be a good hour or two before my body warmed up and gave into the fact that it was another day of paddling. I thought I'd get bored and find the monotony challenging — but, as in Tanzania, that was not the case at all. I was happy daydreaming and listening to music, looking at the scenery and concentrating on my paddling.

When I'd been training for Molokai, a 53-kilometre ocean ski race in Hawaii, I'd struggled with the five-hour training sessions. Here, I was able to give in and accept that it was all-day paddling.

The winds picked up and grew stronger, whipping up waves that broke on me at times, which made my body hurt even more. Now my shoulders were sore, and my right arm was causing me some issues.

As expected, night-time temperatures dropped as we made our way into the desert. During the daytime, it was high 20s Celsius, while at night it would drop to between 10 and 14 degrees Celsius. However, it felt colder at night, and I was sleeping in three tops and tracksuit pants. I think it was sleeping on the sand that did it, despite my sleeping mat.

Each morning, I'd wake at first light, warm in my layers and buried in my sleeping bag. As soon as I woke, I'd grab my paddling clothes and draw them into the warm cocoon of my sleeping bag. While they were warming up, I'd unplug my GPS and phone and pack up the leads and powerbanks. I'd then clean my teeth and face and put on sunscreen, check the weather forecast, then check in with Dave and read the intel report. Finally, I'd go through the route for the day.

When I could put it off no longer, I'd deflate my sleep mat, rolling around on it to expel the air. Then, I'd reluctantly unzip my sleeping bag, take off my night-time layers and quickly put my paddling gear on.

There were lots of layers to my daytime attire: sports bra, sleeveless thermal top, long-sleeve light thermal top, paddling top, a fleece and then paddling lycra pants. Sometimes a windproof jacket was needed too. I feel the cold, and I've always believed I was built for warmer climes. The top layers would then slowly come off as I, and the day, warmed up.

While my body was suffering, I knew it would adapt, eventually, and I just had to push through it. I'd read James Lawrence's biography[40] of his superhuman 50 ironman triathlons in 50 states over 50 consecutive days. He showed what the body could endure, and adapt to, with some serious mental strength. This is a man who, after injuring his shoulder, swam one armed for days on end during this feat of endurance. Reading that book gave me the confidence that my body would come good.

One thing I did do was change paddle. I had two sets that had been donated by Bennett Paddles, Braca-Sport and Canoe Innovations. There were two blade sizes, and it was time to drop to the smaller one. The pain in my right arm and wrist was getting worse, and my left shoulder wasn't great. I had a stash of Mobics (non-steroidal anti-inflammatories), my magic pills, and I was making my way through them. The switch to the smaller blade, along with some magic pills for a few days, reduced the pain.

After a week on the river, we had a full rest day at Atbara. Well, it was a rest from paddling but ended up being a hectic day. We'd paddled 325 kilometres since leaving Khartoum, which was fantastic but I was keen to push the daily distance up. After mooring, Aimun and I went to replenish our supplies. We needed biscuits, bread, sardines, tuna, tomatoes, limes, honey, jam, tea, coffee and pasta. After dropping these provisions off back at the boat, we feasted on grilled meat and bread at a local restaurant, which was a pleasing change after all the fish we'd been eating.

A friend of Aimun's suggested meeting the president of the Swimming Federation for this region. It turned out to be another slightly random experience. We were taken to Atbara's coach terminal, with Aimun's friend talking with great pride about the building. Passing the many coaches coming and going, we entered this smart and modern, blissfully cool building with a large open ticket hall. We were then shown upstairs and into an office.

Behind the desk was an older guy in a safari-style suit. Seated in front of the desk were two military men who, judging by the stars on their lapels and aura of authority, must have been fairly senior.

     PADDLE THE NILE

This didn't seem like a Swimming Federation meeting. For one, there was the distinct lack of any aquatic centre. There were no signs, pictures or anything to suggest swimming was a topic.

I was confused.

I later found out that our man behind the desk was a government minister and former Governor of Atbara. The whole swimming thing was a voluntary side gig. There were piles of papers on the desk, a picture of al-Bashir on the paint-chipped wall, and a cooler containing cloudy, unpalatable looking water.

We took a seat and were given coffee. There was some general chat, mostly in Arabic. It was all quite strange; however, it was another demonstration of the warm Sudanese hospitality. Sure, it was random, but another enjoyable side tour nonetheless.

Back at the boat, it was time to get some washing done. This involved a bucket, some washing powder and river water. I was suspicious of some young guys coming and taking photos of themselves in front of the boat. I tried to avoid being in any pictures; my mind created scenarios of these photos going to some cash-poor terrorists in need of a kidnap-for-ransom target. Slightly paranoid perhaps, but I had been warned to be vigilant here. So, I subtly took a photo of them. The reality was, they were probably more interested in getting a photo of them and the boat, and I was effectively photo bombing.

My body was still aching. I mentioned it to Dave, trying not to sound like I was whingeing. He reminded me to enjoy the experience, pain and all, as it'd be over before I knew it and I'd miss it. He was right, of course, and it was the nudge and change in mindset that helped me reframe things. Plus, I had shortened my paddle, which seemed to help too.

Slowly, my muscles started to adjust, and after about ten days, my body adapted and ached less. However, then the skin on my hands and feet started packing in. Well, when I say 'packing in', I mean 'cracking'. The wind, dry atmosphere and constant alternating between wet and dry was taking its toll. It was like having lots of papercuts. My iPhone no longer recognised my fingerprint. First World expedition issues.

One time, when I knelt, the skin on the bottom of my feet stretched and cracked. *Lovely!* The skin was getting extremely thin and looked like it belonged to an 80-year-old. I couldn't straighten my fingers, and doing up clips and buttons was painful. When you're using your hands all day, these little cuts were less than ideal. I thought trench foot was more likely on this trip. This drying and cracking wasn't something I had anticipated.

The pain was disproportionate to the size of the wounds, and I felt like I was being a sook. In an attempt to fix it, I put Vaseline on at night. One evening, I slathered my hands in Vaseline and put on some surgical gloves from my first aid kit. It helped, but I didn't have enough pairs of gloves to continue with this treatment.

If this was the worst thing I had to deal with on the trip, other than the jigger, then I was stoked. I'd prepared myself for the worst and done remote first aid training for this trip. So far, thankfully, I hadn't needed to put anything I'd learnt into practice.

The winds continued to challenge us as we made our way north. We would move from one side of the river to the other in search of shelter from the wind and into better currents. With the river being a few hundred metres wide, it took a little time to cross, and it was disappointing to get to the other side and find no respite.

I checked the satellite images for the sections ahead to see where there were larger islands and splits in the river to make sure we took the best course. The wind made it cooler, and there were days I'd be shivering by the time I got off the water. But the cold was easier to manage than the extreme heat experienced in summer with average highs of more than 43 degrees Celsius. This was the reason I picked this time of year to do this trip.

One other minor issue was that we weren't getting on the river any quicker, and the breaks during the day were long. After another day of me being ready by 7.30am and waiting over an hour for everyone to be ready, I broached the subject.

Plan A of 'leading by example' wasn't working. So next up was the carrot approach with Aimun. 'If we start a bit earlier, we can make some good kilometres before the wind picks up. How about we aim to start at 7am?'

Thankfully, he agreed.

The next morning, at 7am, he put some water on to make coffee. *Arghhh!*

My slight frustration quickly dissolved once I was on the water, and we were greeted with waves and warm smiles, thumbs up or salutes from the people we passed. Some even fist pumped, and many invited us for food and coffee. One lad showed his appreciation by cracking his bull whip. I wish I'd had more time to stop, take up the kind invitations for coffee or food and spend time with these endlessly hospitable people.

The scenery was amazing. The wide river was broken up with rocky and sandy islands, and its banks were continuously lined with tall date palm trees. It was stunning to witness.

We eventually got into a rhythm of paddling for two and a half to three hours at a time. I'd have short water and food breaks in the kayak every 30 minutes and bathroom breaks as needed.

While the body had adapted, there were still aches. One day, Assam massaged and 'cracked' Captain Salih. He offered to do the same for me. *Yes!* I lay down, and he proceeded to crack my back, elbows, wrists, fingers, knees and ankles with the skills of a highly qualified osteopath. I was impressed and felt a surge of relief and release of energy through my body.

Assam had an interesting background. His father had left when he was a young boy. His mother had then taken him and his brothers and sisters to Libya, where he grew up before returning to Sudan as an older teenager. Assam made me feel safe in the same way Koa had. He was always there, with a quiet but strong demeanour. He had once saved the life of Captain Salih when he was electrocuted in the water. I wish I'd been able to speak Arabic to find out more about him, feeling he must have had a thousand stories to share.

As we made our way north, we approached the great bend and an area that few foreigners get to travel through, as there are military installations creating some sensitivities. We also made it into scorpion territory. This coincided with the zip breaking on my tent. *Bollocks.* I really didn't relish the thought of waking up to a scorpion on my chest, poised to zap me.

What did surprise me was that while I wasn't thrilled with this situation, it didn't bother me much. Contrast this to 28-year-old me who, on thinking she'd seen a scorpion while sun baking on holiday in Turkey, proceeded to spend the next few hours perched anxiously on her sun lounger on scorpion lookout. I'm not sure where this more relaxed and accepting mindset had come from, but it was appreciated. Perhaps this trip had beaten some of my anxiety into submission?

Dave advised that at Abu Hamad, our next stop, there was a shop just north of the market that sold zips. The level of information he had blew me away.

After a total of 13 days on the river since leaving Khartoum, we reached Abu Hamad, home of the zip. And low and behold, there was the shop. I bought a zip, but never quite managed to attach it. I settled for safety pins and the hope that I'd never need to leave the tent in a hurry.

Abu Hamad is a big town at the top of the great bend, and was another opportunity to resupply, have some food and coffee, and for me to get another hoodie. I was getting super cold at night and needed an extra fleece-lined layer.

We were told the next 20 kilometres weren't passable for our support boat due to the rocky rapids. This meant that we'd have to find a way of getting the boat off the water and taken around the section. The guys spoke to some locals, and negotiations started for hiring a truck to take us around. I was gutted, as I really didn't want to miss this section. The quotes for a truck were ridiculous and started at SDG8,000 (US$133) and increased to SDG17,000 (US$283).

Another fisherman came along and on hearing the discussions told us that it would be fine to go by boat; he could even guide us, for a price. The guys questioned the fisherman's confidence, but then deemed he knew what he was talking about, so Assam worked on the price until SDG3,000 (US$50) was agreed. While that seemed reasonable from a Western perspective, for here it was expensive. I was willing to pay, but with my inability to pop to the cashpoint, I had to watch the spending. It was worth it though, as it meant we'd complete this section and have some fun in small rapids. Captain Salih was infinitely less excited at the prospect of taking his precious boat down rocky rapids.

We finally got going on this stunning stretch of river and headed south-west. The area was dotted with small shrub and tree-covered islands with water bubbling in between them. We were also gifted with glimpses of the desert behind the riverbanks. I was looking forward to the change in direction, as we'd have the wind behind us. *But ... no!*

After two weeks of windy days, it dropped. Basically, we were almost wind-free, until we started heading north again. I was doomed. There was no time to lament, as we were off along a series of Grade II rapids. We put the heavy food barrels and jerry cans of fuel in our guide's boat, to ensure Captain's boat sat higher in the water, and we made it through. Captain was visibly relieved to have made it without punching a hole in his boat. We then reloaded our boat, bid our guides farewell and continued on our way.

The further we went, the more remote it felt, with less people and towns. Paddling through the Sahara Desert was an extraordinary experience. I've always had a fascination with the desert. There's something about the harshness, the changing shapes of the sand dunes, the people and animals that manage to live in these seemingly inhabitable lands.

Now I was on a river running through the world's largest hot desert and loving it. It was extraordinary. That night, feeling the warmth of the fire and watching the stars emerge while eating cake and drinking coffee, I couldn't have been more content. Assam commented on how happy I looked. I thanked them all for organising today, and for Captain Salih for taking the chance. 'Anything, Mama Sarah,' he replied. I was filled with gratitude.

CHAPTER SEVENTEEN
DAYS 120–126

*The art of life lies in a constant readjustment
to our surroundings.*

Okakura Kakuzō

Two days later, and sixteen since we left Khartoum, we reached the edge of the reservoir for the Merowe Dam, and it was time for more negotiations. The Khartoum Rowing and Canoe Club had said this was too dangerous to cross, without giving any real explanation. So, we pulled up and it wasn't long before NISS (National Intelligence and Security Services) paid us a visit to find out what we were doing. Another visitor said we'd be fine getting across the reservoir, so we decided we'd give it a crack.

Once NISS gave us approval to continue, I made the most of the early finish for the day and did some washing, of my clothes and me. Washing myself involved getting in the river, clothes on, and bathing respectfully without revealing any skin.

The plan was to set off across the reservoir the next morning, using a local to guide us across, which the guys organised. I thought the need for a fisherman to guide us was over the top. This was basically a lake, right? No, it turned out there were heaps of channels winding between the islands created by the flooding for the dam. On these islands were houses cut off from one another by the waterways. At times there would be a single house on its own unplanned island — no vegetation, nothing. It must be a strange and tough way of life.

In the background, the demonstrations were continuing, and there were rumours that Salah Gosh, the head of NISS, had asked al-Bashir to step down. This was not unexpected, in part because al-Bashir was probably not Gosh's favourite after al-Bashir demoted him from his role as head of NISS in 2009, before reinstating him in 2018. A big focus for Gosh would have been the power play by the various factions — the army, the police, NISS and RSF. Expectations were that each wanted to position themselves to benefit and take power as and when Bashir was gone. It felt like Sudan was sliding ever closer to the edge, given that al-Bashir was on the cusp of being forced to step down. A state of emergency was declared, demonstrations continued, and the heavy hand of the authorities was being widely felt.

All of this meant constantly working on a loose action plan with Dave whose prediction was that, at best, the airports and land borders would be shut. Worst case, there'd be civil war. To spice things up, there was also a new kidnap risk. Some man had been talking about me in a chat room, and Dave was concerned. So, if he was concerned, I definitely was. However, there was little I could do other than be vigilant and prepared. My delays in writing social media posts so people wouldn't know where I was were regularly countered by the Club's well-meaning updates of our real-time progress. When I did post, I would sometimes mention the 'security' with me. Anything to make me not look like a soft target.

Our fisherman who guided us, Ashir, turned out to be a Sudanese Bear Grylls. He got a fire going from next to nothing, boiled water quickly and found us a perfect camp spot on a scorpion-free island. We were gifted with some fish by local fishermen. It was wonderful getting the fish, and the guys were very particular and thorough in how they prepared and cooked it. Not wishing to sound ungrateful, but after a long day's paddling, I'd have happily cracked open a tin of *foul* *and eaten it with bread.

---

* Foul mudammas is a popular Middle Eastern dish of cooked fava beans typically seasoned with cumin and garlic.

Their careful preparation meant it was nearly two hours before we ate, and I was ready to chew my own arm off. Captain Salih and Assam wouldn't accept my help making the fish, so I waited patiently. Well, sort of patiently. As always, it was scrumptious, and it was kind of them to go to such lengths to prepare our dinner. I quicky demolished the food and went to bed.

I'd opted for one of the folding camp beds we had with us, so I could sleep directly under the African sky. The romance of this was cut short when the temperature dropped dramatically, and I retreated with my sleeping bag to the boat.

We were treated to a little wind and chop behind us as we travelled along the next day. I even caught some small waves that were created by the wind and shared some downwind paddling skills with Aimun. The wind assistance didn't last long though. To try and reduce our break time, Aimun asked Captain to prepare some food for the morning break. I was sticking with my oats.

When we got to the break, there was no food prepared, and Captain had wandered off. I was a tad pissed off. He eventually came back, and Aimun pointed out that there was a distinct lack of prepared food. Captain complained that he was ill. He didn't look too ill climbing up on the rocks and dancing on the boat earlier. After this conversation, he suddenly pulled a poor amateur dramatics act of a sick person. It was like watching a child suddenly become 'ill' to avoid doing chores. Aimun explained the concept of delegation to him — Assam could have done this. Anyway, finally food was prepared. And amazingly, Captain's illness didn't impact his appetite, or his desire to smoke cigarettes. It was a miracle to behold.

Stomachs full, we set off and had to keep reminding our guides to actually guide us, after repeatedly going off on tangents. They would go to talk to other fishermen or look at something that caught their interest. On the river, that was fine, but here, we needed to be guided and didn't want to add on countless kilometres following Captain's Brownian motion* path.

---

* 'Brownian motion' is the random motion of particles suspended in a medium (liquid or gas), and it is named after botanist Robert Brown, who first described the phenomenon in 1827.

To ensure we had a landmark to aim for, I asked Assam which way to head. 'Aim for the island,' he said, pointing forward.

If there hadn't been ten islands ahead, that would have been helpful. Sitting at water level, I had no chance of seeing exactly what he was pointing at. I was losing patience; this had been going on for some time.

When the boat seemingly went off on another tangent, Aimun and I decided to stick to our course. It turned out that Ashir was taking us on a short cut, and when they came back, they were cranky at us for not following them. Aimun and I cracked it, saying, 'You're always going off course. Off to talk to random fishermen. How were we supposed to know it was a short cut?'

While Aimun and I were frustrated with the guys, we joked about it and laughed. It was laugh or cry.

The Merowe Dam didn't seem to get any closer, and it was tricky to work out where we were supposed to land. Eventually, we got there.

Aimun warned, 'The moment we set foot on land, we'll find out if Mugahid definitely got the approval we need to land so close to the dam. If we don't have approval, we'll be arrested and locked up. It's a serious crime.' *That was reassuring.*

We tentatively pulled up and a man came over and invited us up for tea in the large shed containing an office where he was based. *Phew.* We were joined by two other men who were clearly NISS, together with a couple of others, so it became a bit of a gathering. Discussions ensued among them on how best to get the boat around the dam. The solution hadn't been agreed by the time we were taken to the dam's workers compound where we were given a house for the night.

For Ashir, our fisherman, this was all a big adventure. He enthusiastically snapped lots of photos on his phone. The guys said he would never have ventured far from the small village he called home. Our hosts generously brought us some food: foul, omelette, pickled vegetables, and bread.

Assam, who was normally very amenable, cracked the shits.

Aimun said the guys were complaining because the trip was taking longer than expected. This was a little frustrating; if we got going earlier and had shorter breaks, as I had repeatedly asked, it wouldn't take so long. Then money reared its ugly head. For this, I had sympathy for the guys. What I had been told I needed to pay, and what Captain had been told he was getting, were not the same. Captain expected more.

On top of these discussions, there were many conversations with Mugahid and the guys in Khartoum about where we'd put-in after the dam and where we'd stay. Then there was talk of Busati joining us. The logistics were a constant challenge, with something new each day to sort out. Just when I thought we had an agreed plan, things changed. There were times I was ready to scream.

Tonight, we were all tired and it was not the time to resolve the issues, so we agreed to have a team meeting at 6.30am. Knowing their lack of enthusiasm for early starts, I should have realised this time was aspirational at best. Turns out my idea of 6.30am and theirs was different.

Come 8am, we started talking. Aimun suggested we start earlier on the water and then take shorter breaks. *What kind of genius is this?*

I agreed and hoped that because this was now their idea, and the fact that there was something in it for them, they would buy into it better. The price for the boat, however, was less easy to resolve. The amounts were going beyond what I had on me, so I threatened to ditch the support boat. I would have paid the extra, but there was no way to access money. We hadn't resolved the issue by the time we were collected and taken back to the dam, where we were met by some local officials and those who had greeted us the day before.

Captain then started telling the people there about the money issues. While I totally understood his vexation, I started to lose patience. 'Aimun, please ask him not to talk to everyone about this.' Aimun calmed me down and managed to quell Captain Salih's public murmurings. I don't know what I would have done without him.

He was an absolute gem with all the negotiations that took place throughout the trip, often mediating between what the Club wanted and my plans. He also bore the brunt of Captain Salih and Assam's complaints. Not speaking the language, I didn't get dragged into the many mindless discussions and, simply got an executive summary from Aimun, as required. He made me laugh too.

In the meantime, the Head of Fisheries for the State (I think) offered me the role of being his second wife with an option for babies. *Too soon.* We'd been chatting over breakfast and photos had been taken. It was a interesting offer, and I wasn't sure he was being entirely serious. Regardless, I politely declined and changed the subject. A couple of the others were also keen to exchange numbers.

The messages that followed over the coming weeks and months were all about asking for help getting to Australia. I could understand the appeal of Australia when they were dealing with such hardships here daily, and I would love to have been able to help them. I tried to explain that it's not like Sudan where someone knows someone who can help or knows the right minister and can slip them some banknotes to help smooth things over.

In Australia, the immigration rules are so strict, and unless you're the Home Affairs Minister, or one of their good mates, then my being an Australian gives me zero clout. I wished it did.

After what seemed like an age, and endless coffees, we were finally on our way in the truck with the trailer being towed. NISS helped us obtain more fuel for the boat. At the time, it was still illegal to fill jerry cans. Up until now, we'd been lucky enough to have contacts who'd been able to source fuel for us. Here, while we had NISS onside, the owner of the petrol station looked deeply unimpressed.

At the put-in, there was a steep, narrow hump on the track leading to the river — not trailer friendly at all. But after a lot of sweating, huffing and puffing and brute strength, the men got the boat over the ridge and down into the water.

Once they'd all been replenished with coffee, tea, and cigarettes, we sat and chatted as a team. It was time to talk money and agree on this once and for all.

We eventually came up with an agreed amount that would clean me out, which was fine. I wished I'd had more money to give them.

A friend of Aimun (he seemed to have friends everywhere we went) brought us some food. It was a feast of fish, chicken, bread and salad, and we sat on the boat and tucked in enthusiastically. This spot seemed to be popular with people coming down to fish or simply watch the river. It included a group of women who we invited onto the boat. They sat with us for a while and talked. Being surrounded by women was a refreshing change.

Our next visitor was the Tourist Police. They'd got wind of a foreign female travelling with three Sudanese men and wanted to check that it was all okay. Copies of the letter from the Rowing and Canoe Club and my passport were handed over. They inspected them closely and called their chief, and all was good. Once again, it was Aimun doing all the talking and smoothing things over.

This had been my intended 'rest day', which wasn't exactly restful. So far, we'd been going nearly three weeks and had only two days off the river. Yet, these were still busy 'doing' days, just not paddling. This ended up being my last rest day until the end of this section in Sudan.

The new plan of start early, shorter breaks went into immediate effect, and we were on the water just after 7.30am. To make things even better, there was no wind. That day, we cranked out 80 kilometres — the furthest yet. When it was time to finish paddling, the terse debating about where we would camp began.

After a day of paddling, Aimun and I were tired, but it was with amazing regularity that, as soon as we wanted to start looking for somewhere to camp, Captain and the boat were on the other side of the river or way ahead and out of shouting range.

When we finally got their attention, they'd pick a spot that was usually inappropriate. Then the debating would begin, which tended to involve us having to paddle further until we found a spot which we all agreed on. This evening I'd been pushing for somewhere with trees for shelter, and with bushes or banks to protect us from the wind. I also wanted some privacy to go to the bathroom, but Captain insisted on a flat open sandy island.

It was still warm when we pulled up, so I made the most of it and had a 'bath' and washed my hair. Looking up, I noticed a thick, dark storm cloud rolling towards us, filling the sky and sweeping across the land. It was a *haboob*, a sandstorm. This thick cloud of sand, rising hundreds of metres in the air, was heading our way, set to blanket us in sand. *So glad I bothered to wash my hair.*

We quickly made some pasta for dinner and ate it while we could before securing everything. We semi-buried the kayaks, and anything loose was either tied down or put undercover. The wind was building, and the skies darkened. It whipped up the river, creating waves that broke over the sides of the boat. There was zero chance of sleeping in a tent, or out on camp beds, so we all took refuge in the boat, wrapping ourselves up as much as possible. I climbed into my sleeping bag and pulled the hood of it tight over my head, but I could still feel the splash of water as the wind created bigger waves. I had the joy of sleeping among diesel filled jerry cans, and the smell seemed to seep into everything.

After a restless night, I awoke the next morning to find everything covered in sand. While sweeping up, a message came through from Dave to say that things were heating up between NISS and the military and I needed to be ready to evacuate. At this point, we were far enough north for the airport at Dongola or the border with Egypt to be my exit points, assuming they remained open.

I found the idea of having to evacuate exciting and was torn between that and getting to finish this section. After all the efforts organising this, and despite my whingeing, I was loving every minute of it, so I wanted to finish this section. 'Best I paddle fast,' I messaged to Dave. He concurred.

As we got underway, I asked Aimun why he'd wanted to do this trip. He said he'd emailed me over a year ago, wanting to join the trip. I'd forgotten about it until he mentioned it then. At the time, I'd replied to say I would consider it and let him know. My preference was to find paddlers through the Club, making everything easier to coordinate, but he hadn't mentioned in that email that he was part of the Club, just that he was a kayaker, swim coach and teacher.

He told me that he had been sure that it was destiny that he join me on this trip and had even had dreams about it. I smiled and was overjoyed that it had worked out.

The scenery as we made our way north became even more magnificent. The desert, in many places, reached all the way down to the river. The sand was soft yellow, the colour of a palomino horse. We were making our way further into Nubia, the seat of one of the earliest civilisations of ancient Africa.

African people from the Sahara started moving towards the Nile in Nubia by around 5000 BC[41]. Much information about ancient Nubia comes from archaeological excavation, monuments and the rock art found here. There are also records from ancient Egypt depicting Nubian history, along with complex relationships between the two lands.

Egyptians referred to Nubia as 'Ta-Seti', or the land of the bow, as the Nubians were known to be expert archers. This skill bolstered military strength for Nubian rulers, and the kings of Nubia ultimately conquered and ruled Egypt for about a century. This Nubian culture is termed A-Group by modern scholars.

Around 3300 BC, the Ta-Seti were conquered, and it is believed they were then harmonised with the Egyptian state, and the A-Group area was almost completely depopulated, probably as a result of migration.

A new culture, termed the C-Group, flourished from about 2500 BC to c.1500 BC. The Kingdom of Kerma arose and battles with Egypt continued and eventually the kingdom was destroyed.

Nubia was mentioned in Egyptian accounts of trade missions from 2300 BC. It was rich in gold deposits and became the gateway through which luxury products like incense, ivory and ebony travelled from their source in sub-Saharan Africa to the civilizations of Egypt and the Mediterranean.

Nubia was home to several empires before being invaded by Ethiopia's Kingdom of Aksum and the rise of three Christian kingdoms. These declined with the influx of Arab traders and the introduction of Islam, which gradually replaced Christianty. The final Nubian kingdom collapsed around 1500. Nubia was divided, and this led to the current split, with Nubians living in southern Egypt and Northern Sudan.

From the river, it was possible to see the difference in culture. The style of the houses changed from being plain mud or cement blocks, to dwellings painted with colourful patterns. There were more women out and about. Before we arrived here, I rarely saw women. Here they were tending to crops and working the land.

People came out to greet us, and kids ran along the riverbanks next to us. There was a different vibe —it was more exuberant.

I too was feeling elated. I was uplifted by the scenery, the progress we were making, and now finally being in a good routine.

CHAPTER EIGHTEEN
DAYS 127–137

Don't limit your challenges, challenge your limits.

Jerry Dunn

Reaching Dongola five days after the dam, I noticed a few people gathered on the riverbank we were aiming for, and I wondered what they were doing. It turned out they were local government officials with a TV crew ready to interview us. Though when I say 'interview', the microphone was thrust into my hand, and I was told to speak to the camera. Fortunately, I was given a few moments to prepare, and I made sure I thanked and acknowledged the people in Sudan who were making this possible.

It was also a short day on the river, so I could have a timeout, which I was ready for. By now, my back was beginning to feel it. I'm used to having a foot plate to push against as I take each stroke, catch the water with my paddle and rotate the body to pull on the blade while simultaneously pressing through the heel on the side I'm taking the stroke. Without a fixed point to push against, I was anchoring from my butt, and my back was taking the strain, particularly when battling into strong headwinds.

The officials took us for lunch. I was never let in on the plans for these sort of stops. It seemed to be a 'need-to-know' basis, and it seemed I didn't need to know. Things like people coming to meet us, or who they were, what we were doing, when we were going back on the water were all lovely surprises. I learnt to go with it, feeling like a nag if I kept asking what was going on and what to expect.

I climbed into the car and was taken for lunch. This generosity never ceased to amaze me. The stops were also a nice break from the food on the boat. It wasn't massively different, but we had the chance to enjoy a few extras, like hummus, salads, meat and foul with more spices and flavour. It was all delectable.

Food in Sudan is generally eaten with your hands, however, I was always offered a spoon. *No, I need the practice!* You would think after two months in Sudan, I would have nailed it — apparently not.

Sated, we were shown back to the car for the next stop on the mystery tour. It was then coffee time before popping into a local market, for what, I didn't know. Oil, as it turned out, to add to the diesel. We made the most of the shops and loaded up with supplies.

In the background, I was arranging the kayak for Egypt and messaging with my fixer there, Youseff, about the approval for entering this area, but I wasn't having much luck in getting the information I needed from him.

The better news was that I had an Egyptian paddler, Nadim Elmessiri, set to join me on this section. We'd been messaging as I'd been travelling, and I was pleased to know I had someone local joining me. At least something was going to plan!

The endless days of paddling, the fatigue that was building, and the pain in my back and shoulders, along with the constant headwinds, started to get to me. While we were regularly punching out 60 to 70 kilometres a day, I felt like the end of this section wasn't getting any closer.

Frustrated and tired as I was, and knowing the guys were ready to reach the end, Assam and Captain Salih still continued to look out for me — 'Anything, Mama Sarah.'

One day, Aimun commented, 'You hear of spoilt children, but not of spoilt mothers.' I laughed. They were giving me preferential treatment, making sure I had the biggest or best fish. They even encouraged me to sleep on the boat if they thought I'd be more comfortable, and offered me blankets if I was cold. Aimun got none of this!

The scenery was changing again. Now there were dramatic mountains in the distance, rising high out of the desert and sand dunes. Dotted along the river was a mix of rocky, grassy and sandy islands. It had been flatwater for a while now, but two days after leaving Dongola, we hit the third set of cataracts, which we successfully negotiated.

Later that day, we heard the rumbling of what sounded like bigger rapids. We pulled up onto an island, and Aimun and I jumped in the boat so we could go and check them out. As we got closer, we saw they spanned the width of the river and were very rocky with no obvious lines to run — well, this inexperienced white water paddler couldn't spot them.

Aimun and I didn't have PFDs or helmets with us, so I made the call that we would have to portage. The question was, what about the boat? There was much umming and ahhing, talking to locals, seeing if there were other options. So, we made camp on the sandy island we'd pulled up on, and slept there.

The next day, under advice from local fishermen, the call was made that the boat would make it through the rapids. The fishermen showed Captain and Assam the line to take and told them to cut the engines as soon as the boat hit the white water ... and pray. Well, I don't think they needed to add that last point, judging by the look of fear in Captain Salih's eyes. I was confident that they said their prayers to Allah. Aimun and I wished the guys a safe passage, and I gave them strict instructions to wear the lifejackets they had. I was worried, particularly as Assam couldn't swim. I asked him to come with us, but he wouldn't leave Captain. Aimun and I paddled to the opposite side of the river and pulled our kayaks out.

Aimun found a lovely local man with a truck. He brought it to us, and we loaded our kayaks on top and then he drove us around the rapids. We reached the edge of the river below the white water, unloaded, and watched nervously upstream as the boat headed into the rapids. It was sucked one way, then the next, the nose dipping down and then rising back up as it rodeoed its way through the white water.

Finally, they made it, and there were sighs of relief all round. Captain and Assam were incredibly thankful to have survived — we all were. And the boat was still in one piece.

The final rapids behind us, we continued north to our next stop, Abri. My spirits were lifted once again by another warm welcome when we arrived. Aimun and I were taken to meet the local Minister for Youth and Sport in his office in the centre of town. After a brief chat, we were whisked away to the new Abri House of Heritage Museum that was due to open to the public a few days later. They even invited me to be the first foreign tourist to see it. It was such an honour.

After a short car ride out of town, we arrived at the museum. Across a few rooms was a mix of displays of local relics old and new, along with information on traditions and use of the objects displayed, as well as information on the local area. They were also building a library for books, historic photographs and documents. The displays would change over time, and they had an outdoor space for local performances and workshops. It had very much been developed with the local community, and I hope it gets added to the tours that go through this northern state.

There was a TV crew present, and once again, the microphone was thrust into my hands, and I was told to speak. It was a chance to express my thanks for this special invitation and for the hospitality shown. All these welcomes were thanks to Mr Abdelrahim.

There was a British woman as part of the team establishing this museum. It was a joy to speak with her, and I was eager to spend more time discussing the work she did there but was soon ushered off to visit a local traditional Nubian guesthouse. It was fantastic to have the chance to see a little of life away from the river. The riverbanks were like walls obscuring these vibrant villages and towns. As much as I enjoyed being on the river, I sometimes felt I was missing out. Once again, I was left with an addition to my bucket list — to come back to the north of Sudan and explore its culture.

We returned to the centre of this big, bustling town and headed to a restaurant for some foul, bread and salads and then to a café for a coffee. Finally, we purchased more supplies at the market and shops, including additional fuel. I even knocked back an ice-cold Coca-Cola. Cold drinks were such a treat. Then it was back on the river — no more stops until Wadi Halfa, which was only a few days away.

We continued to be treated to some amazing camp spots, on sandy islands, sandbanks and the like. Unzipping my tent to see the sun rising behind the dunes and the Nile was extraordinary. I knew I was going to miss this when I left. I also began to wonder how I was going to feel reaching the end. *Paddle the Nile* had been my *raison d'être* for nearly three years. This was my baby, and I was sure I'd feel lost and directionless without it.

What I did know was that there were going to be more adventures. I had never felt so alive or in my element as I had on this trip. Tough and frustrating as it had been at times, I valued having focus and direction to even get to the start line. Then this entire journey had been so different from any other travels. I'd been able to connect with so many different people, their cultures and way of life, in a completely uniquely authentic way. It wasn't the packaged fast-food version of travelling. By learning to have a loose grip on my plans, going with the flow and embracing uncertainty, there was space for random experiences. These random experiences proved to be some of the highlights.

For now, though, it was time to keep paddling.

As we got close to Wadi Halfa, the current stopped. We had hit the start of the Nubian Lake, known as Lake Nasser in Egypt, and created by the dam at Aswan, earlier than I'd expected. This meant that with the headwinds, which were still with us, our progress slowed horribly. At times, it would take us an hour just to cover three kilometres. You could walk twice as fast. It felt like we were literally crawling to the finish line.

As we approached Wadi Halfa, NISS came to meet us. They rocked up in their twin-engine speedboat during our last break, and asked for permits, which we didn't have. We just had the letters from the Federation. However, Aimun answered all their questions, and they advised us that they already knew of our arrival, and our plans. *So why ask us?*

That day, we finally reached the end.

We put the kayaks in the boat for the final stretch across the exposed part of the lake to Wadi Halfa. It was dark by the time we reached the port where we were shown where to dock. Everything had been packed up in advance, so it was a case of me unloading all my gear. I scrambled up the awkward, steep, rocky embankment with the first load of gear.

Reaching the top, somewhat unceremoniously and in a very dishevelled state, I was surprised to be greeted by a round of applause by ten officials there to greet us. I was a little embarrassed by my messy, dirty hair, well-worn clothes, and me in need of a proper clean. It felt like a 'Bridget Jones' kind of moment.

After a discussion with port officials, we were taken to some accommodation that resembled barracks. It turned out to be wonderfully comfortable, with beds and a large living space, along with running water. There was no time for washing though, as we were taken for dinner by the local Minister for Sport and Youth, Mohamed Towfeg, who'd arranged the accommodation.

With a full stomach, and after a quick wash, I collapsed into my bed and fell asleep, smiling with the satisfaction of having made it here. It had been 32 days since we left Khartoum, with 1,500 kilometres covered. I was relieved to have reached this enormous milestone. Now it felt like there was just the homestretch to go. A 1,200-kilometres homestretch, that is.

We spent a day in Wadi Halfa. The guys went to sort out a truck to return the boat to Khartoum and a way to get it out of the water. I was left to my own devices, primarily because the price was guaranteed to go up if I was there for the negotiations. So, I did some packing and worked out what I wasn't going to take on this last leg. I sorted out the money for Captain Salih and then some for Aimun. He didn't expect anything, but he'd given up work to do this trip — no work, no income. I had set some aside when we had renegotiated the price for the boat.

I messaged Youseff, the fixer. Having asked multiple times if there was any further information needed for this next section, he now said that my itinerary and covering letter needed to be translated into Arabic. *Seriously? You couldn't have mentioned this before?*

I messaged Nadim, who was set to join me for the next section. It was a massive favour to ask, but he agreed to do the translation. Aimun was asked to visit NISS for over an hour of questioning. I don't know what they were after. It seemed they wanted to validate his story once again and compare it with what their colleagues had advised them. I felt bad for Aimun having to go through all of this.

That night, I said my goodbyes to Aimun, who was leaving in the early hours for the 12-hour bus ride back to Khartoum. It seemed crazy that what had taken us 32 days, could be covered in half a day by road. I thanked him for joining this trip and for all he had done along the way. He'd been amazing, so supportive, and I thoroughly enjoyed spending time with him. We shared many laughs, and I was sad to say goodbye.

I reflected on all that had been accomplished so far. After hanging out for this end point, I could still hardly believe it was here. It had been an incredible experience. Sudan was a country more spectacular than I expected, starkly contrasted by the desperate political situation faced by these wonderful, kind people.

After saying goodbye to Captain Salih and Assam, Mohamed (the minister) took me to his workplace, and I chatted to several of his colleagues. There was another TV crew present, and it was another case of me trying to say something relevant and intelligent. Finally, I had an audience with the governor of this state. He was an imposing figure in military uniform with many stars on his lapels. He sat behind a grand mahogany desk in his enormous office, and I spoke to him briefly about my travels so far, how much I appreciated all the support I had received and the hospitality.

Mohamed then drove me to the border and helped me through the first part of immigration. It was chaos in the large immigration room, which was crammed with people and luggage, with no indication of what to do or where to go. It eventually involved a few different seemingly disorganised steps (well, that's what this unfamiliar foreigner thought) to get to the other side.

It then wasn't long before it was time to get on my bus, bid farewell to Mohamed and say goodbye to Sudan. I was filled with indebtedness once again for everyone in Sudan who had made my time here so wonderful and helped me make the trip a success. I sighed and smiled as I took my seat in the packed bus.

Now, I just had to navigate a long and painful border crossing to reach the homestretch.

Day 85: Busati and onlookers in Sudan

Day 88: Sarah, Busati & Fahed (L-R) in Khartoum, Sudan

PADDLE THE NILE

Day 107: Mujaheid, Sarah, Hamza, Aimun & Fahed (L-R) at the Pyramids of Meroe, Sudan

Day 114: Captain Salih & Assam and the boat in Sudan

Day 124: Sarah in Sudan

Day 125: Sarah in Sudan

Day 127: Cameraman, interviewer, Sarah, Aimun & government official (L-R) in Sudan

Day 136: Sarah & Aimun (L-R) in Wadi Halfa, Sudan

PART 5

Egypt

Embarking on the homestretch

CHAPTER NINETEEN
DAYS 137–150

Let yourself be silently drawn by the strange pull of what you really love.
It will not lead you astray.

Rumi

Having been hurried onto the bus, we then waited. Then we moved 100 metres, and then we waited. This was repeated until we got to the Egyptian immigration and customs area, not that there were signs to explain this. Fortunately, a Sudanese woman took me under her wing and explained the next steps.

We got off the bus, took our bags and queued to put them through the single x-ray machine. With my heavy dry case full of electrical gear, a 120-litre full dry bag, paddle bag and backpack, it was a balancing act of carrying and dragging my luggage. *Porters would make a killing here!*

All my bags made it through, bar one. I turned to look for my paddle bag to see one of the policemen holding it.

'Is this yours?'

'Yes, it is,' I replied, relieved that it hadn't vanished.

'Do you have a knife in there?' he asked with a serious look and furrowed brow.

'Ah, yes, it's my camping knife,' I replied cheerily. He asked me to open the bag and show him the knife.

'You can't bring this in,' he said in a 'don't argue' kind of way. *Oh, bollocks.*

I really didn't want to leave this behind.

'It's just my camping knife. I'm on an expedition,' I explained.

'Sorry, you can't take it.' He wasn't budging. There was absolutely no point in getting defensive; it looked like he was having none of it. So, I tried one last time …

'But I promise not to stab anyone. Honestly, I won't!' I said, smiling, hoping some humour might help the situation along. He began to soften but was still adamant.

'I'm sorry, but we're going to have to keep it.' *Damn.*

'Okay,' I said, shrugging my shoulders. I started to zip up my bag, relieved of the knife.

'Oh … all right, you can keep it,' he then said, and to my amazement he handed it back. Now I just had to stick to my promise and not stab anyone.

There were still people everywhere, and long queues. It was particularly busy because the ferry that normally took passengers all the way to Aswan, which I wanted to take, wasn't running. Apparently the captain of the ferry had forgotten to renew his licence. I'm not kidding.

After taking my bags, it was time for immigration. The hall was heaving with people queuing for the limited number of cubicles to get their passports checked and stamped. It looked chaotic and was noisy with impatient chattering. I joined what seemed to be the queue.

A man approached me and said, 'This queue is for men, women have their own cubicle.' He took me to a cubicle with no queue. For once, being a woman in a country of segregation had its bonuses, and I was out in a few minutes.

Then there was more waiting around for everyone to get through and back on the bus. I exchanged some US dollars for Egyptian pounds and waited. Eventually, everyone from the bus made it through. I had arrived at the border at 10.30am. By now it was 5pm. We waited some more and then were finally on our way. It was about a 30-minute ride to the ferry, for a one-hour trip to Abu Simbel. Looking at the small, rusty bucket of bolts, I couldn't comprehend how three large coaches were going to fit on board. I was also not going to stay on the coach for this crossing. If this ferry went down, which seemed more than a possibility, I wanted to be able to swim for it.

Once we arrived on the other side, we had time to grab dinner at one of the restaurants. Then it was back on the coach for a perilous ride to Aswan. Along the way, our driver seemed to be engaging his inner Jedi — driving without lights in the middle of the road at breakneck speeds. The coach drivers seemed to be racing to be first to reach their destination. I regretted sitting up front for this white-knuckle ride.

At the end, it was time to get my bags, find a taxi and head to my guesthouse. Around midnight, I made it. I was staying in Aswan, on the opposite side of the river to Aswan city in a fabulous guesthouse. It was pure luxury — a big bed, clean sheets, ensuite bathroom with running hot water. *The simple pleasures.*

After a refreshing sleep, I woke up with a sense of relief. While there was still well over 1,200 kilometres of paddling left, it was counting down. No more borders to cross, teams to build, or approvals to get beyond those for Egypt. The end was in sight. While I was enamoured with this journey, the thought of reaching the end did make me smile.

I caught the ferry over to the east bank and the bustling centre of Aswan. It was a shock to the senses after weeks of being in remote Sudan. The streets were heavy with cars, and the pavements packed with people making their way, ducking in and out of all the shops. There were street vendors and cafés, markets and supermarkets. This slightly chaotic feel was a stark contrast to the last month.

I got some cash and bought the essentials, which included a SIM card and some food. I stocked up on plenty of fresh fruit as well as some sardines, tomatoes, onions, lemons, feta and cucumber. Pieced together, served with fresh bread, it's still one of my favourite lunches.

There was a strong military presence, with Egyptian President Abdel Fattah Saeed Hussein Khalil el-Sisi due to be in town for a few days. There were police trucks and armoured vans surrounded by men wearing helmets and dressed in black, sporting bulletproof vests and guns, looking more like special forces than your standard coppers.

With the shopping done, it was back to the guesthouse and time to enjoy a little rest and relaxation. One thing stood out here and that was the colour of the Nile. Before, it was filled with silt, but here it was blue and crystal clear. The enormous dam at Aswan acts as a giant filter. While it looks good, the lack of silt and nutrients being transported downstream is not beneficial for the farmers.

I caught up on social media and emails, wrote a newsletter, spoke to Mum and Sue, and started creating food lists for this next section. I was going to be near towns most of the way, so I wouldn't need to stock up too much. This was a good thing, as now there was no support boat to carry the load.

It was time to be self-sufficient, and I was looking forward to that.

There was some good news in the form of the arrival of my new kayak, and I moved to another guesthouse, as the one I was at was fully booked and couldn't extend my stay. This one had a fabulous roof terrace overlooking the Nile. It was so peaceful, a little oasis, with the bustling city on one side and the desert behind. It was another excellent spot to chill and catch up on lots of much-needed sleep.

After four days, Nadim, the paddler, joined me for this final section. He arrived with his fiancé, who was here on a trip with her mother, and as soon as I met him, I felt the same positive vibes and enthusiasm I'd felt via his emails. After months on the go, this new injection of excitement and zest was a boost to my spirit. This was a trip that he had wanted to do for some time, and it meant he was very happy to assist with the organising and making sure we got going as soon as possible.

My fixer had done a woeful job of getting any approvals, so we went to the Tourism Police the following day, to see about the approvals needed for our trip. Everyone had told me how hard it was getting approvals in Egypt — I'd get caught up in bureaucracy and it would take an age to sort out. This, however, was not the case.

A week after arriving in Egypt, it was time to put our kayaks on the water. Given that mine was fairly heavy, I very gingerly got in. Thankfully, it didn't sink! We set off on the sparkling Nile, backtracking a little at first, as there were some islands to explore, and we wanted to be close to the dam before heading north. Overall, it was a good day.

That night, we found a nice spot to camp on a sandy bank edged with trees. We had some tinned foul, tuna and bread, and Nadim and I got to know each other better. Nadim was a great guy, with a mix of skills and interests. He was a 24-year-old kayaker, adventurer, talented artist, teacher and engineer. I felt we really connected, and I enjoyed talking to him. I went to bed feeling happy to be sharing this next stretch with him.

My friend, the headwind, was back the next morning. We were slowed even more because of Nadim's kayak, which wasn't suited to this kind of trip and was hard to keep straight in the wind. It was slow to paddle, so I took as much gear as I could to reduce his load. Eventually, we found our rhythm of paddle – break, repeated a few times until we stopped for the night. It was just at a slower pace. Nadim warned me that he wasn't the quickest person at getting going, particularly in the mornings. Even having witnessed it, I'm not sure how it took so long to dress, pack up his gear and load the kayak.

In the meantime, I'd also made our breakfast, had a coffee, washed up, washed my hair, written a few emails and stretched. And waited. I was going to have to adjust my expectations. Clearly, I was doomed to not have early starts on this trip!

The scenery here was very different to Sudan. It was more built up with houses along the river. There were still some beautiful stretches, but they became fewer and further between.

On the fourth day, Nadim started to feel ill in the afternoon. We eventually found a spot to stop for the night. Some local farmers guided us into a place they said we could camp, and it was ideal. They cleared the leaves and lumps and even gave us a big mat to sit on.

On checking my emails, there was one from Mum with some bad news. She was getting cataracts and wouldn't be able to meet me at the end of my journey. With her diminished eyesight, she didn't feel comfortable travelling, and was gutted. While I was sad that she wouldn't be there at the end, it wasn't such a bad thing, and I was fine with it. Having spent six months travelling, as much I as was loving it, I knew that in another month's time, I'd be hanging out for some proper relaxation and Mum's home cooking. It was one less thing to organise and coordinate.

Nadim was still not feeling 100 per cent when he woke up the next day, so I decided we'd have a rest day. I was amazed I hadn't been sick or had gastro during the six months I'd been in Africa. Some was luck, but I was careful where I ate meat and made sure I adopted good camping hygiene and was never too far away from some hand sanitiser or a bar of soap. Fingers crossed I kept this good run going!

The following day, we got going into some headwinds and had our first encounter with the water police. We were getting close to a lock, and seeing the police station, we decided we'd do the right thing and report in. Copies of my passport and Nadim's ID were handed over, and Nadim explained what we were doing. He told me later that he did tend to embellish things a little, mostly around my success as a paddler.

The police were lovely, giving us sweet tea and arranging for the lock ahead to be opened. We got back on the river and my apprehension grew as we approached this first lock. They are massive, designed for the non-stop stream of cruise ships taking people up and down the river from Aswan to Luxor and back. I had images of heavy turbulence and disappearing down the equivalent of an enormous plughole. You won't be surprised to hear that I'd never actually been through a lock before …

CHAPTER TWENTY
DAYS 150–157

Sometimes the best thing you can do is not think, not wonder, not imagine, not obsess. Just breathe and have faith that everything will work out for the best.

Unknown

We went into the first lock. The operators directed us to the side and told us to hold onto one of the ladders attached to the lock's walls. We were like two small fish in a very large pond. The large metal gates then slowly closed behind us and the water started to drain. It was a smooth ride, with the operators watching over us gradually getting further away, until we'd dropped about eight metres — no disappearing down the plughole. With the water levels now equal to the river ahead of us, the doors at the opposite end of the lock unhurriedly opened and we were on our way.

As the gates opened, the wind hit us. Paddling out was like dragging a weight, with each stroke feeling heavy as we pulled against the wind. Our progress was slow, particularly as Nadim hadn't got his strength fully back after being ill. We made the call to finish early when we found a nice spot where some local fishermen were living. There were sandy spots and grassy banks. We were enthusiastically received by the fishermen with waves and smiles, and once on dry land, it was clear they were eager for us to stay.

Nadim called the police we'd seen earlier in the day, as they had asked that we check in at the end of the day. They didn't share our enthusiasm for our chosen camp spot, not trusting the fishermen. Nadim fielded many calls from these police, and despite his best efforts to convince them that we were fine here, the cops were having none of it. Instead, they insisted we paddle to a place they approved of.

With the light fading, we reluctantly packed up our tents and got back on the water. We were still paddling when it was pitch black, keeping our eyes and ears peeled for the big cruise ships making their journey along the river. This was less than ideal.

Eventually, a water police patrol rocked up in a small motorboat and showed us to the back of a mighty water pump station where we tied up the kayaks, and extracted what we needed before being led up a long flight of steps. We were shown into a small standalone brick room. The once white walls were now grey with dirt, the corrugate ceiling thick with dust and spider's webs, and it smelled of stale farts. *Delightful!*

There were two 'beds' — I use that term loosely. I took one that was basically a wooden bench so Nadim could have the marginally more comfortable one. *We gave up our perfect camp spot for this?* The upside was that there was electricity, so we made the most of charging everything.

The next morning, we woke to find the wind had dropped. Nadim chatted about the best approach for the rest of the trip, saying that he didn't mind paddling the long stretches, with a couple of breaks. It just meant he would need more rest days. I reluctantly agreed. I was keen to get this section done as quickly as possible, but I couldn't force him to paddle more, if it was more than he was comfortable with. I was getting frustrated with the low distances covered each day, so I gently suggested we get going a bit sooner in the mornings. An all too familiar suggestion, which he agreed to.

Six days after leaving Aswan, we reached Luxor, where we had a short stop for food and supplies. My plan had been to have a rest day here, as it was somewhere I really wanted to visit. However, having recently had an unplanned rest day and knowing that we were going to have more than I'd planned, I couldn't justify another one here.

We had the first of our police escorts for most of the day. Two policemen were tasked with following us by motorboat. That night, we found a sandy island to camp on, and the police were satisfied with our choice. However, when they called it in with their boss, the boss wasn't so thrilled about it. My teeth clenched, annoyed that we might have to repeat the previous night's performance of packing up and relocating.

Basically, the boss wanted us in the next governorate — off his patch, not his responsibility. This pattern was going to be repeated all the way. I think the issue was that no one wanted anything to happen to me, a tourist, on their patch. *I get it.*

Egypt works hard to protect tourism, an industry they rely on heavily. It's one of the leading sources of income for Egypt, one that they cannot afford to lose. Previous attacks, like the one in Luxor in November 1997, resulted in tourism taking a beating. Consequently, all tourist areas, and people like me, are heavily guarded.

Dave had warned me of their protective nature, and his intelligence briefings and reports were about the terrorism and kidnap risks. Egypt struggles with various terrorist groups, some targeting foreign nationals, and with tourism being such an important part of their economy, they take no risks.

The police and Nadim were fielding calls back and forwards with everyone getting uptight and pissed off, until eventually, the boss agreed we could stay, but we needed more protection.

Two armed police were sent, one with what looked like an AK-47, the other with a shotgun. Neither of them were in uniform.

So, there were four police, guarding the two of us, well me really, on this tiny island. It seemed like overkill, but I wasn't complaining. I was relieved we could stay put. While I didn't think I was in much danger, this security made me feel very safe.

As a peace offering, we gave the police some food, which seemed to do the trick, and they softened despite the prospect of an uncomfortable night away from home. I got into my tent, thankful, until some loud violin-type music signalled the start of a big celebration in a nearby village that was set to keep me awake until the early hours.

I was awakened by the police trying to rouse Nadim at 6.20am. *Good luck with that!* They wanted to get going, and I didn't blame them. When they'd set off the morning before, they hadn't banked on being away overnight.

We were blessed with a wind-free start to the day. The land around us was mostly flat, with grass, a few palm trees, and bushes on the gently sloping riverbanks. There wasn't much to see other than the river ahead. There were less of the cruise ships and *feluccas*, which are the traditional wooden sailing boats, now we were north of Luxor. It was good to have less of the ships and the larger wake they created. The heavy load on my kayak meant it wasn't super stable, and it was sitting low in the water.

This kayak was good though. It was more comfortable than the last one and had fixed points I could push from my feet. We stopped for lunch on a sandy bank and chowed down on pasta with Nutella — the food of champions! Our escort from the day before had left us, so we were on our own, enjoying the peace and quiet.

The mobile coverage was better too, so I listened to podcasts and audiobooks. I went off into my own world, enjoying the rhythm of paddling, distracted by the stories I was being told. The weather was wonderfully sunny, with just a gentle breeze. Nadim and I then decided we needed a better strategy with the police. 'Fun' as these nightly negotiations were, we decided to try to negate them by calling the cops before we started making camp.

That afternoon at around 4pm, we found a great spot to camp, so Nadim called the police, seeking their approval. Initially, the police said it was okay. Then they said no, we should paddle to Qena. These calls took an hour! I lost count of how many conversations poor Nadim endured with various police departments and locations.

With the sun setting and temperature dropping, I threw on a couple of extra layers, and we reluctantly started paddling towards Qena. *So much for our cunning plan.* We were compensated with a stunning sunset as the sky turned pink and orange. There's something extra beautiful about a sun setting over water, the colours reflecting in the ripples.

However, once again, we were paddling in the dark until we reached Qena at around 8pm. By this point, we were both tired and cranky. The police suggested we sleep in the public park and leave our kayaks without any security, but Nadim and I were adamant this was not a good idea. Nadim called the boss and said we weren't going to back down on this. He even checked I was supportive of the bad cop approach. *Abso-bloody-lutely. You go!*

So off he went to find the local police and talk to them face-to-face.

I sat, holding his kayak with one hand, the other holding the steps leading up from the river, trying not to get carried by the current. A couple of local men came down the set of steps to where I was. They tried to chat, but their English was limited. However, one managed to get his point across, saying, 'I fuck you.'

'I beg your pardon. What did you say?' I replied, not believing what I'd heard.

'I fuck you,' he repeated. While he wouldn't have understood the words that came out of my mouth in response he would have got the gist based on the tone in my voice. I waved over one of the policemen at the top of the stairs. I explained what happened, and the men were taken away. When Nadim came back, I said under no circumstances were we camping out in the park. Thankfully, Nadim had reached an agreement with the police.

We paddled upstream to the water police station and secured our kayaks there, taking what we needed for the night. A taxi was called for us, and we were given a police escort to a nearby hotel.

They even came in to make sure we checked in. It had been nearly five hours from when we first made a call to the police, to now being settled for the night. We desperately needed to change our approach again, because repeating this each night was going to send us over the edge.

A positive was that I got to have a hot shower and make use of the electricity to power everything up once again. Nadim popped out and got some chicken wraps, which we inhaled before turning in for the night.

Cunning Plan B was to agree with the police *before* getting on the water each day.

          PADDLE THE NILE

After getting a taxi back to the river the following morning, Nadim spoke to the police to agree on a place to stop that day. We were given a choice of a shortish paddle to Dishna, or 60 kilometres to another area. There was no way Nadim would make 60 kilometres, so we agreed on the shorter distance.

We set off eagerly, and I was back to doing the maths, working out how many kilometres to go, how many kilometres per day, how many rest days, and when I'd reach the end. At that point, I estimated another 25 to 28 days …

Shortly after setting off, a new police escort arrived. The police had sticks of sugarcane on board and gave us some. I loved sucking on the cane, getting the sugary liquid out and chewing on it a little. Again, we were treated to a warm, wind-free day, optimal for paddling. After a couple of hours, the police escort advised us that their boss said we couldn't stay in Dishna, because he felt it wasn't safe. After trying to do the right thing and agree to things upfront, this was maddening. The police escorting us were lovely, and on our side, so they tried to get a reasonable agreement.

We continued to Dishna, where we pulled up and were greeted by the big boss who was making the calls. He had slicked hair, aviator sunglasses and a stern look. The stars on his lapels suggested he was senior, and he came across as not the kind of guy you'd mess with.

We were at the bottom of a steep concrete bank that stretched along the river for 50 metres or so. There was a narrow, flat piece of land between the river and the bank, so we pulled our kayaks onto that. We then climbed the bank to talk to the 'boss'. A large audience of men quickly gathered, watching our discussions intently and looking at our equipment. After some deliberation, it was agreed that we'd leave the kayaks here and they would make sure they were secure. Then the police would take us by boat to a point 30 kilometres downriver so we could stay at a hotel.

At 7.30am, they would bring us back and we'd set off again. It wasn't ideal, but we didn't have a choice, and this was better than missing a section, which was what they initially suggested.

We took the gear we needed for the night and climbed in the boat that had been escorting us. It was a rubber boat, like the surf rescue boats back home in Australia, but dark green instead of bright red. We sped down the river to the next water police station, talked to the police and agreed that we'd stay in a hotel overnight. The plan was to then return to our kayaks in the morning and paddle back to this point and stay in the same hotel the following night. It meant a short day of paddling, but no arguing with police, and we could leave some gear in the hotel. So, we took it. It was all turning into a logistical shit show.

We went to the hotel, ordered some food, and after a shower, we called it a night.

The next morning, we returned to the police station, and some police kindly took us to our kayaks. I was keen to get the 30 kilometres done speedily and then have more downtime. The agreed approach of paddle – break, repeated a few times, was now paddle – break, repeated countless times. I wanted to get the paddle done quickly, but Nadim preferred to take it slow. While Nadim and I had the same goal — to paddle the length of Egypt, which we were equally excited about it — our execution style was different.

There was nothing wrong with either approach, it was personal preference, but it created challenges for both of us. I have no doubt Nadim found my approach wearisome, wanting to push harder, and on top of that, he was having to deal with the police. The good thing was that Nadim seemed great at ignoring my crankiness, which never lasted that long.

The difference in approach, combined with having no control over the start time and the kilometres covered, made me feel like I'd joined someone else's trip, which I found frustrating. Frustration then gave way to a feeling of despondency.

So, it was time for some self-talk, and I did my best to change my attitude. I was suffering because I was resisting a situation I couldn't change. Everyone was doing their best and helping me. I reverted to my 'control the controllables' mantra once more. What was in my control was how I chose to respond to the situation — what I felt, thought and did. The 'suffering' was optional. I took some deep breaths and thought of all the good things about this trip and this situation. I focused on gentle paddling and listening to some uplifting music, and my mind softened.

We reached our destination and returned to the hotel, which we were escorted to, despite it being a short walk. This was a conservative area. Nadim pointed out that the man on reception had set up a mirror so he could see down the corridor and make sure we weren't going into each other's room. We weren't even allowed to eat together in one of our rooms with the door open!

Egypt has a population of over 100 million, of which over ninety per cent are Muslim with most being Sunni[42]. Unlike Sudan, Egypt is not under Sharia Law, so there is diversity of interpretation of their religion. Some areas were more conservative, and others more liberal. There was a mix of women wearing the *burqa*, some the *hijab*, and others with no head covering. Egyptian unmarried couples are not allowed to share a room, and in some cases, unmarried foreign couples are not permitted to either.

We had dinner in the hotel restaurant, which was a strange place. There was no one else there. The restaurant was a mezzanine floor overlooking the big function area that looked like the last event was an eighties wedding. Faded pink covers graced the tables and chairs, and large bows decorated the lofty pillars that reached up to the ceiling. Nadim reckoned it would be a good setting for a horror movie — he was right.

I'd sent out a newsletter before setting off from Aswan, and reading the email replies gave me a lift. I'd put a post on Instagram and Facebook to say 'thank you' for all the comments on my posts and for the emails and direct messages. It was always encouraging being in contact with my mates, as it made me feel less alone, and it was wonderful to hear that people enjoyed following this expedition.

The next day, it was super windy, and poor Nadim had a struggle ahead of him. His kayak kept filling with water as the wind whipped up little waves, making his life even more difficult. The wind kept pushing his kayak one way and then other. It was painful to watch and would have been far more painful for him to endure.

By the time we reached the next lock, we'd covered just 17 kilometres in five hours. We made our way through it, relishing the protection from the wind as it slowly drained. When the gates opened, we were greeted by strong gusts and a new set of police. They were stationed on a boat at the bottom of a steep bank.

Our next potential stop was 45 kilometres away. There was no way we'd make that before midnight, so I suggested we stop here.

Nadim put his awesome negotiating skills to use, and it was agreed that we could stay where we were. The front of the boat was moored next to a triangular cement platform with a thick cement pillar at each corner. It was covered with a similar cement platform about five metres above, and one side of the platform was enclosed. There were a series of these platforms running next to the riverbank, and it wasn't clear what their purpose was. This first one was going to be our room for the night. Well, at least we had a room with a view, and it was certainly well ventilated.

Mind you, getting to the loo was an endeavour. It meant climbing onto the boat, walking along it, disembarking down a rickety set of steps, climbing up all the boulders and rocks that made the steep riverbank, then walking 200 metres to what was a surprisingly respectable loo. *Here's hoping I don't have a dodgy tummy tonight!*

Two police armed with guns were sent to provide protection. I almost felt like travelling royalty and wondered whose army was coming to get me. The basic accommodation kept my feet firmly on the ground. Nadim spoke to the police who had arrived and asked why they were here. Nadim paraphrased their response, 'They reckon the police stationed here are pussies and would run at the first sign of trouble.' *Fair enough.*

We cooked some pasta, tuna and foul on the camping stove, chatted and laughed about the crazy situations we found ourselves in each day. Nadim was wonderful company, and we got on fantastically. After some tea, we rolled out our sleeping mats, put on some layers to stay warm and wriggled into our sleeping bags at one of the most random places I've ever slept. I loved the strangeness of it all.

When I woke, I noticed that the wind had dropped a little, which made for an enjoyable paddle. We didn't have far to cover, so had time to prepare and savour a pre-paddle coffee sitting up on the platform watching the Nile drift past. I prepared breakfast which we had once we got going – floating along, eating the standard oats special, watching the landscape unfold in front of us. We made it to Al Balyana by midday. After storing our kayaks with the water police, we were ushered into a police van. There were two armed police with us, and then another van behind with more police, who were also armed. While at times the lack of freedom could be a little irritating, I was grateful for the security the police provided as the kidnap risk continued.

Our hotel for the night was four-star luxury, the likes of which I hadn't experienced for ... well ... a very long time. There was wi-fi, spacious rooms that had fluffy towels, a big TV, and there was a swimming pool, a great restaurant, and the list went on. It was US$100 for two rooms, which was a bargain. Nadim's room was cheaper than mine.

In Egypt, there are generally two prices in hotels — one for the locals and one for foreigners, as many locals wouldn't be able to afford it otherwise. We tucked into a buffet lunch and then wandered up to the Temple of Abydos for a step back in time.

Egypt has a long history, tracing its heritage back to the 6th–4th millennia BCE and is considered the cradle of civilisation. Its heritage and rich culture are part of the national identity.

Abydos has been a sacred site to the Egyptians since predynastics times and is one of the oldest cities of ancient Egypt. It was a burial site for Egyptian royalty of the 1st (2925–2775 BCE) and 2nd (2775–2650 BCE) dynasties. The area was also a pilgrimage centre for the god Osiris and considered a gateway to the underworld, and many Egyptians desired to be buried as close as possible to the tomb of Osiris. It is considered one of Egypt's most important archaeological sites[43].

We walked up to the temples through the ruins of the First Courtyard. The remnants were large stones dotted around, some creating low walls. We made our way into the temple, across what could be described as an expansive ancient verandah, the roof of which was held up by 12 large pillars. This main temple of Seti I dates to around 1300 BC and was built as a memorial to King Seti I and dedicated to the pharaohs and gods. Walking through the large doors into this immense hall built from sandstone and limestone with 24 towering columns supporting the roof above was breathtaking. The walls and the columns were all decorated with intricately coloured reliefs of kings and scenes from the time; they were stunning. I wondered what it would have been like in those days.

In total there were three main temples. Nadim and I wandered in awe through these incredible buildings. I couldn't help but be amazed by how the people had created these gargantuan temples and decorated them with such exquisite, detailed carvings.

I appreciated seeing a little of Egypt's sights. It was going to be the only opportunity on this expedition. After an hour or so in the temple, we headed slowly back to the hotel, buying an ice-cream on the way.

Nadim then called the police to make plans for the next day. He optimistically suggested we camp, but the policeman laughed. We were going to have to stay in Sohag. We were both keen to put in a big day on the water after many short ones. It didn't feel like we were making much progress. We joked about how long it was taking. When Nadim told his fiancé the estimated arrival in Cairo was over ten days away, she nearly cried. Another policeman called Nadim offered to send us some hash in a tuk-tuk. *How very thoughtful of him.*

There was the usual waiting around for the police to take us back to our kayaks the following morning. Nadim asked one of the policemen what they would do if we went off on our own and got a tuk-tuk. 'You'll be arrested,' the policeman replied. *Okay, so let's bin that idea.*

To reiterate, they weren't doing this to be arseholes, it was all about my safety. For Nadim, however, it was exasperating not being able to move around as he wanted in his own country, and I got the impression he was not keen on being told what to do, which I got. Plus, now we weren't allowed to camp, something which he was really looking forward to. It wasn't quite the adventure he had anticipated.

We travelled back to the river in a taxi, escorted by a police van and motorbike with their sirens blaring. Reaching the river, we loaded the kayaks and put our paddles in the water and then proceeded to knock out 60 kilometres, which was an improvement, and we arrived at Sohag around 5pm. We then had to have a taxi with police escort to go the 500 metres to the hotel, and we were told that we (or really me) would need a police escort if we left the hotel.

We did, however, manage to sneak out and get some dinner and a few supplies. It felt like I was back breaking out of boarding school, and it made something ordinary kind of fun.

CHAPTER TWENTY-ONE
DAYS 158–169

You may not control all the events that happen to you,
but you can decide not to be reduced by them.

Maya Angelou[44]

The next day was short and sweet — just 35 kilometres. It was wind-free, and we launched our kayaks onto the glassy water.

The Sohag governorate was more scenic, and there were longer remote stretches. Pale-beige cliffs to our right rose steeply out of an equally pale-yellow desert, with a narrow strip of palms and greenery between them and the river, creating a line between the two. The towns we passed were small, with red brick houses and small blocks of flats. Many looked like they were unfinished with rebar protruding from the top floor, ready for additional floors to be added. With no pressure to complete a big day, it was time to breathe deeply and take it all in. We also made the most of the weather and scenery to take photos and videos.

Next was Assuyt, followed by a rest day — and a productive one at that, spent catching up on emails and speaking to Mum. She now had a date for her cataract operation, and I was keen to get home well in advance of this. It would mean having a short stop in Cairo and then a big push to the end with some long days of paddling. The downside was, I would have to go solo to cover the required distances.

So, I began to look at flights, and suddenly the end of the trip was becoming real. For the first time, I felt close to the finish.

I washed my clothes in the bathroom, replenished my cash reserves, and got more data for my phone. One email put a smile on my face — it was from a journalist who wanted to write an article about my trip, for Red Bull. We exchanged some messages, and a few weeks later, the article was released on the Red Bull website.

The following day began with an early start. We'd estimated it was a 70–80-kilometre day. The steep cliffs continued on the right-hand bank. A dip between the cliffs revealed a resplendent walled Coptic church built from smooth cream stone. It was stunning, and I would have loved to have taken a closer look. With the distance we had to cover, there was no time. At the 80-kilometre mark, we were handed over to a new police patrol, which wasn't a good sign.

We had to do another 12 kilometres, as it turned out, and it was my biggest day on the water for the trip. But the police weren't able to give us a clear indication of how far we had left to paddle. Darkness fell, the temperature dropped, and I was feeling like crap. All day I'd felt like I was coming down with a cold, my eyes were sore and I began to shiver. Not knowing whether it was minutes or hours to go, made it mentally more challenging.

So I focused on taking one stroke, then the next, then the next and tried to take comfort that it was taking me closer to the end. Wherever that was. Finally there were lights ahead and we paddled towards the police station. Relieved to finally be able to put our paddles down for the day, we pulled up next to the riverbank, and secured our kayaks.

Then, it was an awkward unpacking process from the steep, grassy bank. We took what we needed for the night, and the police showed us into one of the offices in the single-storey complex of white cube buildings. Walking out of the dark night into a brightly lit office, Nadim asked, 'Are you okay? You don't look so good.' He noticed my bloodshot, puffy eyes. I felt as bad as I looked.

The police who greeted us were lovely and gave us sweet tea while arrangements were made for our transport to a hotel. It was basic, but joy of joy — it had good wi-fi. It was a relief to walk into my room, close the door behind me and, after a hot shower, climb into bed. Chilled to my core, I donned a hoodie and pulled two thick blankets over me. However, this wasn't enough to warm me up, and I went to sleep still feeling cold.

Nadim wanted a rest day after 92 kilometres, which I understood, but given the choice I would have pressed on, having only just had a rest day. However, it was a chance for some self-exploration, so I tried to dig into why I was struggling so much with going slowly. I felt that I was being inefficient, and that time was being wasted.

It was also about the need to feel that I was accomplishing something and that I had physically pushed myself. I wasn't looking to sprint, but instead do the best pace and distance possible, that could be backed up day after day. I wanted to feel the fatigue in my muscles, like I had in Sudan, and a sense of accomplishment. It helped to understand a little of why it was so challenging.

Unfortunately, this insight didn't take away the desolate, heavy feeling. I was nervous this feeling was a step towards a bout of depression, which has been a part of my life for a long time, although it took me too long to realise. In the past, depression, with a side order of anxiety, has taken me close to a breakdown.

Back in 2005, it was an incredibly stressful time at work, following on from some fraudulent trading and a sizeable program of remedial work. We were preparing for a vital set of meetings with the financial regulator. And in the background, I had recently broken off a ten-year relationship with my fiancé. This stress built to a crescendo of depression and anxiety, with external signs such as my hands shaking uncontrollably. I went into a meeting room with my boss and uttered a sentence that seemed unthinkable for so long. 'I can't cope.'

It turned out to be one of the most liberating moments of my life. I admitted I couldn't cope, yet the world kept spinning. And what do you know — I still had a job. No one thought less of me.

I briefly tried antidepressants, which did nothing for me. I band-aided myself back together. It was still years before I got much-needed and overdue help, thanks to the encouragement of a friend. Even then, I was by no means out of the woods. I don't think you ever are fully. The cloud is always there, ready to grow and darken the sky.

When I first started therapy, the worst was still ahead of me. I hit a rock bottom that scarred me. I ended up so deep in the pit of depression, so much so that the thought of getting out of it scared me, because I knew how far it was to fall back down. I didn't want to get out of bed, see anyone or do anything. The joy was sucked out of my life. My energy levels plummeted. This occurred during the time I had my own personal training business. I would drive to my sessions in tears and then use every ounce of energy I had to be the bright-eyed, bushy-tailed, enthusiastic PT they were paying for. It got worse, to the point where every time I got in my car, I wished a car or truck would jump a set of traffic lights and plough into me and end the pain. I wouldn't do it myself, but someone else snuffing out my flame, at that time, would have been welcomed.

This, however, came with feelings of enormous guilt. I had the jackpot: physical health, security, my own beautiful home, friends, food in the fridge, and lived in a country I loved. There were some slight financial challenges, but I wanted for nothing. So, how dare I want this blessed life to be over?

Hours of therapy, learning about myself, being given tools to help, and gaining a greater awareness of the signs that I was slipping back into the pit, have meant I have never ended up as deep in it. Yes, I have periods of depression still, but so far, not for as long or as dark.

One of my concerns coming on this trip was having a depressive episode and not having access to my therapist. My therapist, pre-empting this, said that she was always on hand and could chat or email at any time. *Bless her.* The thing was, despite the physical and mental challenges, I never felt even close to depressed in a clinical sense. I was down at times, like I was now, but not depressed. I hoped it would stay that way.

In the meantime, I had a day off and left the hotel to go for a wander. It was a hustling, bustling, tourist-free town, made up of narrow streets with old buildings reaching up high. I found a market and bought some fruit and then grabbed a coffee. Actually, I had two, it was so good. Decent coffees were few and far between on this trip, other than in Sudan. As a self-confessed Sydney coffee snob, it had been one of the few things I missed from home.

Back on the river, I told Nadim that once we got to Cairo, I was going to have to press on, as Mum was having a cataract operation. He was totally cool about it, and I was happy with the prospect of paddling solo for the last 250 kilometres. I was going to finish the expedition on my terms.

Nadim seemed pleased too; he would be able to finish on his terms, going at his own pace, camping, and not dealing with the police all day every day. The result was, we were both upbeat and more relaxed.

     PADDLE THE NILE

Two days later, we arrived at Bani Mazar where I was advised that I could sleep in an old police boat and Nadim in the police station's mosque. It was the closest to camping we could get and were both happy with the outcome. We cracked open the stove and started cooking. It was all going well until a more senior policeman visited us.

We couldn't stay here. *Seriously? Here we go again.* So, we grabbed what we needed and were taken to the main police station. I have never spent so much time with the police. Up until then, my interactions with them had been random breath tests, and getting arrested as a university student. A big misunderstanding that resulted in a night in jail, an interview with some detectives, an adult caution and an entertaining story to share.

After a short drive, we arrived at the station and were shown into the boss's impressive office and asked to wait for him.

Sitting on the sofa, we were given tea until he finally arrived, barely acknowledging our presence. Some other people came and went. One, a local doctor, did talk to us, and I discovered that Nadim had gone with a 'me being a world champ story'.

The doctor asked me, 'Have you been to the Olympics?'

'Sadly, surf ski paddling isn't an Olympic sport,' I replied, hoping to shut the conversation down. Eventually, the big boss started talking to us. By now, Nadim and I were totally over it all. After some short discussion establishing what we were doing on this trip, we were on our way. I was slightly bemused as to why this had all been necessary. A taxi was called, and we got in, and finally reached a hotel at 11pm.

We were now getting close to Cairo and the scenery on the next stretch was beautiful. There were more palm trees and greenery along the riverbank, and gradually the buildings gave way to steep, sandy banks.

The next day, I was unexpectedly emotional and just wanted to cry for a reason I couldn't quite pinpoint. I was tired after a crappy night's sleep. The end was in sight, but not quite close enough. There was still plenty to organise and uncertainty as to how the last section from Cairo to the end would play out and whether the police would even let me proceed without Nadim.

Messaging one of my best mates back in Australia about my homecoming party prompted homesickness for the first time. Seeing the river, shimmering in the sun, distracted me and lifted my spirits.

Another emotional boost was booking my flights to the UK, placing a bookend on this trip. For the next couple of days we continued slowly making our way towards Cairo and on the way, I received an email from the British Embassy in Cairo, inviting me to meet the Ambassador. *Yes, absolutely!*

This was a blessing, as it forced me to have a rest day. I foolishly had planned to crack on to the end, but, I needed to get more supplies before the long days ahead. I am my own worst enemy at times.

Nadim and I checked out the hotel options for the final section to Cairo, which were very limited. He then suggested we do the last two days in one day. *Hell yes!*

The headwinds ensured it was a long, slow day, and it was dark by the time we reached our end point. We were both relieved to have made it. For Nadim, he was home and some friends were there to meet him. I gave the police, who had escorted us, some money as a thank you for the dull day they had endured.

We then pulled our kayaks out of the water and unpacked them, this time taking everything with us. We stored them there, and Nadim and I said a brief goodbye, as it was late, and we were both shattered. We'd catch up again before I left Cairo. I got an Uber to my hotel, where I fell into bed and a deep sleep.

The end really was in sight now.

CHAPTER TWENTY-TWO
DAYS 170-176

Adversity is an opportunity for us to grow.

Omar Samra

First order of the day was moving my kayak closer to where I'd be starting the final stretch. It was a chilled ten-kilometre paddle to the Kayak Royal Club. I also decided some retail therapy was in order, and, when I walked into a shopping mall, I almost grew teary at the sight of all the shops. This trip had given me a new appreciation for living where everything you need is just a stone's throw away. I left on a shopper's high, the upbeat owner of a new pair of trackpants, a T-shirt and a hoodie. My limited space in the kayak kept my retail therapy under control. There was a supermarket for supplies and even a sports shop for some tennis racquet grips for my paddle. Most paddlers don't seem to use a grip on the paddle shaft, but I've always found it more comfortable, and it provides a better grip.

Next was a visit to the British Embassy, a stunning, refined colonial-style building. I was pleased to have a new and clean T-shirt for the occasion. After making it through security I was guided to the grand entrance, up the steps, and into the deliciously cool entrance hall. We then made our way through the white painted high-ceilinged corridors with its walls lined with pictures of former ambassadors, the British Royal Family, and many other dignitaries.

I was shown into the Ambassador's, Sir Geoffrey Adams KCMG, office where I was offered tea, coffee, and homemade shortbread. Sir Geoffrey was lovely and seemed genuinely interested in hearing about my trip. It was such an honour to be talking to him. We had a quick photo on the lawn, and then said our goodbyes with Sir Geoffrey wishing me a safe finish to my journey.

I then headed up to the Australian Embassy. Their set-up in an office block, however, wasn't as impressive, which is to be expected, having a smaller presence there and far less history. I met the Deputy Ambassador, Samuel Allen, and then returned to the hotel. Ahead of me now was the final four days and 250 kilometres to bring it home.

It hardly seemed possible to be so close.

On the 15 April 2019, I packed up my kayak and was ready to go. It was an emotional moment standing there on the pontoon. I had been at this very spot 20 months earlier on my reconnaissance trip.

Back then, I'd thought, 'Wow, when I get to this point it will be the homestretch, just 250 kilometres to go.' Then it had still seemed like an out of reach dream. Now, here I was — it felt surreal – with everything that had happened — to finally be so close to the end.

Being able to set my own timetable now, I was on the water by 7am. The police were waiting for me not too far away. The wind picked up and temperature dropped. I zipped up my waterproof jacket, put a cap on and tried to warm myself up by paddling.

The river splits into two branches, one goes to Damietta, and the other to Rosetta — or Rasheed, as it is called locally — and this is the one I chose. The next three days were long and tough going. I was on the water for to up to 11 hours a day, battling headwinds for most of it, with chilly starts and ends to each day.

Toward the end of the second day, one of the police escorting me pointed to his shoulders and grimaced in sympathy. To make things a little more mentally challenging, my GPS was playing up, making it difficult to know how far I'd come and had to go. It didn't matter though, knowing I was so close to the end kept me going. Hard as the days were it felt good to be putting in the long hours and feeling the satisfaction in the fatigue and ache in my muscles as I crawled into bed each night.

After three long days and 185 kilometers, I made it to Desouk, where I was taken to the nearest hotel which was in Damanhour, about 30 minutes away. I was now just one day away from the finish and the anticipation within me was mounting.

Fahed, who I had stayed with in Khartoum, had a stopover in Cairo on his way back to Sudan from Europe, and he drove up for dinner. It was awesome to see him. We went out for dinner, and it was a lovely way to spend the night before the final 65 kilometres. We said our farewells once again, and I went to sleep, excited at the prospect of my last day on the water.

At 1.30am, I woke up with a dodgy tummy. It started with diarrhoea, and after an hour or so, the vomiting followed. *It's okay, if I'm only sick once, I can still paddle tomorrow. I can finish it.*

A few more vomits and regular trips to the loo, it was clear that today was not going to see me on the water. Instead, I was lying on the bathroom floor, with thoughts of *take me now*. On standing, I realised how weak I felt and began to feel light-headed. I messaged Dave, and he was amazing. He got in touch with my insurers and advised me to head to hospital to get an IV and some fluids into me. I knew he was right, but decided to wait it out a bit, hoping that I'd start to feel better. But I got worse.

Dave then suggested getting an ambulance. Summoning all the energy I could muster, I packed up my grab bag and started shuffling towards the lift, clutching the bathroom bin in case I was sick again. I made it downstairs, and with no one at reception speaking English I used Google translate on my phone and showed them 'hospital' and 'ambulance' as it appeared in Arabic on my screen.

I received some concerned looks, but there was a distinct lack of action. So, I just lay down on the marble floor. The coolness on my back felt wonderful. This seemed to create some urgency, and after ushering me to a chair, the police were summoned and an ambulance called. When it arrived, I shuffled in, with one policeman joining me, and off we went careering around the streets of Damanhour, sirens blaring, me hanging on for dear life as I lay on the stretcher.

I thought about Google translating that it was okay, we didn't need the sirens and breakneck speeds, but that fell into the 'too hard' basket. It would also have meant relinquishing my grip that was keeping me on the stretcher as we hurtled around another corner.

We arrived at the hospital where I was shown into an examination cubicle, relieved to be somewhere with help on hand.

After a few minutes lying on a bed, a doctor arrived, who took my blood pressure. It was super low, and my heart rate was high. 'You're very dehydrated and need to be put on a drip and given antibiotics,' he concluded. *Sounds good to me, let's do this.*

By now there was a small group, all crowded into this little cubicle. Among them was a nurse. At one point, she gently put her hand on my knee and looked at me with kindness and compassion and smiled. I can't tell you the difference it made. Feeling warmly cared for, I sighed and smiled back. In hindsight, I think it might have been more of a grimace.

I was then told I needed to pay before they would treat me. This was a cause for concern, as I was due for a trip to an ATM. They asked for 100 Egyptian pounds (EGP), about US$6, but I thought they must have meant EGP1,000. I handed over EGP100, expecting to be asked for more; they took it away, only to return later with EGP60 in change.

I had an ambulance ride, fluids, antibiotics, and anti-nausea meds for the princely sum of US$2. *Bargain.*

I was shown into a small women's ward and given a bed to lie on. A group of nurses came in to watch a cannula being put into this foreigner's hand.

She tried in the back of my hand, but the veins had collapsed with dehydration. She then tried my arm, repeatedly. It's rare that I get faint with needles, but this was pushing my limits. I started to feel faint. At that point, unconsciousness would have been a welcome outcome. There was no such luck, and instead, intense nausea took over. Just as they got the cannula in, I started retching and sat up while some quick hands grabbed a bin, just in time for me to vomit into. I simultaneously clenched my butt cheeks with everything I had to avoid both ends being evacuated. This was definitely the low point of the trip.

The nurse hooked me up to the IV, and the fluids entering my body had a near instant effect. The policeman stayed with me until the bag of fluids was empty about an hour later, and then it was time to head back to the hotel where he saw me to my room.

I crawled into bed and called Mum, as I needed some verbal TLC. She also had some good news — the BBC were interested in doing a story about my journey. She had contacted them by email, telling them what I had achieved and that they should do a story on me. *Go Mum! Who needs a PR agent when you've got Mum on the case?*

I then practically passed out, with my tummy grumbling and still feeling like I was running a temperature. The hotel owner's wife called. Apparently, the police were concerned that I hadn't eaten all day and requested that she ask if I needed anything and if I wanted a nurse to stay with me. *Bless them!* No, I was fine. After an apple and biscuit, I went back to sleep.

The next day I felt so much better, but disappointed. The plan would have had me finished by now. Instead, there was a rest day.

And when I spoke to Dave, he recommended that due to my weakened state, I should take two days to paddle the final distance, instead of completing it in the one day, as originally planned. The hotel owner's wife even helped with the logistics, organising hotels for those two days. She explained to the police that the final day was being split over two days.

In the background, I was arranging for someone to meet, and take me back to Cairo. I also had to get my kayak shipped to Sudan. I was donating it to the Khartoum Rowing and Canoe Club as a small 'thank you' for everything they'd done for me.

As I started to get ready the following morning, a small knot started to grow in my stomach. The nausea was still there. Even splitting this final stretch, it was still a 50-kilometre day with a less than friendly 30 kilometres per hour headwind. Getting underway, I took things very easy. No music, just listening to my body and dreading potential diarrhea episodes. Goodness knows how'd I deal with them with any decorum and decency. I was also dreading paying the price of pushing myself and getting sick again.

Come midday, I'd done 25 kilometres and my body was surprisingly feeling stronger as the day progressed. In the back of my mind, Plan B was to get in the police boat if it was too tough; however, Plan B disappeared when I went around the final lock to find no police escort on the other side.

I was finally on my own.

As I approached the end of the day, a policeman called me, which was a little pointless, as I couldn't speak Arabic and he couldn't speak English. I phoned Nadim, and he, of course, sorted it all out, telling me to look to the left, as that was where the police were. They had been following me by car. All I had to do was meet up with them and they would take me to the hotel. *Too easy!*

The day had fallen into place perfectly.

I arrived at the hotel, which was cheap as chips, and ordered some food. I desperately wanted vegetables and rice, but the idea of not having meat seemed to be an alien concept to the personnel there. So, I got chicken, rice, bread … and some vegetables.

Dave had imparted some final day advice: 'Stay safe, don't lift anything stupid, break an arm or get kidnapped. Switch the fuck *on* — early night and no dancing.'

He had a knack of making me laugh when I needed it. It was also some sage advice. As I'd been approaching the end, he had been reminding me to stay 'switched on'. On expeditions, things often go wrong at the start while people are still finding their way and adjusting, or at the end when risk fatigue and complacency take over.

I was so close to the end, now was not the time to make a stupid mistake.

CHAPTER TWENTY-THREE
DAYS 177-178

> *I need to believe that there is more to this world than what we know. I need to believe there is magic out there. I cannot believe these things blindly, though, and maybe that is why I had to do this mission — to prove to myself that we can do things which are bigger than ourselves. I needed to walk through a minefield to feel protected.*

Hendri Coetzee

Come 4am the next morning, apprehension woke me up. This was it. The final day. I felt seriously wobbly, more emotionally than physically. I felt on the verge of a mini-breakdown and had to look in the mirror and quite literally say to myself, 'Sarah, fucking keep it together.' Now was definitely not the time to lose it.

Waiting downstairs, I felt utterly spent, physically and mentally. There was nothing left in me. I just wanted to get to the end. Having been away nearly seven months, constantly on the go, dealing with varying levels of stress and constant uncertainty, I was ready for this to be done.

And there was still uncertainty — where would I be able to finish, would I get onto the Mediterranean Sea, where would I meet the car to take me to Cairo? The 15 kilometres I needed to cover that day seemed like a long way, overwhelmed with amplified emotions and fatigue.

The police were a couple of hours late, so I had to rearrange the timing for the pick-up. The person organising this was Roy — the man I'd purchased the kayak from. He arranged for his driver and company car to collect me and my kayak, even though I couldn't tell him exactly where I was going to finish, or when, for that matter. Sarah of old would have stressed massively about this. Now, I rolled with it, confident that everything would work out, somehow.

On reaching the river, seeing the water sparkling in the sun gave me an overwhelming sense of joy. This was it; it was time to bring this expedition to a close.

I loaded my gear into and onto the kayak for the last time, putting the dry bags in the storage hatches and tying others down onto the deck forward and aft. The satellite phone and last remaining snacks were zipped into the deck bag, so I could access them easily once on the water. I then pushed the kayak out onto the river, got in and attached the spray skirt to the deck. I took the first stroke and did my best to take in every one of those final 15 kilometres, ensuring I relished every moment.

The river was busier here, with fishing trawlers coming in and out. I started to smell the sea air, and soon I could see the breaking waves on the Mediterranean. The only real problem was that because the wind was whipping up big waves, paddling onto the Mediterranean Sea was going to be out of the question. I paddled as close as I could to the Mediterranean, smiled and called it — the end — raising my paddle above my head, whooping and hollering as I recorded this historic moment on my GoPro with a jubilant, 'I've finished!'

This was it. I had made it. I had completed a seemingly impossible dream.

The obstacles, fears and self-doubt that had to be overcome; the 1,100 kilometres of rafting; the 3,000 kilometres of kayaking, and the patchwork of transport that made up the rest of the trip ... it was all behind me now. I experienced a whirlpool of emotions. There was immense happiness and satisfaction that had me beaming, contradicted by sadness that this incredible journey was over. There was also tremendous relief and total exhaustion. I'd pushed myself, particularly this last week, and my body was feeling it. I was ready for a very long rest.

I'd barely put my paddle back down when my phone rang. It was Dave, 'Congratulations Sarah, you did it!' After everything he'd done, our doing this expedition together, even if he was a few thousand kilometres away, he was the first person I wanted to speak to, and the sound of his voice made me feel even more elated. I couldn't have done it without him. As well as keeping me safe, he helped keep me sane and made me laugh. I was looking forward to a proper catch up when I got back to Australia*.

I took some photos and video, then turned around and enjoyed a brief downwind paddle until I found a spot to pull up. Some men came to help me. It turned out they were a group of co-workers who'd come to Rosetta from Alexandria for the day and were enjoying a quick coffee before heading home. They were fantastic and turned into my unexpected welcome party. They got me coffees, gave me cake, asked a hundred questions, and took numerous photos. It would have been a lonely, anticlimactic finish if I'd had to sit there on my own waiting for transport to turn up. They made it for me!

We laughed and chatted, and they insisted on staying until my transport arrived and I was safely on my way. When the car pulled up, the guys quickly loaded my kayak. I said my farewells to my new friends and got in the car, one ecstatic paddler.

I wanted to sleep on the three-hour drive back to Cairo, but not a chance. Despite my exhaustion, I was too filled with emotion and still buzzing. I shuffled deep into the back seat of the very comfortable car, looked out of the window, slowly letting it sink in that I had finished. A few hours later I was back in Cairo, where I treated myself to some celebratory ice-cream and then crashed at 7.30pm.

The next day, it was time for my final check-in with Dave. I was feeling separation anxiety! We had conversed in some way, every single day for the seven months I'd been in Africa, usually multiple times a day.

There was one last treat in store before leaving for the airport. I had the great privilege of meeting Omar Samra at the British Embassy for a filmed interview. Omar was the first Egyptian to climb Mount Everest, the Seven Summits, and to ski to both the Geographic South and North Pole. On top of his incredible achievements as an adventurer, he is an entrepreneur and speaker. It was fantastic to chat to him.

---

* Dave and I met in person when I got back to Australia, and we have kept in touch since.

Then it was back to the hotel, where I grabbed my bags and headed to the airport. It was a hasty turnaround, with my planned day or two in Cairo to unwind thwarted by the last days spent being ill.

Sitting in the back of the taxi, I saw the Nile for the last time. Instantly, tears streamed down my face. They took me by surprise and I couldn't pinpoint the exact trigger, there were so many. A big one was sadness and grief — I was desperately sad to be saying goodbye to this mighty, beautiful river. The Nile had been my purpose, my goal and focus for years. I had been travelling along it for many months.

There was grief that this journey was at an end. It seemed like such an abrupt finish and farewell. At the same time, there was a huge amount of relief that this goal of mine had finally been accomplished, that there was no more planning, problems to solve, obstacles to overcome or the constant physical demands that had exhausted me physically, mentally and emotionally. There was also an enormous amount of pure joy. I was ecstatic to have made it and so incredibly thankful to have been able to go on this amazing journey.

In the process, I had become the first women to lead an expedition down the Nile. I had done it. Or rather *we* had done it. It was a very long list of people that made this expedition possible.

This had been the most extraordinary, life-changing journey. One that I knew would take some time to really process and fully appreciate. When I set out on this adventure, I had no idea what was ahead of me or any real expectations. It had turned out to be better than anything I could ever have imagined — an amazing adventure that challenged me on every level. I was gifted with not just seeing, but really experiencing the incredible countries this trip took me through.

I learnt about myself as well as what it takes to plan and execute an expedition. I came away with new friends, hundreds of wonderful memories, so many life lessons ... and a few thousand photos!

As I sat at the airport, looking out at the planes on the tarmac, I was wistful that my travelling was concluding. There was no longer a feeling of excitement of heading somewhere new, launching into the unknown, the anticipation and the adventures to be had.

However, when I boarded my flight, and the plane began taxiing down the runway, while it signalled the end of this expedition, I knew in my heart that this was just the beginning.

Day 158: Sarah in Egypt

Day 163: Sarah & Nadim (L-R) in Aswan, Egypt

Day 163: Sarah & police escort in Egypt

Day 177: Sarah at the end in Egypt

PADDLE THE NILE

EPILOGUE

Experience is the teacher of all things.

Julius Ceasar

People have asked me whether this journey changed me.

I have found it hard to distil real changes in me, the core of who I am. It was more about developing who I am and experiencing personal growth rather than me 'changing'. I think of the journey as being like the nourishment we give our plants. That food will help your roses grow and blossom, but it doesn't change them into orchids. We don't change who we are, instead we explore who we are.

This trip allowed me to explore what I am capable of, my strengths, what I enjoy and what I can overcome, as well as where there is room for growth. My confidence and courage grew, and all of this has had a ripple effect across my life. My world feels like a far larger place. Adventures that may once have seemed out of reach are now achievable. It's like my comfort zone and boundaries have expanded from a back garden to a national park.

Eight months after reaching the end of the Nile, I completed a 2,500-kilometre expedition down the Murray River in Australia. Having completed the Nile, this felt like a comparative 'walk in the park'. Then in 2021, I cycled 4,700 kilometres across Australia.

I have a long list of more expeditions I plan to do! The lessons and takeaways from this trip are still rising to the surface in my consciousness, but these are my top five.

1. BACK MYSELF

Going into this trip, I was racked with self-doubt, not trusting my capabilities, particularly as I was venturing deeply into the unknown. I learnt to not let self-doubt be in the driving seat. I gradually learnt to, instead, let it be my co-driver to fuel my preparation and then focus on backing myself and not letting the voice of self-doubt take over.

A few things helped me and what I take with me into future exploits. One was investing time in researching and planning. The next was the support around me – having Dave with me along the way, and being surrounded by 'believers' from the day I announced my plans. There was no one saying I couldn't do it.

Then it was taking action, because that took away the power of the questions in my mind. When we're *doing*, we spend less time *thinking*. This made a massive difference; it was like creating a distraction for a child.

2.   FOCUS ON WHAT I CAN CONTROL

My mantra, 'control the controllables' served me well. It's easier said than done, particularly when dealing with challenges such as hippos, which scared me so much, or things outside of my control that I thought might really impact the trip. Regularly putting it into practice helped and is something I come back to often.

This trip was one big lesson in not wasting my energy on things outside of my control. It was disempowering to focus on what I couldn't control or influence, and it created unnecessary stress. When I was able to focus on the things in my control – how I felt, what I did and what I thought - I took the power back. It helped me accept the situation rather than resist it. When we resist, we suffer more.

3.   FACE THOSE FEARS

Fear is a natural human response designed to keep us safe. There was so much that terrified me. I wouldn't say I'm a particularly brave person, and have been held back by fear many times and certainly by things less scary than what I faced on this trip.

Having a strong 'why' — wanting to do this expedition so much — was the greatest enabler to overcoming my fear. It got me back in the raft after the hippo attack. As Friedrich Nietzsche said, 'He who has a why to live for can bear almost any how.'

Fears aren't facts. Fear can involve assumptions and some creative imagination, which can result in unrealistic scenarios that can stop us in our tracks. The risk management approach aided me in unpacking the fears, taking away the assumptions and getting to the reality.

It helped direct my preparation by doing things like the Swift Water Rescue Technician course, wilderness survival, Krav Maga, and the Hostile Environment Awareness Training.

Then it was just getting on and doing it, and taking a step towards those fears and then another step. As with overcoming self-doubt, taking action was key. So much of what we want is on the other side of fear. Fears can turn us into excuse makers — to face them, we must be action takers.

4.   THE VALUE OF HAVING PURPOSE

I knew real 'purpose' was missing from my life, but I underestimated the value it would bring. I've always had goals to work towards, like the races I train for, but this was next level.

From the moment I committed to this expedition, I had a future that excited me and a purpose that fired me to my very core. The expedition was tough, yet despite the challenges and the physical pain, dropping out never once crossed my mind. The suffering and challenges were buffered by the meaning I assigned to the expedition.

This trip was a reminder to me to never settle for less, and to live with purpose – and to keep finding things that light me up. Life is too short not to. It wasn't about the destination; the whole journey, the experience and the struggle was the purpose. It gave me meaning, feeling like I was moving towards something, creating my life and living intentionally.

5.   FIND RISKS WORTH TAKING

There were many risks wrapped up in this trip – from the obvious physical risks, to financial and reputational.

Having a strong risk management approach was critical to the success of this expedition and staying safe. That was why I engaged Dave, did the training, took the meds, chose the craft I did, and so on. This approach created boundaries of what I was getting into.

Most, if not all, of the greatest experiences of my life have involved taking some kind of risk. We are biologically programmed to take risk — without it, humans would never have explored new lands, traversed the seas, learnt new skills. We have a choice — to settle for the seemingly safe and familiar or we can step away from the accustomed and open ourselves to challenges and the unknown and see where that takes us.

PARTING WORDS

My final words are this: 'You don't need to be amazing to start, but you need to start to be amazing.' *Thank you, Toyota ad.* Take the first step and launch into the unknown. We tend to regret the things we don't do. If you can dream it, you can do it. There'll never be the perfect time, the planets won't line up just as you need — only you can make it happen.

Take action every day, persevere and you will experience the adventure of your life.

THANK YOU!

No one who achieves success does so without the help of others.

Alfred North Whitehead

This trip was only possible because there were so many people who helped to make it happen.

My Sponsors:

- *Shaw and Partners Financial Services* came on board as a sponsor from the day I announced my plans. Not only that, but they raised funds and donated money to CARE Australia, the charity for this trip. Earl Evans and Allan Zion — I can't thank you enough — without the generosity of Shaw and Partners, I would never have been able to even start this trip.

- *Big Water Rescue Equipment* supplied all my vital white water safety equipment — the best there is on the market – and there was a lot of it! Alan and Catherine Carrette – thank you!

- *Kathmandu* was where much of my camping equipment came from and the all-important GPS.

- *Braca-Sport, Bennett Paddles and Canoe Innovations* provided the paddles. Braca are the best paddles on the market — the choice of everyday paddlers through to those for Olympians. I had two sets with different blade sizes put together for me by Bennett Paddles (the place to get your paddles in Australia! Thanks, Greg).

- *Vaikobi* provided my super comfortable and durable paddling clothing. I highly recommend them for all the paddlers out there — it was certainly tested on this trip! Thanks, Pat Langley.

- *Nile River Explorers* gave me all the rafting gear to use, the repair kits and put me in touch with the team for the rafting sections. On top of that they allowed me to stay at the fabulous Explorers River Camp — a gorgeous place overlooking the stunning Nile. Thanks so much, Jon Dahl — I couldn't have done this without your support.

- *Dick Smith AC* – your support meant so much to me as well as being such a financial help

- *Peak Dynamics* provided assessments of my decision-making capacity as the physical and mental stress took their toll throughout the trip. Very insightful and valuable assessments to go through — thanks, Sandy Loder.

- *Borika Mounts* put mounts on the kayak for the GoPro. They offer a variety of mounts for all types of boats.

- *Mayo Hardware* donated money to my expedition. Thank you, James Mayo.

- *Nurmi Accountants* also donated money to the expedition. Thank you, John Nurmi.

- *Nuzest* gave me a selection of incredible supplements.

- *Sportslab* helped make sure I was in tip-top condition before undertaking this challenge.

The Paddlers

Having local paddlers with me was an essential part of the trip for me. I knew it would bring a far richer experience. I was blessed with an incredible bunch of men who joined me. I walked away from this trip with new friends who I will be forever grateful to.

- Paulo Babi — our leader on the water for the rafting sections. Paulo, thank you for joining the expedition, bringing together the *Dream Team*, for the jokes and your constant support.

- Peter Bagaga — part of the *Dream Team*. Peter, thank you for your calmness under pressure, for coming up with new solutions for the most treacherous of situations, for being the spokesperson and doing so much to help make that section a success, and getting us to the end in one piece! You have a wonderful, wicked sense of humour — thank you for the laughs!

- Koa Bahazi — part of the *Dream Team*. Thank you for making me feel safe, for being our safety kayaker, for your support, and for being such an important member of the team.

- Fahed Belali — who gave me somewhere to stay, who fed me, helped me organise my time in Sudan, provided ground support and joined me on the water for the first section in Sudan. Fahed, I loved our time together, the chats and for your friendship.

- AbdelRahman Mubarak (Busati) — the paddler with me for the first section in Sudan. He was a talented and patient paddler who valiantly tried to teach me Arabic, and who also had a fabulous sense of humour. Busati was in a car accident at the end of March 2020 and tragically died a few days later. His passing is a great loss to all who knew him, felt deeply by the Khartoum Rowing and Canoe Club.

- Aimun Abu Shamela ('Coach Aimun') — who joined me from Khartoum to Wadi Halfa. Thank you for coordinating everything as we went, for keeping me sane and making me laugh. It was such a pleasure to spend 32 days with you!

- Nadim Elmessiri — who paddled with me throughout Egypt. You were amazing at dealing with the police and were such great company. I'm sorry for my crankiness, and I thank you for your patience. It was great getting to know you!

While not paddling with me, the following people were instrumental in my time on the river:

- Mr Abdelrahim Hamad Ahmed, Head of the Sudan Rowing and Canoe Federation and Khartoum Rowing and Canoe Club, who with Mugahid Obeid and Hamza Abdalla ensured I had paddlers with me, the boat support, the official approvals as well as publicity. You welcomed me into your paddling family and made me feel a part of it. Your kindness, hospitality and generosity were next level. I miss sitting with you next to the beautiful Nile.

- Captain Salih and Assam, who provided the boat and support from Khartoum to Wadi Halfa. Thank you for looking after 'Mama Sarah'. You were so thoughtful and kind. It was wonderful to share the journey with you both.

Friends and Supporters

To my friends who agreed to be on the 'crisis team': Sue Watts, Daniel Sadecky, James McInerney, and Nina Malmström. Knowing that you were there gave me confidence, and you did so much along the way, particularly Sue. Thank you.

So many of my friends donated money and bought equipment for me – the generosity was astounding. You are legends; that you donated to help me go on this expedition still blows me away. Thank you! It meant the world to me that you helped me turn my dream into a reality.

I can't tell you how much all your comments and messages along the journey meant and the difference they made to me. At times, it was lonely and tough going. Your messages lifted my spirits when I needed them the most.

Then there were all the people who gave me advice and helped me organise things as I went. As much as I tried to have everything lined up before I left Australia, there was much to arrange 'on the fly'. Throughout, people aided me in organising various things, overcoming problems, all the while giving up their time in the process and putting in an impressive amount of effort to make my dream a reality.

A few other mentions

- Ben Griffiths, for believing in me and giving me so much help and advice on finding sponsors.

- Nicci Mostert and Paul Ferguson from Basecamp – your support and advice was very much appreciated and Nicci, for your help getting the kayak through customs and getting the all important glue to me!

- Joanna Nicholas — thank you for being 'fixer extraordinaire'! So much more to 'fix' than we could have imagined – you were amazing.

- Steve Venton and Dan Folta for your valuable advice through the Rwandan section.

- Georgie and Chris Higginson — for allowing us to stay at Murchison and for giving us a lift to save us from a guaranteed hippo attack.

- Rob Davies – thank you for your friendship, the dinners and support (and thanks to your mum Eileen too!)

- Shirray Knight – thank you for giving me accommodation at All Terrain.

- The Egyptian police — so many of the police endured some long boring boat rides next to me or uncomfortable nights guarding me. Thank you for allowing me to complete my journey through your wonderful country.

- North Bondi Surf Life Saving Club for introducing me to paddling, without which I would never have considered this trip. I was given so much support from the Club and its members.

- Mat Morris did an exceptional job of creating a video introducing me, the expedition, why I was doing it and what I wanted to achieve with it.

- James Anderson, thank you for great promotional photos.

Finally, thank you to the FCO and DFAT for their support, particularly during my side trip into Burundi, and to the FCO in Egypt for their hospitality.

Special Mention

Dave and the team at TCG — not only did you help get me to the start line with training, advice and support, you kept me safe and got me out of some sticky situations.

Dave, you went above and beyond. You were an essential sounding-board for decisions, you made me laugh, you encouraged me, and you gave me the confidence to complete this trip. You helped with PR ideas, and you kept family and friends in the loop when I was out of communication range. You were with me the whole way and made more of a difference than I think you could ever realise. I couldn't have done this without you. Thank you!

To everyone

I am indebted to you all, and I couldn't pay you back in multiple lifetimes. So many of you contributed financially – your generosity blew me away. The words THANK YOU do not feel enough. I am eternally grateful to you all.

Now, go follow your dreams.

REFERENCES

Prologue

1.   World Atlas 2019, The Longest Rivers in the World, viewed 5 December 2021, <https://www.worldatlas.com/articles/which-are-the-longest-rivers-in-the-world.html>.

Chapter Three

2.   World Bank 2020, Poverty & Equity Brief Sub-Saharan Africa Uganda, viewed 19 February 2022, <https://databank.worldbank.org/data/download/poverty/33EF03BB-9722-4AE2-ABC7-AA2972D68AFE/Global_POVEQ_UGA.pdf >.

Chapter Four

3.   Rwanda Development Board 2021, Nyungwe National Park, Visit Rwanda, viewed 19 November 2021, <https://www.visitrwanda.com/destinations/nyungwe-national-park/>.

4.   United Nations, Rwanda, viewed 5 December 2021, <http://data.un.org/en/iso/rw.html>.

5.   Statista 2021, Proportion of seats held by women in the national parliament of Rwanda from 2000 to 2020, viewed 19 February 2022, https://www.statista.com/statistics/1248551/proportion-of-seats-held-by-women-in-rwanda-national-parliament/.

6.   World Economic Forum, Global Gender Gap Report 2021, Insight Report March 2021, viewed 22 February 2022, https://www3.weforum.org/docs/WEF_GGGR_2021.pdf.

Chapter Five

7.   World Atlas, What languages are spoken in Uganda?, viewed 19 February 2022, < https://www.worldatlas.com/articles/what-languages-are-spoken-in-uganda.html>.

8.   Esther Smitheram, How one charity is working to prevent child sacrifice in Uganda, The Guardian, viewed 19 February 2022, <https://www.theguardian.com/global-development-professionals-network/2015/mar/04/child-sacrifice-uganda-mutilation-witch-doctor>.

9.   Visit London, Famous bridges in London, viewed 5 December 2021, <https://www.visitlondon.com/things-to-do/sightseeing/london-attraction/bridge>.

10.   Rwanda Facts 2021, How is banana beer brewed?, viewed 5 December 2021, <https://www.rwandafacts.com/fact-sheets/rwandan-life/how-is-banana-beer-brewed/>.

11.   Anne Marie Helmenstine Ph.D 8 July 2019, Nile Crocodile Facts, viewed 19 February 2022, <https://www.thoughtco.com/nile-crocodile-4691790>

12.   Bryan Haines 2020, 57 Huge Hippo Facts: Complete Guide to the Massive Hippopotamus, Storyteller.travel, viewed 5 December 2021, <https://storyteller.travel/hippo-facts/>.

Chapter Six

13.   Australian Institute of Institutional Affairs, 24 January 2021, Burundi vs Rwanda: potential for future genocide, viewed 19 February 2022, <https://www.internationalaffairs.org.au/australianoutlook/burundi-vs-rwanda-potential-for-a-future-genocide/>.

14.   Britannica, History of Burundi, viewed 19 February 2022, <https://www.britannica.com/place/Burundi/History>.

15.   South African History Online, Burundi, viewed 10 April 2022, <https://www.sahistory.org.za/place/burundi>.

16.   Britannica, Ruanda-Urundi, viewed 19 February 2022, <https://www.britannica.com/place/Ruanda-Urundi>.

17.   World Happiness Report 2018, viewed 5 December 2021, < https://s3.amazonaws.com/happiness-report/2018/CH2WHR-lr.pdf>.

Chapter Seven

18.   Immaculée Ilibagiza with Steve Erwin, Hay House Inc., (7 April 2014) Left to Tell: Discovering God Amidst the Rwandan Holocaust, p80.

19.   United States Holocaust Memorial Museum, Genocide Fax Part i-III, viewed 19 February 2022, <https://www.ushmm.org/genocide-prevention/countries/rwanda/turning-points/genocide-fax-part-i>.

20. Lt Gen Romeo Dallaire, Arrow books, (2003) Shake Hands with the Devil: the failure of humanity in Rwanda, p6.

21. BBC 2019, Rwanda genocide: 100 days of slaughter, viewed 19 February 2022, <https://www.bbc.com/news/world-africa-26875506>.

22. United Nations, Outreach programme on the 1994 genocide against the Tutsi in Rwanda and the United Nations, viewed 19 February 2022, <https://www.un.org/en/prevent genocide/rwanda/supporting-survivors.shtml>.

Chapter Nine

23. Joshua Rapp Learn 2021, The Source of the Nile River: A Mystery That Spanned Three Millennia, Discover, viewed 5 December 2021, < https://www.discovermagazine.com/planet-earth/the-source-of-the-nile-river-a-mystery-that-spanned-three-millennia>.

24. Uganda Local Governments Act 1997 Chapter 243, Act 49. Functions of the parish and village executive committee.

Chapter Eleven

25. Visit Uganda Now, Murchison Falls, viewed 5 December 2021, <https://visitugandanow.com/listing/murchison-fall/>.

26. StMU Research Scholars, Felipe Macias, Fuel for His Pen: The Two Consecutive Plane Accidents of Ernest Hemingway, viewed 19 February 2022 < https://stmuscholars.org/two-consecutive-plane-accidents/>.

27. BBC 2018, Josephy Kony – child kidnapper, warlord, 'prophet', viewed 5 December 2021, < https://www.bbc.com/news/world-africa-17299084>.

Chapter Twelve

28. New Vision, Jinja regains its glory, viewed 5 December 2021, < https://www.newision.co.ug/news/1509422/jinja-regains-glory>.

29. BBC 2018, Uganda profile – Timeline, viewed 5 December 2021, < https://www.bbc.com/news/world-africa-14112446>.

30.	Patrick Keatley 2003, Idi Amin, The Guardian, viewed
5 December 2021, <https://www.theguardian.com/news/
2003/aug/18/guardianobituaries>.

31.	The Conversation 2020, Insights into why Uganda's strategy
to create jobs for young people hasn't fully worked, viewed 19
February 2022, < https://theconversation.com/insights-into-
why-ugandas-strategy-to-create-jobs-for-young-people-hasnt-
fully-worked-149576 >.

32.	reliefweb 2019, South Sudan Humanitarian Needs Overview
2020 (November 2019), viewed 5 December 2021, <https://
reliefweb.int/report/south-sudan/south-sudan-humanitarian-
needs-overview-2020-november-2019>.

33.	UN Refugees, South Sudan Refugee Crisis, The UN Refugee
Agency, viewed 5 December 2021, <https://www.unrefugees.
org/emergencies/south-sudan/>.

34.	Biomedical Central, BugBitten, Jiggers: a painful infestation,
viewed 19 Febaruary 2022, <https://blogs.biomed
central.com/bugbitten/2019/05/31/jiggers-a-painful-
infestation/>.

Chapter Thirteen

35.	World Population Review, Sudan Population 2021 (Live),
viewed 5 December 2021, < https://worldpopulation
review.com/countries/sudan-population>.

36.	BBC News 2019, Sudan Profile – Timeline, viewed 5 December
2021, https://www.bbc.com/news/world-africa-14095300.

Chapter Fifteen

37.	Sufi dancing, Ala Kheir, John Burns and Ibrahim Algrefwi
2016, The psychedelic world of Sudan's Sufis – in pictures,
The Guardian, viewed 5 December 2021, <https://www.
theguardian.com/world/gallery/2016/feb/05/the-psychedelic-
world-of-sudans-sufis-in-pictures>.

38.	Allen Carr, Sterling Pub Co Inc (25 December 2005),
The Easyway to Stop Drinking.

Chapter Sixteen

39.   Sorin Furcoi 2015, Pictures of Sudan's forgotten Nubian pyramids, Al Jazeera, viewed 5 December 2021, <https://www.aljazeera.com/gallery/2015/4/5/pictures-of-sudans-forgotten-nubian-pyramids>.

40.   James Lawrence, Iron Cowboy – Redefine Impossible, Iron Cowboy (15 May 2017), viewed 5 December 2021.

Chapter Seventeen

41.   Black History Month 2021, Nubai and the Noba people, viewed 19 February 2022, < https://www.blackhistorymonth.org.uk/article/section/pre-colonial-history/nubia-and-the-noba-people/>.

Chapter Twenty

42.   Britannica, Egypt, viewed 5 December 2021, <https://www.britannica.com/place/Egypt>.

43.   Britannica, Abydos, viewed 5 December 2021, <https://www.britannica.com/place/Abydos-ancient-city-Egypt>.

Chapter Twenty-One

44.   Maya Angelou, Little, Brown Book Group, (12 June 2014), Letter to my daughter.

ABOUT SARAH

Sarah Davis is a professional risk manager with a passion for risk taking.

She is a British born Australian, an award-winning adventurer and accomplished sportswoman, who at the age of 44, keen to explore what was possible, decided that she needed more out of life.

Always in search of a life less ordinary, she struggled to discover just what it was that she craved so badly. After delving deeply and exploring countless options, she hit upon an idea – she was going to paddle the Nile, from its source to the Mediterranean, a gruelling challenge that would involve over 4,000km paddling. Sarah became the first woman to lead an expedition down this mighty river.

It was the escape from her corporate environment that she had been seeking, and it transformed into the most incredible, life-changing adventure she could ever have imagined - one she has described as being equal parts fun, tough and terrifying!

It sparked something in Sarah, and she has gone on to complete a source-to-sea descent of the Murray River in Australia and cycled 4,700km across Australia.

Away from her adventures, Sarah is now a speaker, writer and coach, helping and encouraging others to 'explore their possible'. She also has a long list of adventures to pursue, including a source-to-sea descent on each continent. Find out more at www.sarahjdavis.com and you can follow her on Instagram at @sarahpaddles.

Manufactured by Amazon.com.au
Sydney, New South Wales, Australia

15243437R00141